MANAGING LOCAL GOVERNMENT

MANAGING LOCAL GOVERNMENT

John Fenwick

Principal Lecturer in Government
University of Northumbria at Newcastle
UK

CHAPMAN & HALL
London · Glasgow · Weinheim · New York · Tokyo · Melbourne · Madras

**Published by Chapman & Hall, 2–6 Boundary Row,
London SEI 8HN, UK**

Chapman & Hall, 2–6 Boundary Row, London SEI 8HN, UK

Blackie Academic & Professional, Wester Cleddens Road,
Bishopbriggs, Glasgow G64 2NZ, UK

Chapman & Hall GmbH, Pappelallee 3, 69469 Weinheim,
Germany

Chapman & Hall USA, 115 Fifth Avenue, New York,
NY 10003 USA

Chapman & Hall Japan, ITP-Japan, Kyowa Building,
3F, 2–2–1 Hirakawacho, Chiyoda–ku, Tokyo 102, Japan

Chapman & Hall Australia, 102 Dodds
Street, South Melbourne, Victoria 3205, Australia

Chapman & Hall India, R. Seshadri, 32 Second Main Road,
CIT East, Madras 600 035, India

First edition 1995

© 1995 John Fenwick

Typeset in 10/12 pt Palatino by Florencetype Limited, Stoodleigh, Nr. Tiverton, Devon
Printed in by Great Britain by The Alden Press, Osney Mead, Oxford

ISBN 0 412 49720 4

A catalogue record for this book is available from the British
Library.

Library of Congress Catalog Card Number: 95–68505

∞ Printed on permanent acid-free text paper, manufactured in
accordance with ANSI/NISO Z39.48–1992 and ANSI/NISO
Z39.48–1984 (Permanence of Paper).

Dedicated to the memory of my Mother and my Father

CONTENTS

viii   **Contents**

LIST OF CASE STUDIES

PREFACE

In writing this book, I have sought to fill a gap. In the course of teaching and researching in local government, and indeed in my own experience of practice, there has seemed to be a gap between those books dealing with the structures and functions of local government, but saying little of the **processes** which make local government come alive, and those books applying social science theorizing to local government, but saying little of the issues and problems of day-to-day **practice**.

This book has also been motivated by a wish to identify the key areas of **current change** in local government, and to analyse the impact of such changes on local authority management. If there was ever a time when local government was an uneventful backwater where little ever happened, that time is long gone. The rapid pace of change in local government has been directly related to debates about the kinds of local public services we want and to arguments about how those services are to be run. This book is intended as a textbook, dealing with processes and themes rather than structures. It seeks to examine what it means to be involved in running local government today. Reference is made to current and recent research wherever possible, and it is assumed throughout that the process of managing local government must be considered in its political context if it is to make sense at all.

Managing Local Government has been written to be of use to students of public administration and of political and social science, but also to be relevant to the needs of non-social science students such as those in business studies and management.

The book is also designed to be a teaching tool, each chapter including questions and exercises suitable for use as assessment, examination or project topics, with additional notes on how to approach each question and where to look for relevant material.

Additionally, readers involved in the practice of local government should find the text to be of use in linking the specifics of running a particular service to general themes of local authority management, in a style which is relatively jargon-free, applied and accessible.

Thus the book has been written with a number of audiences in mind, and it is hoped that the importance of local government today is brought home to some new groups of readers too.

John Fenwick
University of Northumbria at Newcastle

ACKNOWLEDGEMENTS

Many people have contributed, in their different ways, to the completion of this book. I would like particularly to acknowledge the patience and support of my family during my immersion in this work, the word processing skills of Caroline Ede, the constructive comments of Professor Michael Connolly on an earlier draft, and the time made available by my University in the final stages of manuscript preparation. The opinions expressed are, of course, my own, and I remain responsible for any errors which may be present.

Grateful acknowledgement is also recorded to the following for permission to reproduce table or figures: the Organization for Economic Co-operation and Development for Figures 4.1 and 4.2; the Local Government Management Board for 'Performance Standards and Targets: Libraries Department' in Case Study 5.2, and for Figure 1.2; the Public Finance Foundation for Figure 5.2; Jessica Kingsley Publishers for Figure 5.1 and G. Quicke for Figure 6.2.

MANAGING THE CONTEMPORARY LOCAL AUTHORITY

1

This first chapter begins to explore the process of managing the contemporary local authority. The key themes of the book – competition, listening to the public, comparative local government management, performance measurement, and information and intelligence – are introduced. Managing local government is considered according to different perspectives drawn from traditional managerial theories and from studies of organizational culture. The political dimension is emphasized throughout, including the growth of the non-elected local state and the lasting implications for accountability.

Introduction: key themes

This book has been written to resemble its own topic of enquiry in the senses that a textbook and the management process alike should both imply:

- clear objectives;
- a structure for their implementation;
- critical self-examination.

The overall aim of the book can be expressed simply. It aims to help the reader to understand the process of managing local government today. Yet this apparently straightforward statement of intent contains terms which need a little elaboration.

- **Process**: running local government is not a matter of mechanical procedures, nor is it a series of (e.g. legislative) events. Process denotes instead the dynamic and changing nature of managing local government.
- **Managing**: a broad definition is adopted throughout of what constitutes management, and in the course of the book the growth (for instance) of contract management in place of traditional line management systems will be discussed. At

a time when the role of the public sector is contested, when resource decisions drive decisions about need, and when private provision is a characteristic of public service as never before, the process of managing local government is as much about politics as about managerial theory. This is assumed, and self-evident, throughout the book.

- **Local government**: this term no longer describes a stable set of institutions with established functions and a fixed structure. The thrust of central government policy since the beginning of the 1980s has undoubtedly been to reduce the scope and scale of local goverment *per se*. However, the changes are more complex than a shrinking of local government's direct service role. As private provision of certain local services increases, so local authorities have new roles in 'enabling'. A range of non-elected but publicly-funded bodies has taken over other functions, particularly in relation to planning and the local economy. The structures of local government itself are continuing to change under the terms of the reorganization of the 1990s.

The book seeks to understand these processes of managing local government by a principal concentration upon **key themes** in running the contemporary local authority, supplemented by (rather than lead by) a focus upon salient aspects of legislation, structure, and administrative procedure.

The key themes to be addressed are as follows.

- **Competition**: the growth of competition is of crucial significance in contemporary local government. Managing competition includes the direct management of the process of Compulsory Competitive Tendering (CCT), the implications of localized managerial regimes such as the local management of schools (LMS), the new relationships with the private sector and with the Health Service implied by 'community care', and the difficulties implied for the corporate and strategic management of the local authority by an increasingly fragmented pattern of local provision. It will become evident on one level that increasing competition requires new managerial skills. More fundamentally, the redefined relationship between public and private provision in and around local government implies that the nature of bureaucratic line management must be recast.

- **The public as consumers**: the 'rediscovery' of the public has taken several forms, open to interpretation as either threats or opportunities to those responsible for running local government. The perceived threat of the public is in its challenge to the paternalism of a local state which aimed or claimed to know best. The opportunity is in the strength which local public services (and public service deliverers) may derive from the public, either in genuine defence of local services or in a more calculated invoking of a local public to help fend off a hostile central government. The terms **consumer**, **citizen** and **community** will be seen to imply rather different notions of the public: with different implications for management. The discussion of a 'consumer perspective' will be both critical and constructive.

- **Comparative local government**: professional practice in local authorities has increasingly become part of an international framework, in several senses. First, European legislation and regulations have provided standards – which, again, may be viewed as threats or as opportunities – for services and for managerial practice. Second, the active role of local authorities in economic development and the reality of a global economy have widened horizons dramatically – driven by the search for resources. Third, industrial societies as a whole face a common agenda of achieving a new balance of taxation, public spending and service provision – and can learn positively or negatively from the example of other countries. Additionally, the academic disciplines of public management and administration are undoubtedly less parochial, less ethnocentric, than has traditionally been the case. A comparative perspective has become essential in seeking to understand the problems of running British local government.

- **Performance management**: it is impossible to understand public services – in local government, the National Health Service and central government agencies alike – without an understanding of how organizational performance is now measured. The growth of performance measurement will be examined from its origins as something imposed by central government upon local authorities into a vehicle by which local government as a whole now examines not only the cost but also the quality and effectiveness of its services. It will be seen that relatively uniform and coherent indicators now exist for the key areas of council activity, but that problems remain in assuming that all such activity is quantifiable and measurable. Problems also exist in linking up performance measurement to performance management – that is, in making an informed use of performance measures as tools of managerial practice rather than as ends in themselves.

- **Information and intelligence**: the broad theme of information contains several distinct elements. First, **access** to information provisions have implications for the work of council managers – implications for time and cost most obviously, but perhaps with more significant implications for the culture of public service provision. Secondly, the **growth** of information (and of the technical means of processing and presenting it) relates directly to the opportunities provided by management information systems. Thirdly, information as **intelligence** forms part of another crucial area: local authority research. This includes the central policy function, strategic intelligence, and support for the corporate planning and management functions. The importance of information in all these senses is clear enough, but information has a cost, it requires organization, and above all it must be the right kind of information at the right time.

In the pages to follow, each theme is explored in turn. These are taken to be the key themes in understanding the changing nature of contemporary local government, in relation to practitioners and to students of local government alike. The interlocking nature of these themes is to be emphasized. It will become evident, for instance, that the growth of competition implies new information needs; or that the growth of a consumer perspective implies that performance measures of public opinion are needed; or that comparative study suggests different approaches to competitive tendering. It is intended that taken as a whole the chosen themes can include all salient developments, for irrespective of political and economic change in the rest of the twentieth century and beyond, these themes will continue to constitute the agenda for local government.

Finally, some points about general approach and general assumptions can be made. Within each of the thematic chapters:

- **case studies** will be used to illustrate and elaborate where appropriate; these are separated from the text as a whole and thus can be consulted readily in considering a specific topic;

- **politics** and the ideological bases of contemporary debates in local government will be recognized fully in seeking to understand current practice;
- **practical implications** will be drawn out from a sometimes necessarily complex and ambiguous reality.

At the end of each chapter, detailed questions and exercises are presented. These have several possible functions. Students may use these as key revision questions or as tools for drawing together the arguments and issues from a particular chapter. Tutors may wish to use these as direct assignment or examination topics. Practitioners may consider these as a lens through which to view practice, or in some cases as a practical design or development exercise. It may be noted that each exercise is followed by an elaboration of possible lines of enquiry, suggestions for reading, and indications of what may lie behind some of the terms of debate.

The contemporary local authority

How can we characterize today's local authority? A standard text on the structure and functions of local government (e.g. Elcock (1994), Byrne (1994)) tells us of formal duties, administrative structures and relevant powers, and of course all these are important. How, though, do we characterize what is **going on** within local government – the day-to-day process of managing change, the practical activity of local government based in the tension with central government? In this task, a knowledge of the structures of local government is necessary but insufficient. We need to dig deeper.

A fundamentally important aspect of running the contemporary local council is the legacy, from 1979, of hostile relationships with central government. Irrespective of political developments from the 1990s onward, local government has been reshaped by the agenda of Conservatism and by an ideological stance unsympathetic to local government values. This legacy matters in several senses.

First, long- or even medium-term financial planning has been undermined by changes to the rules by which central government funds local government and by which local councils are allowed to fund themselves, in addition to the continuing effects of the change from the rating system to the poll tax and then to the council tax.

Secondly, an ever-increasing proportion of local council services has been subject to **compulsory** competitive tender with private companies, thus transfering services from public to private sector without naming the process one of privatization.

Thirdly, local councils have found their duties and powers being transferred to non-elected bodies, publicly funded but based on appointees rather than elected representatives. Wilson and Game (1994) point out, citing the earlier creation of the NHS and the setting up of bodies such as New Town Development Corporations, that while non-elected local government in itself is not new

> What is new is the rapid growth of additional non- elected or indirectly elected bodies **at the expense of** directly elected councils. Throughout the 1980s service responsibilities have been removed from local authorities and given to mainly single purpose Government-appointed agencies (Wilson and Game, 1994, p. 13, emphasis in original).

Whatever the merits or otherwise of these changes, the point is that they have had an immediate impact on the practical matter of running a local council: resources are not only limited (of course they are) but the basis on which they are allocated is highly uncertain; competition is present throughout significant layers of council activity; and the existence of the elected local authority itself cannot be taken for granted.

For some, perhaps, this high degree of change and uncertainty can be held up as desirable, as somehow approximating to the real-world market of the private sector and thus productive of tough efficient management in local government. Yet this argument rather neglects the fact that the best private-sector companies actively seek to **replace** the kind of uncertain environment so deliberately created for local councils by stable conditions more conducive to service quality, employee care and, indeed, efficiency.

As will be seen throughout the discussion to follow, running local government has undergone a **cultural** change. Whether or not councils stand in opposition to the drift of central government policy, and whatever the local mix of public and private service provision, the culture of local government management has changed. In looking, for instance, at compulsory competitive tendering, this change can be regarded as one where a 'commercial ethos', a 'business awareness' or, less approvingly perhaps, an 'accountancy culture' have grown in significance (Shaw, Fenwick and Foreman, 1994, p. 211). This does not mean that public sector management has simply become akin to private-sector management. However, the public–private mix has changed, and the social–public service values of the local government sector have had to adapt.

The exact way in which public-sector management has adapted is the subject of current debate among both theorists and practitioners. A summary of debates such as that provided by McKevitt and Lawton (eds, 1994) reminds us that perspectives on public-sector management range widely across the political spectrum and that notions such as that of organizational culture itself are contested. Painter examines the management of change in local government, pointing to an uncertainty in some councils about their 'primary mission' but, equally, a greater emphasis upon strategic planning and management (1993, pp. 50–1). If this is an accurate depiction of the current direction of local authority management, the problem would seem to be that as the need for strategic management grows, so the difficulty of achieving it grows too. **The very forces – financial and political – which propel local government toward thinking strategically prevent it from acting strategically.**

This dilemma will appear again in subsequent discussion. For now, the problem of strategic planning can be noted as one of the key issues for corporate management. It potentially pulls a local authority in quite a different direction from the equally strong pressures to extend project management around particular cost centres or specific items of work.

Stewart's review (1994) of local government management considers – in addition to some of the issues already raised – the scale of **social** change, including the decline of traditional industries, persistent mass unemployment, growth of the elderly population, growth in numbers of single-parent families, the reality of a multi-ethnic society, environmental concern, social division, and the extra-national nature of problems and solutions (1994, p. 3). All these aspects of change in society would impact upon local government even in the absence of the financial and political factors already mentioned.

> It is commonplace to state that local government faces a rapidly changing society, yet it is not the rapidity of change that should be emphasized but the number of dimensions on which change is taking place (Stewart, 1994, p. 3).

The scale of change has brought with it concrete organizational changes within which the process of management takes place. These changes include the development of a flatter structure, control by contract in place of control by hierarchy, arm's-length organization of commercial functions, the client–contractor split, independent inspection, decentralization, the changing role of the centre, the decline of traditional service committees and the growth of management boards, new cycles for council activity within the traditional undifferentiated annual cycle, new ways in which the council itself may meet, and corresponding changes to the structure of political leadership on the local level (Stewart, 1994, pp. 17–18). In addition, there has been increasing attention to 'subnational government' as a whole, rather than to local government in isolation (e.g. Gray, 1994).

These are all aspects of what is 'going on' in local authorities today – the **context** within which the practical matter of running local government occurs. It is now appropriate to focus upon perhaps the most significant feature all. This is the **fragmentation** of local authority management.

The fragmentation of management

The consequence of successive changes made to the local government sector via legislation, competition, political pressures and financial uncertainty is that management has become fragmented. By fragmentation, we mean the replacement of traditional forms of direct service provision by a more complex oversight of various forms of delivering services. Figure 1.1 sums up old and new styles and methods of management.

Figure 1.1 summarizes key features of the move away from unified hierarchical management of direct service provision: by far the most significant feature of 'fragmentation'. The old and new forms of management also have their local **political** counterparts. Traditional service committees have tended to give way to a client–contractor/purchaser–provider form of organization on the level of the elected councillor too, or a cross-service form of committee organization based around particular user groups.

What then are the **consequences** of this changed pattern of local authority management? It is evident that this more diverse pattern of service management requires rather different **skills** from the ones associated with traditional line-management, a point which will be developed further below. Identification of further consequences depends on how we evaluate, rather than merely describe, these changes. For instance, the move toward employment of the professional manager to head a major service department depends on judgements about the nature of public services and the responsibility of the senior manager. In the public sector, these judgements are contested. This is not a matter of managerial theory. It is, like much else we will encounter, a political question.

Old

• Direct provision of all stages of service direct to user

Characteristics

• Hierarchical system of line-management
• Manager as professional qualified in the area of service delivery
• Real budgetary control retained at the centre of the authority
• Monopoly
• Stability of expectations from staff and public
• Public funding and public provision with peripheral charging element

New

• Provision of some services direct; partial provision of some services via other public and private agencies

Characteristics

• Management by contract (i.e. around a preset specification for a particular service)
• Management by project (i.e. around a particular initiative, development or area of work)
• Manager as skilled in 'management' *per se*, transferable to various professional settings
• Budgetary devolution
• Partial competition
• Changing expectations of public services
• Public and private funding and provision

Figure 1.1   Old and new management in local government

This is a suitable point at which to reintroduce the importance of the changing **culture** of local government. The fragmentation of management reflects and is reflected by this cultural change. It has been a part of central government's agenda since the late 1970s to effect a cultural change in the way public services are run and delivered, based around a particular view of how the private sector goes about its work.

> Many of the changes sought by the government can be seen as attempts to change the cultures of the public services, dominated as they have been by the traditions of administration, hierarchy and professionalism (Stewart and Walsh, 1992, p. 508).

Indeed, the culture **has** changed along with managerial structures, although not always in the way central government has intended. It will be seen in the discussion of performance measurement, for instance, that in discovering the 'performance culture', local government discovered a powerful weapon in its battle with central government for resources. The fragmentation of managerial structures and the changes in organizational cultures in contemporary local government are of central importance and are closely interlinked.

Yet 'structure and culture' may seem mere abstractions. What does fragmentation **mean** in practice? To address this question, the first case study considers the arrangements for 'community care' implemented from 1993 under the terms of the National Health Service and Community Care Act 1990.

CASE STUDY 1.1 Managing community care

'Community care' has both a **general** meaning relating to care and support outside of institutions, perhaps specifically within the family or through informal neighbourhood ties, and a number of **specific** formal meanings relating to particular government policies such as people with a mental illness moving from hospital to 'community', or people with a mental handicap or special needs moving from residential care to substitute family care. The government's perspective on community care as a whole is set out in its White Paper 'Caring for People' (1989). In this case study, community care is taken to refer to the provisions of the National Health Service and Community Care Act 1990, implemented in April 1993, which govern a range of domiciliary (i.e. provided at home) services but, particularly, set up new residential care arrangements for the elderly and for people with disabilities or with needs for continuing nursing care, and new arrangements for paying for those services.

Community care in this specific sense incorporates a number of themes of general importance including:

- **public and private**: residential care is not directly provided by the local authority alone; it is provided by both private and public sectors;
- **multi-agency provision**: the links between health services and local authority, as well as between public and private providers, are extended;
- **management by contract**: private institutions enter into contracts with their local council to provide care to a certain specification at a certain price;
- **extending choice**: it can be argued that public choice is increased by the ability to select the preferred accommodation, up to a cash limit.

These themes correspond to the changed public service model of the local authority 'enabling' and providing a framework for a service. Under community care, the local council is still responsible for assessment of individual needs, for a 'care plan', and in this capacity the local authority arguably has a greater role than before. However, the actual provision of care passes substantially to those privately owned institutions under contract to the council.

The council determines the terms of the contract (some of which were, on implementation, initially subject to appeals from private owners). In addition, there continues to be as before a private sector outside the scope of the scheme, charging its own rates, though subject to whatever inspection arrangements exist – as there is, indeed, for health care or education.

The changed **management** of community care is evident on a number of levels:

- at the corporate/planning level, a greater emphasis on resource management;
- at the level of providing individual care, a greater emphasis on co-ordination of staff and agencies involved;
- at the local political/policy level, a statutory framework which reduces direct provision and reduces local authority control overall.

Whether this signifies an efficient economical service based on arranging packages of care to meet individual needs, or a disjointed service which reduces the quality of care and also reduces the role of the local council is a separate matter –though eventually the most important one.

As an indication of general changes in local authority management, this example of community care is of general relevance. It illustrates how a relatively fragmented form of managing the service overall has come into being, involving as it does the local authority (and within this distinct staff at the levels of professional care, corporate mangement, resource allocation etc), health service liaison, private sector providers, and central government, in its determination of the overall framework.

So far, some general changes in the nature of local authority management have been suggested, with particular illustrations, and the continuing importance of changing organizational culture has been identified. These issues form the basis of the book as a whole. Before considering the first specifc theme, however, it is necessary to consider the process of management itself a little more closely.

What does it mean to 'manage' local government?

So far:

- a broad definition of local authority management has been advocated

and it has been suggested that

- there has been a decline of line management based upon monopolistic direct service provision;
- there are changed skills associated with the growth of project and contract management;
- there is a tendency toward the (often fixed-term) appointment of senior managers possessing general 'management' skills rather than expertise in the area of professional activity associated with work in their departments or units;

- while the direct influence of the private sector on methods of delivering services and of running departments, and the indirect influence of private-sector models of organization are significant, there has been no simple or straightforward adoption of private-sector approaches in local government.

Developing the initial depiction of local authority management a little further requires some consideration of what it means to be a 'professional' manager in local government. Gyford (1993b) identifies the growth of two distinct challenges to professionalism in local government – one managerial, the other political. The managerial challenge to professionalism in its early stages was expressed as a corporate challenge to departmentalism, a critique of narrowly defined professional interests; the political challenge to professionalism was expressed in a refusal of sections of the public to accept the legitimacy of professional solutions (Gyford, 1993b, p. 13).

Loughlin links the challenge to professionalism to the growth of more precise performance measures (1992, p. 21). More recently, notes Gyford, the political critique of the 'professional' in local government could be seen to subdivide into distinct New Right and Left versions, each unhappy with the alleged expertise and actual power of professionals, but offering different solutions. The managerial critique of professionalism has developed further too. As will be discussed later, the 'new' public management and the consumer perspective represent critical approaches to professional competence *per se*, whether departmental or corporate.

By the 1990s, argues Gyford, the 'managerial' approach increasingly emphasized the applicability of private-sector techniques, and overall three 'styles of decision-making' had evolved in local government: the **professional**, the **managerial** and that of **democratic politics** (1993b, p. 15). Gyford's characterization of how each of these three modes of making decisions embodies different assumptions – we might say, different **values** – is presented in Figure 1.2. It helps to address our task of defining what it means to 'manage' local government today. It also illustrates once again the interconnectedness of management and politics which is important throughout.

Within this matrix, where does the individual manager in the local authority stand? The new public management may seem to reflect an attractive 'apolitical' approach,

	Professionalism	Managerialism	Democratic politics
Perception of public	Clients	Consumers	Citizens
Basis of evaluation	Professional standards	Performance indicators	Interest defence
Ethos	Mystery	Clarity	Ambiguity
Mode of evaluation	Judgement	Measurement	Argument

Source: Gyford, 1993b, p. 15.

Figure 1.2   Modes of decision-making in local government

yet perhaps the private-sector inspired 'managerialist' is really only implementing the political agenda of the New Right (Gyford, 1993b, pp. 16–18).

To draw some of these strands together, it would seem to be beyond argument that the individual manager in a local authority is working within a **framework**, making **decisions** and to some extent using a **vocabulary** which have all been politically generated, i.e. generated on the level of values, interests and power. The complications arise because these very values are today in dispute. What is significant, then, is not that the council officer works in a political environment but that the politics are non-consensual in nature. Battles between local and central governments accentuate this further. The 'new' public management and an assertive 'managerialism' both embody particular values. Yet traditional 'professionalism' represents a specific set of values too. By this account, any discussion of managing local government as a set of techniques – as an essentially neutral process of implementing generally applicable management theories and models – is inappropriate.

Yet it has been the claim of management theorists that general management techniques not only exist, but may be scientific in nature. Such an approach continues to be influential. The principal approaches are well-known, but may usefully be summarized here as a reference point.

- **Scientific management** assumes (a) that a given job can be broken down into its constituent parts, with each part measured, timed and analysed irrespective of context, and (b) that there is an objectively best way of doing the job, again irrespective of context. Taken literally, such 'scientific' management – also known as Taylorism, after its founder – is concerned with universal principles and methods just as applicable to local government as to any type of private company. In practice, no-one today would sensibly propose such a crude application of scientific management, but as a perspective it has influenced critiques of local authority management, particularly those from the Right. Its emphasis on employees acting rationally, and being differently rewarded according to results, fits in well with latter-day market-based theories.

- The **human relations** school, associated with Mayo, assumes that the social group, and in particular the interpersonal relations of the workgroup, are just as important as the actual organization of the job in determining output and performance. The well-known Hawthorne experiments in the United States in the 1920s and 1930s appeared to demonstrate that the solidarity of the workgroup at the Western Electric Company, and for that matter the seemingly benign interest shown in the group by the researchers, had a greater impact than physical conditions or economic incentives had on output. The assumptions of the human relations approach clearly run counter to those of the rational economic actor embodied in the scientific management model. It may also be noted – of some relevance today – that scientific management is an individualist theory of organizational behaviour, while human relations emphasizes the group.

- **Systems theory** focuses exclusively upon neither the task nor upon the actor, but instead, not surprisingly, upon the organization as system. The 'system' includes both structure and culture – that is, the formal organization, and its culture and values – consistent with some of our opening remarks above on understanding local government systems. The 'system' also includes internal and external components (e.g. local and central government). A characteristic of any system is that change in one part has an effect upon other parts of the system. A development of systems theory is **contingency** theory which:

highlights possible means of differentiating between alternative forms of organization structures and systems of management. **There is no one optimum state**. For example, the structure of the organization and its 'success' are dependent upon the nature of the tasks with which it is designed to deal and the nature of environmental influences. The most appropriate structure and system of management is, therefore, dependent upon the contingencies of the situation for each particular organization (Mullins, 1993, p. 52, emphasis added).

Such perspectives, and others, have influenced the development of thinking about both private- and public-sector management. The relevance of such perspectives to the **contemporary practice** of **public management** is a matter for personal assessment, but some connections are fairly obviously there. The systems approach is widely drawn and dynamic enough to inform, to some extent, our own discussion of change in local government. However, the discussions below tend to place relatively more emphasis upon culture than upon structure.

More generally, the growth of 'human resource management' in contemporary local government could hardly have occurred without the initial development of the human relations school. Scientific management too continues to have an impact. Pollitt (1990) has discussed the rise in public-service management of a 'neo Taylorism' which dressed the original emphases upon economic self-interest and individualism in a manner suitable for the prevailing political and economic conditions of the Thatcher and Reagan years. Arguably the process has continued in the post-Thatcher/Reagan era too. Further, on a more everyday level, elements of scientific management have attained a general currency. Techniques which are relatively commonplace in public and private sectors alike, including work study, organization and methods and payment by results derive directly from scientific management (Mullins, 1993, p. 39).

Let us sum up so far. We have been considering, at this initial stage, **what it means** to talk of local authority management. A broad definition of management has been proposed and the decline of traditional line management has been referred to. It has been argued that the growth of competition and the influence of private-sector perspectives have changed not only the environment of local authority management but also the skills required of the manager. The critiques of the 'professional' manager from both Left and Right have also created additional pressures for change, many of which will be explored in the following chapters.

The traditional theories of organization and management in their original forms propose universal techniques of management which seem to be of very limited value in local government today. However, some elements of these theories have a continuing relevance which must be addressed within current debates, including for instance the rediscovery of scientific management in the agenda of the New Right and, particularly, in some of the challenges to the perceived welfare ethic of local government.

This brings us once again to the importance of the changing culture of local government. As argued above, the characteristic fragmentation of management in local government today is linked to cultural change. An attempt to describe what it means to manage local government inevitably returns to cultural change. This cultural change can take in the critique of professionalism, the growth of a 'new' public management, the partial rehabilitation of traditional management theories and the changing skills of the council manager.

The general importance of organizational and managerial culture has long been recognized. Handy (1985, pp. 186–96) refers to the links between organizational culture, structure, and subsequent system, identifying:

- the **power culture** of the entrepreneurial organization (perhaps enjoying something of a revival);
- the **role culture** of the bureaucratic organization where formal role is more important than the person who happens to occupy it (perhaps applicable to unreconstructed local government in its 'paternalist' phase of expansion);
- the **task culture** of the group or the project team around a specific task (of increasing importance in the public sector as project and contract management grows);
- the **person culture** of a group without any overarching, superordinate, objectives where a 'cluster' of individuals is more important than the formal organization (with little immediate applicability to local government today).

Such a terminology of organizational cultures is still valuable. Within such a framework can be added the vocabulary of latter-day public management. For instance, there is now a **quality culture** – or there is at least talk about a quality culture – across many public-service organizations. This may take the form of a search for 'total quality management' (TQM) across the organization as a whole, or perhaps through the setting up of 'quality circles' of employees (and users) to guide the process. Individual departments of local councils may seek their own formal quality recognition, for instance the particular ways in which BS5750 as the British standard of quality **assurance** can be achieved in local authority social services departments (Patel, 1994). As Patel points out, BS5750 was formulated originally for manufacturing industry not for public services, and it has undergone recent modification for this rather different environment (1994, p. 6).

The general question is raised here once more of the applicability of private-sector methods to the public sector – a continuing theme. In addition to a culture of quality there is of course in all public services a culture of **the market**. Again, this is a recurring theme. It can be argued that public service management now somehow straddles 'state' and 'market' and, related to this, that the very boundaries between public and private are increasingly blurred. When, say, a National Health Service trust enters into co-operation with a private provider it would seem difficult to distinguish public from private provision with absolute precision.

> The new management of the public services involves an attempt to have the best of the market and government, through the development of market mechanisms within the state (Walsh, 1993, p. 7).

Quality culture may be talked about but not achieved. Market culture may be a rhetoric for increased centralism. These conceptual ambiguities are also problems of practice. The gap between what these terms seem to mean and what they actually deliver is something to be 'managed' too: within the new culture of local government.

Concluding comments

In this summary of the scope of the book, and this initial sketch of what it means to talk of 'managing local government', considerable emphasis has been placed upon cultural change and upon the inter-relationship of the managerial and political levels. The task in the following chapters is to link this to practice through exploration of the key themes already defined.

Wilson and Game's discussion of the developing internal management of local councils emphasizes culture, values, 'enabling', listening to the customer, and, once more, refers to debates about the 'professional' which remind us of a long-standing tension between departmentalism and corporatism:

> departmental dominance is increasingly being questioned as a more customer conscious ethic develops. Professionally qualified staff are not necessarily good managers. Often they have a very narrow focus of interest and fail to think in authority-wide terms (1994, p. 315).

Departmental and **corporate** remains an important dichotomy in any local authority. The dichotomy between private and public is even more important. The differences and similarities between private and public management will be something of a background issue throughout the book, but an important difference to identify at this stage is that of accountability. As we will see, the process of compulsory competition for defined local services and the considerable number of other changes to local government generated by the Conservative years have been in the name of a greater 'accountability' which seems to have meant a **budgetary** accountability and a fairly vague accountability to the public, conceived as a collection of individuals.

Yet resistance to the very same changes has also been couched in terms of preserving a **political** accountability, through the local democratic process, to the community, defined as a collectivity. The many meanings of accountability in local government –administrative, legal, political – are dealt with by for instance Loughlin (1992).

Whatever interpretation of accountability in public management is offered – and differences of interpretation are largely determined politically – the differences with the private sector are evident enough. The private-sector concept of accountability is largely one defined by ownership. The local government manager however is not accountable to a group of shareholders, nor to an individual private owner. Patterns of accountability in local government are to the local population through elected representatives, to central government through its increasing volume of direct regulation, to formal specifications for contracts, and to budgets. The particular nature of **public-sector accountability** is the final element of our initial characterization of what it means to talk of managing local government today.

Summary

In this initial review, public sector management in the contemporary local authority has been described as requiring particular skills based on the growth of competition and contracts, changes in political accountability, the decline of traditional public-service paternalism, and cultural changes in the way the public is perceived. The boundaries of public and private are rapidly changing, and there is a trend towards the fragmentation of hitherto monopolistic direct service provision by local councils. A critical view has been taken of perspectives which propose that managerial skills and methods can be defined in common across public and private sectors. Decision making in local government has been considered in its managerial and political senses, to be more fully explored in the following chapters by reference to the book's key themes and case studies.

Discussion questions and guidance

1. *What do you consider to be the most significant changes in local authority management in recent years? Illustrate with a detailed example with which you are familiar.*

This question, general in its approach, is designed to help you to examine your own view of the changing management of local government before proceeding further. Additionally, it may be productive, after answering this question, to come back to it again on completion of the book. Your definition of 'recent years' should be spelled out at the beginning. Several general changes in the way local government is run have been discussed in Chapter 1, including the growth of management by contract and the decline of hierarchical line management systems. Do you agree?

Your answer may well also include an assessment of the changed balance of private and public sector management. Remember that 'management' in local government potentially includes the section head and the chief executive, operational managers, corporate planners, and in-house contractors. Clearly, some roles may have changed more than others, and in different ways. To prevent over-generalization, and to keep answers grounded in practice, note also that the question requires a specific worked example from your experience, or from your own reading and research.

2. *In the age of the non-elected local state, is local government irrelevant?*

The question invites a discussion of whether local government remains important in the light of the expansion of appointed rather than elected QUANGOs and single-purpose boards. It was noted in Chapter 1 that Wilson and Game (1994) pointed to the growth of non-elected agencies 'at the expense' of local authorities. Does this matter, and, if so, why?

A critical response should extend to the terms of the question itself of course. Not everyone would accept that this is 'the age of the non-elected local state' – though, if not, supporting arguments need to be aired.

For a critical discussion of central government strategy toward the local state during the Conservative years see Cochrane (1993, ch. 2).

It will be necessary to consider suitable examples of non-elected public agencies, for instance the Urban Development Corporations whose planning powers override those of the local authorities for the area, the growth of the TECs (Training and Education Councils), or the Funding Agency for Schools which from April 1994 began to take over spending on grant-maintained schools. The Local Government Information Unit (1994b) points out that the public money spent by QUANGOs exceeds that spent by local government. These figures include health service spending within the QUANGO total, since the elective element of health authorities (via local councils) disappeared in 1991.

Moving from specific examples, the question more fundamentally is about the relevance of local government on the level of **values** and local public accountability.

Do local authorities and non-elected agencies represent different value systems, and does this impact upon styles and methods of management?

3. *'Have the new public management class (consciously or unwittingly) allowed themselves to become vehicles for a particular (narrow) set of political values?' (Painter, Isaac-Henry and Barnes, 1993, p. 184).*

The quotation raises the uncomfortable but very important issue of the relationship between political values – in this case, those of central government – and management practice. Later in this book, aspects of the 'new' public management such as responsiveness to the customer, quality and managerial devolution will be discussed. For now, however, the question implies a general discussion of how the agenda and methods of local authority management are determined politically, and some of the dangers inherent in this. It may be useful here to **define** the dominant values of central government, and contrast these to what you consider to be the values underlying local government services. There is of course a point of view which would accept that the new public management does indeed embody a narrow set of political values, but that this is functional and desirable as it leads to greater efficiency. The question could be tackled with reference to Chapter 1 alone, especially the discussion of the **themes** of the book, but it would be preferable to read more widely, perhaps starting with the paper by Painter, Isaac-Henry and Barnes (1993) from which the quotation is taken.

4. *Do the available theories of organization and management help us to understand the problems of running a local authority today?*

An overall assessment of the applicability to local government of the standard theories of management is sought here. Note that an assessment is not just a description. An attempt is required here to evaluate which of the existing theories (if any) are useful in understanding contemporary local authority management.

The 'available theories' are those referred to in Chapter 1, including scientific management, contingency theory, human relations and other schools of thought or management models with which you are familiar. For a summary of these theories see for instance Mullins (1993). A critical set of readings such as that of McKevitt and Lawton (1994) takes the discussion a little further.

As with question 1 above, it may be useful to come back to this question again on completion of the book, in order to re-examine your initial conclusions.

Suggested further reading

Byrne, T. (1994) *Local Government in Britain: Everyone's Guide to How it All Works* (6th edition), Penguin, Harmondsworth. This concise account of contemporary local government is a useful reference source, either for readers unfamiliar with British local government or those who require an update of the local government system.

Wilson, D. and Game, C. with Leach, S. and Stoker, G. (1994) *Local Government in the United Kingdom*, Macmillan, London. A critical discussion of issues and problems in local government today, with supporting examples.

Blackman, T. (1995) *Urban Policy in Practice*, Routledge, London. An account of services on the local level in urban areas which examines the role of local government and other service providers. Includes relevant detailed case study material.

Flynn, N. (1993) *Public Sector Management* (2nd edition), Harvester Wheatsheaf, London. An effective introduction to public sector management as a whole which provides a useful context for examining the specifics of local government.

Cochrane, A. (1993) *Whatever Happened to Local Government?* Open University Press, Buckingham. A series of essays which sets the problems of local government in the ideological and theoretical context of overall welfare restructuring.

Farnham, D. and Horton, S. (eds) (1993) *Managing the New Public Services*, Macmillan, London. Readings which refer to different aspects of running the 'new' public services, again providing a context for understanding the particular role of the local authority.

MANAGING COMPETITION

2

Although local government has never been the monopoly provider of every local service, it enjoyed until the 1980s a freedom from significant commercial competition in relation to its main areas of activity. Private provision of education, or of residential accommodation for elderly people, is not new, but the **relationship** between local authority and private sector has changed. It can no longer be assumed that the large-scale provision of educational services, social services, housing, environmental services and the range of technical and support activities will continue to be the responsibility of local government. Local authorities have been compelled through central government legislation to participate ever more fully in the marketplace. Thus the senior council officer increasingly has to **manage within a competitive environment**.

Introduction

Competition has a number of distinct meanings in the context of local authority management. It is important – both for clarity of analysis and for effective practice – to identify the different connotations of competition, while bearing in mind that politicians (local or central) may seek to blur these same distinctions.

First, competition may denote a direct contest between public sector (the local authority) and private sector for provision of a specific service – one of the 'defined activities' within the terms of the Local Government Act 1988 (and subsequent regulations) such as refuse collection and school meals. The development of Compulsory Competitive Tendering (CCT) is discussed below, with examples of practice, together with a review of whether local authority management becomes fragmented as a result.

Secondly, competition may be seen to result from an obligation upon the local council to sell off public assets – such as council houses – into private ownership. A more competitive housing market results (according to central government) in the sense that a fundamentally different **mix** of public/private provision comes to prevail. Here, it is assumed that the market and the service concerned become more competitive as a direct consequence of a greater element of private provision.

Thirdly, competition may denote the introduction of a market **mechanism**, even where the public/private balance is unchanged. This form of quasi-market competition is perhaps most clearly developed within the internal market of the National Health Service. Within local government, the Local Management of Schools (LMS) – following the Education Reform Act 1988 and subsequent DES Circular 7/88 – sought to introduce market characteristics such as budgetary devolution and responsibility, and the delegation of powers to hire contractors and suppliers, into the running of schools. LMS also began to imply competition between schools, insofar as formula-led funding tends to encourage schools to maximize pupil numbers. Schools which opt out of local authority control altogether (not to be confused with LMS which obtains in all schools) of course take competition a step further, for LEA schools then compete (for pupils, and for resources) directly with their central government grant-supported counterparts. LMS is considered in more detail below.

Thus, competition in contemporary local government refers to a range of processes, not a single phenomenon. Further, competition is not invariably about greater choice at the point of use. In the case of CCT, competition is not about greater user choice at all. In such cases, why is competition then held to be desirable? The advocates of greater competition tend to argue its merits in terms of greater efficiency, through the driving-down of producer (and, hence, consumer) costs. Competition is, in these circumstances, presented as cheaper. When **this** is not so, the virtues of competition tend to be argued as those of quality: the quality of service will improve.

What, then, is the guarantor of this quality? Consumer choice. These arguments tend to be rather circular, and there are no established criteria for evaluating the overall success of benefits of competition in local government in all its forms. It must be remembered that the main thrust for increased competition has been ideological: the relevant legislation has derived from the clearly stated political priorities of the then Thatcher administrations. The discussions of competition in this chapter must refer to this essentially political context. It makes no sense to try to understand competition as an administrative or procedural topic. It involves management at its most politically exposed.

Furthermore, the management of competition is not only about direct service-provision. Even where the local authority no longer provides a particular service, it may still 'manage' the (public or private) provision of that service. The local authority provides the framework, the initial specification (in its 'client' role), and provides the monitoring and evaluation. The local authority constitutes a system of infrastructure, of which direct service provision is only one part. This implies the development of new skills of the part of council managers, perhaps more closely linked to project management and resource management than to traditional local authority line-management. This too is discussed below.

Managing competition is not only about acquisition of new skills. It is also, more fundamentally, about the nature of public and private provision. Even where a local authority retains a service in-house by successful tendering, it may have done so by changes to the service, or to working conditions, which more closely resemble a private bid than one from a local authority. In short, local councils may begin to resemble private contractors in order to win contracts. The fact or fear of competition may considerably affect the management of the particular service: crudely, a commercialization of the service in question.

Significantly, competition may increase **management** choice, even where consumer choice is not extended. On the everyday level, managers may become increasingly free to buy-in their support services, choose their suppliers, or control their budgets. However, it is equally important to realize that competition constrains management choice, by the very discipline of the market which is held initially to be so desirable.

Competition also affects the accountability of the local authority to its electors. The examples of CCT and of LMS change the traditional responsibilities of the elected councillor via the council officer to the public at large. This can be portrayed as a healthy democratization – a handing back of power to individuals alongside an attack on the unresponsive bureaucracy of local government – as central government claimed for LMS. However, it could equally be seen as a transfer of power from local government to central government rather than to the public, given that the point of competition is not the individual user, and given that the rules of the game are centrally determined. Thus an ostensible 'competition' may amount to centralization, not decentralization. Both sorts of consequences can be claimed for the 'competitive environment' in local government. Whatever view is taken, managers have to work with the fact of competition.

This chapter explores key aspects of competition, together with examples of practice and some enduring problems.

The impact of Compulsory Competitive Tendering (CCT) on the culture and management of local government

Local authorities, historically, have been able to **choose** to engage private contractors (e.g. for environmental services or transport) in competition with their own workforce, or indeed in preference to retaining the service in-house. Such voluntaristic outside provision tended in the early 1980s to be strongest amongst those local authorities ideologically committed to the priorities of Thatcherism. Southend, Wandsworth and, later, Bradford, are usually regarded as leading examples of a move to greater private provision where the freedom (in contrast to the obligation) to contract-out exists. The motive force was ideological and political as much as it was economic. A model of how local government with a significant private-sector involvement could henceforth conduct its affairs was, it seemed, being offered for all to emulate. The priorities of the political leadership led in turn to the kinds of managerial change consistent with an entrepreneurial and commercial model of management for local government.

The contracting-out of services – where no obligation to do so exists – has continued throughout the 1980s and into the 1990s. For instance, Berkshire County Council privatized its corporate finance function (Coppell and Brown, 1993) and transferred its highways Direct Labour Organization to the private sector (Morris, 1992).

Alongside the patchy and uneven growth of private contracting by choice, the first moves were made toward **legal compulsion** upon local councils to submit certain services to outside competition. The Planning and Land Act 1980 introduced Compulsory Competitive Tendering (CCT) for certain building, highways, construction and housing maintenance activity. The council's Direct Labour Organization (DLO) – as it was then known – was compelled to compete with private contractors for part of its work, and for its own jobs. The significance of the 1980 legislation was not in the **quantity** of work actually contracted-out, nor even the quantity subject to contracting, but in the **qualitative** change to how local services would henceforth be organized and delivered. Specifically, these changes were:

- the compulsion to offer specified services to outside tender;
- the obligation to keep separate trading accounts for in-house contracts, and to make a return on these;
- the beginnings of a distinction between the local authority as client (specifying the service requirements on behalf, one might say, of those who will use the service) and the local authority as contractor (providing the specified service) and the possible tension between the two;
- the growth of a commercial culture in the running of local authority services.

Thus, the organizational, managerial and cultural changes associated with CCT were already underway when the Local Government Act 1988 was enacted. The 1988 Act, however, took all these changes much further. A new range of 'defined activities' was made subject to CCT. These activities include: catering, street cleaning, building cleaning, grounds maintenance, repair and maintenance of vehicles, leisure management and refuse collection. The list can be extended by Order under the 1988 Act without the need for further legislation – leisure management was added by this method at an early stage. Some of the implications of the further extension of CCT to white collar services and to housing management will be discussed below. In addition to the prescriptions of domestic CCT legislation, local government in the UK is also bound by European regulations: specifically, by the provisions of Public Procurement Directives which apply when services are subject to tender. Significantly, as Baddeley puts it, 'British Local Government is experiencing the simultaneous pressure of **two** regulatory systems' (1992, p. 5, emphasis in original).

Where services are contracted out, the total activity of the local authority is of course reduced: a simple **quantitative** effect of CCT. This is important, not least for jobs, and without doubt it has been part of the agenda of central government to reduce the scope of direct council provision. However, a more significant and fundamental consequence of CCT is that even where services are won in-house, the nature of provision has changed. Reduction of wage costs, a 'businesslike' management and the growth of a commercial culture are increasingly features of successful bids whether these originate from the private sector **or from the in-house council contractor.** If this perspective is accurate, the political goals of CCT have largely been achieved irrespective of the particular division between public and private provision, for the cultural change has already happened (Fenwick, Shaw and Foreman, 1994, p. 11).

The cultural changes in local government provision under conditions of CCT should not be over-simplified. The suggestion is not that local authorities are becoming indistinguishable from private companies. As discussed in Chapters 1 and 7, the **values** of local government continue to be distinct from those of a purely commercial enterprise. However, local government management is taking on features hitherto characteristic of the private sector, and increasingly there are common skills in resource management, management of cost centres, marketing and 'customer care'.

CCT and the client–contractor split

A particular complexity in responding to the demands of CCT is the distinction between management of the contractor side (where it has remained in-house) and management of the client side (the Department or other part of the authority which has specified the service it wants).

CASE STUDY 2.1   A clear client–contractor split under CCT

Research into local authority responses to compulsory competitive tendering, conducted in the north of England in 1991–2, suggests that although a clear client–contractor split tends to prevail, there are numerous variations in organizational and managerial arrangements (see Shaw, Fenwick and Foreman, 1993; Fenwick, Shaw and Foreman, 1993).

On the contractor side, a single Direct Service Organization (DSO) covering all services may exist, or the DSO function may be carried out by separate contracting units for each service (or group of services). Some of the implications for 'managing the split' are discussed in Shaw, Fenwick and Foreman (1993). The DSO and its consequences for managing the local authority are also reviewed by Hender (1993).

A clear organizational separation of the client and contractor roles exists in the following urban authority, one of the councils included in the study of CCT in the north of England referred to above.

In this council, the decision to have one large DSO (for all services except one) was made in 1988. The trade unions were very much 'incorporated' into the planning processes of this (Labour) authority and although staff had been lost, national agreements had been maintained – in contrast to many other authorities. The DSO buildings were physically separate from the main council offices. As the Director of the DSO noted: 'we moved the Department up here as I wanted to get rid of the Civic Centre mentality'. He did not consider that this change of attitude had yet spread to the rest of the authority.

Thus, a distinct split existed on the physical level, in managerial structures – strong line management within the contracting operation – and also on the elected members' level in the reorganized committee structure. The same senior officer noted that the authority wishes to be 'seen to be whiter than white' in its organization of the split and in its monitoring arrangements, perhaps leading to a split for its own sake in some areas. Partly to compensate for this, the customer services part of the DSO monitors contracts, and investigates complaints/comments, but is funded by the client-side via service-level agreements. To some extent this softens the impact of a strict client–contractor split.

At least one view from an officer within this organization felt 'the split is wasteful and inefficient ... the DSO has the council's best interests at heart and produces surpluses it can use'. Only if there was an outside (private) contractor would this separate client role be seen to be so necessary.

This example of a fairly strict client–contractor split also contained mechanisms for managing some of the tensions which arise from too harsh a division of functions. There is also the question of how far the local authority maintains a corporate identity in this potential clash of structures and cultures within the council itself. The DSO manager commented: 'we have to seek the best of commercialism, **but at the same time retain traditional local government values'.**

As CCT has developed, an identifiable split between client and contractor sides within the local authority has tended to be the norm, consistent with the guidelines of the Audit Commission and the accepted spirit of the initial legislation (Fenwick, Shaw and Foreman, 1993, p. 24). The Local Government Act 1992 has subsequently reduced the scope for avoiding such a split still further. Nevertheless, the formal client–contractor 'split' is not identical in every local authority. The in-house Direct Service Organization (DSO) may be entirely separate structurally and geographically, or the split may be relatively less distinct. Case study 2.2 provides a detailed illustration of a local authority which under the terms of the 1988 Act chose to avoid a strict client–contractor split.

CASE STUDY 2.2 Keeping the client and contractor functions together under CCT

The Local Government Act 1988 did not create a statutory obligation to split the client and contractor functions under conditions of CCT, although it became the practice of most local authorities to do so. Subsequent regulations governing 'anti-competitive' practice (issued under the legislative authority of Section 9 of the Local Government Act 1992) reinforce the likelihood of a client–contractor split by prohibiting officers at any level below chief officer from having dual client–contractor responsibilities at key stages in the tendering process (Local Government (Direct Service Organizations) Regulations 1993).

Research into local authority responses to compulsory competitive tendering, conducted in the north of England in 1991–2, located some authorities where a formal 'split' of client–contractor functions had been avoided under the terms of the 1988 Act. Departmental managers were 'two-hatted', having both client and contractor responsibilities (see Shaw, Fenwick and Foreman, 1993; Fenwick, Shaw and Foreman, 1993).

The client and contractor roles had deliberately been kept together in the following urban authority. In this council, CCT brought some reorganization as trading accounts were set up, and the disparate elements of some services were centralized into particular departments. Chief officers became responsible for the contract side of services, the actual contract being delivered by one of several DSOs within the authority. 'We did not want to set up a big separate contractor' as a senior officer remarked.

The two principal reasons advanced at a senior level within this council for a combined client–contractor structure were, first, the lack of capable managers in sufficient number to go round a 'split' organization and, secondly, the disadvantages of too many contractual arrangements within the authority, i.e. 'too many contract claims with people trying to make money out of each other and too much energy being wasted'. On the elected councillor side, this authority opted for minimal change too.

As for the big separate DSO which this authority decided to avoid, a senior manager commented 'it's logically wrong for [us], it can be too powerful and you may not know what's going on inside it and you've put all your eggs in one basket'.

In general, the councils which chose to keep together the client and contractor functions, so far as legislation allowed, seemed either to be authorities which emphasize their traditional values as coherent unitary local authorities, or authorities which like to retain a strong centralized influence over the whole council. Both motivations are aspects of a 'corporate' approach. As the same senior officer commented: '. . . **CCT has been managed within the corporate context from the centre and run as one process**'.

Pressure upon local authorities to differentiate the management of the client and the contractor functions has certainly increased since the Local Government Act 1988. The 1993 regulations (discussed in Case study 2.2) restrict the activities of officers in having client-side as well as contractor-side responsibilities (see Dobson, 1993). There is increasing pressure from Government to curtail 'anti-competitive' practice. The typical local authority is increasingly likely to be charactered by separate contracting and client elements, and **not just for services subject to CCT**. It is becoming the normal mode of organization for local authority services. This gives rise to various methods of 'managing the split' (Shaw, Fenwick and Foreman, 1993). A crucial element here is the precise role of the Direct Service Organization.

Research in the north of England has found that where separate DSOs have been set up, the usual form is that of an organizationally distinct DSO responsible for all council contracts, but that in some local authorities the leisure management contract side is excluded from the general DSO (Fenwick, Shaw and Foreman, 1993, p. 25). The Association of Direct Labour Organizations (ADLO), in their study of client–contractor relationships for grounds maintenance, consider the strengths and weaknesses of a 'client service agency', which is responsible for contract letting and client functions across the whole range of defined activities, while client officers remain within recreation: a 'split' within the client-side itself (ADLO, 1993). The ADLO study suggests that practical disadvantages of confusion over budgetary control, and lack of overall guidance, were features of this model within the particular authority studied (1993, p. 9). The study reminds us, however, that organizational and structural variations in responding to CCT legislation can and do exist, and need to be assessed on their merits.

Where the DSO is relatively separate, so too is the client-side.

> Where there is a clear separation, client-side responsibilities have continued to be exercised by the individual client departments (Fenwick, Shaw and Foreman, 1993, p. 26).

Important as the distinction between the contractor (DSO) side and the client side may be in any analysis of the management of competition, there is an additional dimension to consider too: i.e. **corporate** management. The corporate level, within which we might include central policy co-ordination as a whole, has so far been given relatively little attention in the analysis of CCT. The following discussion thus examines the three strata of local authority management under CCT.

Client, corporate and contract managers: the three Cs of local authority management

The client-side manager and the in-house contractor, although part of the same local authority, tend in practice to pursue distinct objectives arising from their distinct roles in the CCT process. The client-side manager is concerned with service to the individual user, value for money from the client point of view, monitoring and also with local authority policy as a whole. The contractor is concerned with cost, efficiency and value for money from the contractor's point of view, with a lesser interest in the policy context of the council as a whole. This is not to say that the client-side manager and the in-house contractor are necessarily at odds. However, the perception of **divergent interests** between client and contractor within the authority does arise. This derives from the structural arrangements of CCT rather than the personal attitudes of individual managers, although the latter may be relevant too where an entrepreneurial culture has been particularly encouraged within the DSO.

The possibly divergent interests of client and contractor sides, even within the same authority, have implications for **management skills and methods** on both sides.

● The **client manager** may be involved in efforts to be 'closer to the consumer' (see Chapter 3). As Walsh notes, there has under CCT been a growth in user panels and in complaint mechanisms (1991, p. 49). Certainly, client-side managers under CCT have fewer staff, but potentially greater resources to manage, implying a shift in styles of and training for such management. The traditional style of line-management within a bureaucracy, with which many client-side managers will be familiar, is of limited value in the new world of CCT.

● The **contract manager** retains a need for effective line-management, internal accountability and for making a financial return on contract activity. Methods are closer to those of an outside commercial organization, although this does not imply adoption of a crude private-sector model. Total quality management (TQM) and the quality standards of BS5750 will be familiar and important to many DSO managers too.

> It is likely then that competition in general and CCT in particular are leading to distinct client and contractor forms of management, with styles and methods of their own. The question is raised of whether this diversity enriches local government, or is just another element in its continuing fragmentation. . . . do the client and in-house contractor management belong to the same organization, the local council, any more? (Fenwick, Shaw and Foreman, 1994, p. 9).

The possible divergence between client and contractor management, and beyond this the more general fragmentation of local government discussed in the previous chapter, imply an increased need for co-ordination and strategy in the form of the third 'C': the corporate or central manager. 'The division into client and contractor roles and the greater autonomy of DSOs and service departments raises questions about the corporate nature of the authority' (Walsh, 1991, p. 134). Yet as the need for corporate management increases, the means of realizing it become more elusive for local authorities. The pressure of CCT is against effective corporate and strategic management, as the co-ordinating mechanism of competition is, ostensibly, the market not the planner. Yet, as senior officers in all local authorities will recognize, CCT brings with it the need for more rather than less central administration. A similar contradiction will be encountered below in the discussion of the local management of schools (LMS).

How then do local authorities preserve and extend corporate management in a competitive environment? One option is fundamental reorganization of the officer and member sides in order to 'design out' departmentalism and the divergent interests of client and contractor in a structural sense. The organization of North Tyneside Council (see Case study 7.2) attempts a corporate approach through a non-departmental structure. However, structural reorganization has costs, and in itself does not denote corporatism. There are obvious dangers in solely structural responses to problems of process. The real issue is preserving and extending a **corporate culture and ethos** when the pressure from CCT and other changes (including LMS and community care) is in the opposite direction.

The corporate management task under CCT has – like the other two 'Cs' – its particular methods and skills. The effectiveness of corporate management is likely to be reinforced by explicit recognition of and support for those skills, for instance through training.

● The **corporate manager** is not significantly a line manager. Key skills are in the co-ordination of resources, the management of the relationship between the political and administrative centres of the authority (see Chapter 6), the technical, intellectual and political acumen to deal with information relating to (for instance) performance review (see Chapter 5), and the articulation of authority-wide and strategic goals in the face of pressures for a service-specific approach.

Central services are part of authority-wide corporate support functions. However, as the Audit Commission has pointed out in its second report on CCT (1994b), central 'support' may be perceived by headteachers under LMS or contract managers under CCT as central **control**. The Audit Commission recommends a clear-cut distinction be made between 'corporate' and 'support' roles of central departments, and that the nature of the support role be defined in a Service Level Agreement, recognizing that support services may not necessarily be provided from within the authority (1994b). The 'centre' may continue to be distrusted by departmental or contract managers on the grounds that it is out-of-touch and irrelevant, or, alternatively, too powerful and too interfering. In addition to the difficulties of the central support role, Walsh and Davis point out that the **skills** associated with the central support manager are not always easy to find (1993, p. 31).

The future growth of CCT

There are two senses in which the further growth of CCT is of relevance. First, there is the specific matter of additional 'defined activities', adding to the range of services already subject to CCT: most significantly, 'white collar' services and housing management. Secondly there is the general sense in which the new relationships – the new patterns of organization and management engendered by CCT – will continue to grow as a feature of local government (for instance, the client–contractor split) irrespective of particular additions to current 'defined activities'.

Against these pressures for growth are certain constraints on the further development of competition in the form of CCT. First, there are legal constraints in the form of European employment protection. Second, there are political constraints arising from the ideological stance of central government.

Let us now consider both aspects of growth and both forms of constraint.

The extension of defined activities

The growth of CCT in the mid- and late-1990s includes a range of professional white-collar services, and housing management as a whole. A governmental consultation paper in relation to housing management (Department of the Environment, 1993) envisages that the first management agreements for housing management CCT will operate from the financial year 1996/97. The legislative authority to introduce CCT for housing management derives mainly from Section 2 of the Local Government Act 1988 under which, as explained above, the list of defined activities may be extended by order of the Secretary of State. The subsequent enactment of the Leasehold Reform, Housing and Urban Development Act 1993 provides the basis for detailed aspects of the implementation of CCT for housing management, including 'provisions for comprehensive tenant consultation before a management agreement is entered into and for tenant involvement in the subsequent monitoring of the contractor's performance' (Department of the Environment, 1993, para 13).

The government clearly distinguished the client and contractor sides in its planning for housing management CCT, placing the wider strategic and policy aspects within the client side, and the 'day-to-day management' on the contractor side (Department of the Environment, 1993, para 17). Noting that authorities need a strong client-side, and a strategy and policy function, the report concludes that 'the defined activity should consist of the contractor function only' (Department of the Environment, 1993, para 18). This is explored further in Case study 2.3.

CASE STUDY 2.3 CCT and housing management

The government's consultation paper *Compulsory Competitive Tendering of Housing Management* (Department of the Environment, 1993) follows earlier papers which had set out the possibilities for extending CCT into the management of housing services. This is the first instance of a **management function** rather than a direct service being made subject to compulsory competitive tendering. It represents a qualitative extension of the scope of CCT rather than merely an addition to the list of defined activities.

> Housing management covers a wide range of responsibilities, involving policy and strategic issues, alongside the day to day management of the housing stock and its residents. The process of CCT recognizes the requirement to split housing departments into two components, the client and contractor sides. The former will retain the strategic and policy functions whilst the latter will assume the role of day to day management. The contractor role may be carried out in-house (subject to CCT) or contracted out through CCT or voluntarily (Department of the Environment, 1993, para 17).

Thus, housing management CCT involves a client–contractor split from the start, defined much more clearly than it was for the original defined activities of the Local Government Act 1988. Further, under housing management CCT, it is very clear that the 'strategic and policy functions' are not available to potential bidders.

The housing management 'defined activity' is taken to include

- rent and service charge collection;
- allocating properties and arranging lettings;
- enforcement of tenancy agreements;

- management of vacant properties;
- management of repairs and maintenance;
- management of caretaking and cleaning (Department of the Environment, 1993, para 27).

Implementation: the introduction of housing CCT is a staged process, based on the size of an authority's housing stock – the authorities with the largest housing stock being able to phase in the process over two/three years. The extension of CCT to housing management follows the experience of several 'pilot authorities', each concentrating on arrangements for one aspect of housing CCT, as follows:

1. Rochdale: consulting tenants prior to management agreements being drawn up
2. Westminster: monitoring management agreements
3. Derby: the boundaries of the client–contractor split and of the defined activity
4. Brent: contract specifications
5. East Staffs: 'management and cultural change' following CCT
6. Newham: implications for capital programmes
7. Mansfield: warden services under CCT
8. Mid Suffolk: the effect of housing CCT on the smaller housing authorities (Department of the Environment, 1993, para 5).

In addition to housing management, the separate provisions for 'white-collar' CCT are of considerable significance for the future of local authority non-manual functions. The services specified in the government's 'competing for quality' document (Department of the Environment, 1991) will be subject to CCT by April 1997, although it is not inconceivable that the timetable may be varied. The first professional service to be contracted-out is planned to be legal services (commencing June 1994, with 33% subject to tender by October 1995). Secondly, 80% of computing services start to be subject to contract in October 1996. Thirdly, 25% of financial services, 25% of personnel, and 15% of corporate administration face tender by April 1997.

'Construction-related services' (engineering, architectual services and property management) will face CCT from July 1994: 90% of these services, in three blocks, to be subject to tender between then and October 1996. Local councils which are being reorganized under the 'rolling programme' of the Local Government Commission will have extra time to implement CCT for each of these services. It is impossible to speculate usefully upon the patterns of organization and management which will characterize local government once all these changes are in place. Conceivably not every planned change will occur in this form, by these dates, or at all. However, the characteristic changes to the way local government is run – resulting directly from competition – are here to stay.

The growth of new patterns of organization and management

Managerial change – project management, internal trading accounts, 'service level agreements', professional 'managers' imported from the private sector, fixed-term contracts – is not likely to recede, irrespective of the specifics of how defined activities are or are not extended. This is partly because, even for the initial group of defined activities set out in 1988, the changes still have a long way to go: local councils are still developing their responses; contracts will have to be won or lost again (and again) in a setting where public and private bidders alike are more experienced, and new modes of organization (particularly around client and contractor) are still being consolidated (even for non-CCT services). These structural – and cultural – changes are not dependent upon any particular additional services being subject to tender, but they are at the heart of 'managing local government' today.

As already noted, however, there are also constraints on the expansion of competition which may counteract the tendencies toward growth.

The applicability of European law

This may yet undermine not only the further expansion of CCT, but also the existing provisions of the Local Government Acts 1988 and 1992. The Transfer of Undertakings (Protection of Employment) Regulations (Statutory Instrument 1981/1794) – known usually as 'TUPE' – were introduced by the British government as a way of putting the European Commission's Acquired Rights Directive (1977/187) – ARD – into practice, or, as critics might argue, not putting it fully into practice. Much controversy has followed. It has been argued that the ARD, and TUPE, mean that employees transferring from one employer to another must retain their agreed pay and conditions – which clearly they do not under CCT – and must be consulted about any such transfer –which, under CCT, they are not. However, the argument has been advanced that when contracts are won under CCT, workers do not 'transfer employment' in the sense meant by TUPE, so the protection does not apply.

To complicate matters, there is the separate question of whether TUPE adequately reflects the provisions of the ARD in the first place. The European Commission Report no. 2 of June 1992 (Local Government Information Unit, 1993a, p. 3) has stated that UK legislation does not follow the ARD satisfactorily in terms of consultation, and in relation to exclusions from the scope of this protection. In response, the government's Trade Union Reform and Employment Rights Act 1993 (part II) to some extent meets the ARD requirements more adequately.

Over a long period there were confusing signals from government about the applicability and meaning of TUPE. The government's powers under the Local Government Act 1992, Section 9, to instruct councils against 'anti-competitive' behaviour –discussed above – are also relevant. A local authority's prior insistence on a contractor's adherence to a particular interpretation of TUPE might yet be judged anti-competitive by the Secretary of State. The recent debates (and the specific effects of CCT on employment) are discussed by Kerr and Radford (1994).

Meanwhile, successive legal cases have tested the applicability and meaning of TUPE in local government and other areas of the public sector. Workers in Eastbourne won such a case in relation to their refuse collection jobs in July 1993, but in August of the same year hospital cleaning workers in Essex lost an apparently similar case. In June 1994, a ruling in the European Court of Justice finally established that employee representatives do indeed have a right to be consulted about proposals for redundancy, or for transfer of employment from one owner to another. Although the provisions of the ARD and their translation into TUPE thus now apply to cases where services are privatized, the implications of this for the practice of CCT have by no means been clarified fully. Testing of subsequent cases is likely to establish with whom 'consultation' needs to occur before transfers of employment take place, arrangements where appropriate for compensation, and the effect on future proposed extensions of privatization including CCT.

Political constraints

There is a political question mark over the future of CCT. A general election is due within the period specified for the extension of white-collar CCT. The policy of a non-Conservative government to CCT cannot be known with any certainty. Perhaps as important as the speculative possibility of a change of government are the shifting ideological trends within successive Conservative administrations. The ideological commitment of the first Thatcher governments to the rhetoric of the market gave way to a less strident tone from successive admistrations, but the legislative programme for CCT as in other areas continued unabated.

The internal dynamics of Conservative government have, however, changed in the post-Thatcher years. The Parliamentary majority of the fourth Conservative government, elected in 1992, made it **relatively** less secure in political terms, obliged to take some account of critics within Conservative ranks. The initial plan for Post Office privatization, itself a compromise proposal, was abandoned in November 1994 before reaching the Queen's Speech. It remains to be seen whether housing management CCT, and the contracting out of the white collar and professional services discussed above, represent the final instalment of a process which has now run its political course.

Concluding observations on CCT

CCT is but an **example** of competition within local government. The competitive ethos is manifested in other ways too, for instance in the delegation of budgets and hence managerial responsibility within education via the local management of schools (LMS), discussed below. Competition has many other manifestations too. It is worth emphasizing, in drawing together some strands of the discussion so far, that both CCT and LMS were **imposed upon** an unwilling local government. It may be that some local councils initially hostile to CCT began to perceive that it had a political value in blurring the responsibility for cutbacks; and it may be of course that some councils were from the start ideologically receptive to the call of the market. Nevertheless, it remains true that, in local government overall, compulsion has been central to the expansion of competition.

The managerial implications of CCT have been seen to include a possible fragmentation of activity across the three Cs: the client, contractor and corporate managers. It has been noted above that the three layers of management require distinct skills. These skills are linked to cultural change within the organization. Other than this, there are few definitive pointers towards specific managerial structures for the new competitive environment of local government. Rigg and Trehan talk about the importance of 'defining **core values** and communicating these through the organization, thereby helping to build a new sense of purpose' (1993, p. 85, emphasis added). Clarke and Stewart refer to the need to 'encourage experiment and diversity', and tell us that 'new forms of organizational structure and approaches to management are being experimented with' (1991, p. 54). These organizational and structural adaptations vary considerably: some are considered in Chapter 7.

Kingdom points to CCT as very much a part of the Thatcherite attack on local government as a whole, along with the sale of council houses, deregulation in general, school opt-outs (grant maintained status), privatization, and the removal of the former polytechnics and subsequently the further education colleges from local authority control (Kingdom, 1991, pp. 41–2). This is the widest context of 'competition'. Ironically, of course, when these processes result in private-sector monopoly, 'competition' is hardly extended. Additionally, Government powers to determine 'anti-competitive' practice by local authorities will directly affect the extent to which competition will continue to be centrally driven.

Finally, competition of course has a cost. It is not possible to produce a precise balance sheet relating to the costs of CCT, much less to the benefits. Consequently, much debate remains politically speculative. However, real staff in local government have to deal with real costs. The Audit Commission (1992), certainly in favour of the principle of extending competition, made the following observation in its response to the government's 'competing for quality'. It registered 'a concern for the costs of exposing activities to competition. The benefits to be gained from competition must, over time, outweigh the likely costs' (Audit Commission, 1992, pp. 5–6). As yet, it is impossible to reach a balanced judgement of the costs of competition within local government. It is particularly difficult to quantify the effect of competition on **people** within the local authority.

Managing competition and managing people

> Whatever the nature of the work organization, a manager achieves results through the performance of other people (Mullins, 1993, p. 574).

As a work organization, local government is very labour-intensive and, notwithstanding technological development, is likely to remain that way (Leach, Stewart and Walsh, 1994, p. 185). As most local government spending is on staff, the implications of competition for 'resources' denote human resources as well as the financial costs normally associated with discussions of competition. The managerial changes discussed throughout this chapter impact directly upon people employed by the local authority, as well as upon people in the community.

What kinds of people?

All staff employed within local government are affected by competition, but there are specific differential effects. It is clear, for instance, that front-line staff in education and social services are still predominantly female, their managers predominantly male. The devolution of management characteristic of LMS (or of the changes associated with community care) reflects this: it is not a devolution in equal measure to all staff. It is also of course significant that part-time posts are largely female-staffed, and that part-time work is most vulnerable at a time of diminishing financial resources. Maysey (1992) suggests that, as a result of CCT, women are particularly affected in terms of their lower pay, terms and conditions, weakened Equal Opportunities provisions, reduced access to employment, lack of training and reduced promotion prospects.

The differential impact of competition is not, however, uniform. The first defined activities for CCT purposes included male-dominated services such as refuse collection and grounds maintenance as well as those characterized by a high proportion of female employees such as catering. The salient point is that competition impacts upon different people in different ways. Gender is one, but not the only, basis of differentiation: age, ethnic group or disability may also compound the general impact of competition. As noted below, management is about different degrees of power, and clearly power is unequally distributed.

However, the impact of competition may be more positive. The divergent management skills arising under the impact of competition may broaden the base from which local authority managers come to be drawn. New people, not necessarily coming up through the route of specific professional training and progression through the hierarchy, may for instance find a role in client-side management or on the corporate level, while staff from a private-sector background may find their way into contract management: in these senses, competition may eventually serve to extend opportunity.

What kinds of management?

The pressure of competition is to some extent away from direct formal management control, towards a greater emphasis on contract management and on specific projects. These new arrangements embody new forms of control. The changing skills of management under competition have already been referred to, but it is to be noted that the specific skills of managing **people** are changing too.

There are, for instance, greater moves toward local pay deals, delegated management and individual appraisal. Individual reviews of pay may be linked to individual performance measurement. A direct consequence of the competitive environment is that senior managers are subject to the market rigours of time limited contracts and a direct responsibility for performance, though normally for a greater financial reward in the short term. This is an international trend. The pressure of public-service management is almost universally toward budgetary devolution, individual accountability, and 'results' as may readily be seen for instance in the discussion of the United States and the Netherlands in Chapter 4.

Griffiths, writing of Kent County Council, notes that the Chief Executive in this local authority is no longer first among equals in a Chief Officer team, but is instead 'on a fixed-term contract and is sharply accountable' for resulting performance (1993, p. 39). At the same time, his Chief Executive 'has nevertheless to combine this with a continued commitment to public service and its essential values' (Griffiths, 1993, p. 39).

Three questions are thus raised.

1. What are the 'essential values' of local public service?
2. Does the 'results' orientation **work** in local government?
3. Can a 'results' approach be combined with the values of local government service?

To deal with the first question, there remains a persistent normative difference between local government and the private sector. The fact that local government does indeed have a distinctive set of values, defined by its historical experience and its public-service role, is a recurring feature of this book. Some overall observations are made in the concluding chapter. The resilience of public-service values is especially notable in the context of central government policies since the 1970s dealing with competition, local government finance and reorganization.

The second problem – whether the 'results' culture translates readily or successfully to the employment terms of local government – is a matter for further debate. Performance-related pay, for instance, has not been conclusively demonstrated to link directly to subsequent individual results or to organizational performance as a whole.

The third issue – the combination of a results-orientation and an emphasis upon the traditional values of local public service – will define the future course of local authority management. The tension between between two normative systems lies behind several themes considered in this book, including competition, consumerism, and performance measurement.

Personnel and human resource management

The personnel function, whether named as such or termed 'employee relations' or part of a wider human resource management (HRM), is an integral part of managing people. It is important that this function is not sidelined as an entirely separate specialist unit, of relevance only to recruitment or staff turnover. It would generally be held now that personnel matters cannot be the exclusive province of a few staff, but are properly the concern of staff throughout the organization (Mullins, 1993, p. 579).

Competition has a significant impact upon the capacity of the personnel function to co-ordinate human resources across an increasingly fragmented local authority. Indeed, as a central support service itself, personnel is also subject to the direct pressures of competition. Griffiths, writing of his role at Kent County Council as one which has expanded from leading the personnel function to take in the strategic management of the central policy capability, the client-side, information, property and finance as well as personnel, emphasizes the 'pivotal' position of personnel and its 'full involvement in the process of corporate decision making' (1993, p. 37). The difficulties of achieving a corporate approach under conditions of competition are, however, already very clear from the preceding discussion of CCT.

Personnel management is but one element of HRM as a whole. Rigg and Trehan (1993) point to the ways in which **'collaboration'** (i.e. inter-agency and internal–external relations), **decentralization** and the growth of **internal markets** (including

CCT) have affected the HRM function in local government. Several implications are identified (Rigg and Trehan, 1993, pp. 85–92):

- a move from administration toward **management**, including risk-taking, innovation and resource management;
- a redrawing of traditional boundaries between departments and between the council and other organizations, including the split between client and contractor generated by CCT;
- changes to employment terms and conditions under the impetus of competition, including wage cuts, fixed-term contracts and a more general increase in job insecurity;
- the centrality of the personnel function in managing future change, based upon a closer relationship between personnel and service-delivery functions;
- the threats to equal opportunities policies through the impact of CCT and the minimizing of contractor costs;
- the need for coherent, strategic, management development policies, linked to clear statements of where the organization is heading.

Managing **human** resources is thus a process which extends far beyond a specialist personnel function. Indeed, it is a process which goes beyond HRM professionals and HRM units altogether. Under the cumulative influence of competition, financial devolution and performance measurement, the management of human resources has become the responsibility of an ever broader group of staff throughout the local authority. The specific human resource responsibilities of the manager vary, being closely linked to the role occupied (e.g. contract-side, client-side, profession-based) but in general these responsibilities are increasing, especially on the contract-side.

Managing people: some overall observations

The general effect of competition has been to **individualize** the relationship of employee to the employer in local government –as it has elsewhere. Individual pay negotiations, individual appraisal, and the emphasis upon individual responsibility for performance are general and lasting consequences of working in a competitive environment. This does not mean that all those working in local government will become uniformly subject to such arrangements: local political circumstances vary. However, the overall trend is towards such an individualization. Farnham points out that since 1979 there has been a move toward a 'harder' market-oriented approach, a more flexible and localized basis to negotiation and a more individualist 'fractional' form of managing people in the public services (1993, p. 99). This has eroded the former, and explicit, claim of public-service employers to provide a 'model' of standardized good employer practice.

> Public service employers can no longer universally claim to be model or good practice employers, setting an example for other employers to follow. They, like their private sector counterparts, are now far more likely to be concerned with efficient human resource utilization, effective employee performance, flexible working arrangements and widening pay and benefits differentials amongst employee groups (Farnham, 1993, p. 122).

For some, of course, the changed nature of people-management in local government is a new paradigm in itself, not the abandonment of good practice. As always, the values of public sector management are politically defined.

Managing people in local government is also about differences of power. However enlightened, supportive or responsive managers may see themselves as being, they largely manage people who are less powerful than themselves. Competition extends and diversifies the layers of management in a local authority, as we have seen, but it also, especially in relation to CCT, sharply differentiates those without power. As Wilson and Game (1994) point out, a number of different cultures and perspectives exists in local government, and the views held by senior staff do not necessarily resemble those of other (perhaps most other) staff.

> A local authority viewed from the perspective of a school cleaner is a very different organization from that viewed by the chief executive, the Director of Education, or even a headteacher. Indeed, it may be very difficult for senior managers and councillors to know all the different cultures or perspectives of the employees they oversee (Wilson and Game, 1994, p. 233).

There are differences of perspective between the different layers of management too. The views of senior managers may be at odds with those of more junior mangerial staff, and the effect of competition in pushing down managerial responsibility to lower levels is likely to compound this problem.

A related consequence of CCT in particular and of the competitive culture as a whole is the weakening of collective trade union influence in local government, a consequence consistent with the ideology of central government during the Conservative years. The 'right to manage', unrestrained by the collective agreements and bureaucratic constraints of the past, has increasingly become a feature of public-sector management (Farnham and Lupton, 1994, p. 102). This does not mean that collective representation has evaporated altogether: where local political conditions permit, trade unions may, for example, seek an active role in the preparations for CCT (Shaw, Fenwick and Foreman, 1994, p. 205). Yet the general trend of managing people in local government continues to be the further development of individualism, not least in the 'modernized' trade unions and the Blair-led Labour Party themselves.

Let us now consider a further specific extension of competition and managerial devolution in local government.

Initial steps: local financial management (LFM) in schools

The major growth of delegated powers and responsibilities in the finance, staffing and management of individual schools has, like CCT, fundamentally affected the role of the local authority. At best this has reinforced an 'enabling' role for the local council. At worst, it has reinforced the fragmentation of local government coupled with a budget-led reduction in service quality.

What became the local management of schools (LMS) derives directly from the provisions of the Education Act 1988, refined by subsequent statutory guidance, in particular Circular 7/88 (Department of Education and Science, 1988). LMS did not arise in a vacuum. During the 1980s there had been several voluntaristic efforts by local authorities to achieve greater delegation of spending power for individual schools, and the term local financial management (LFM) was coined to describe these disparate schemes. One of the best known early examples of LFM was the Cambridgeshire scheme, starting with relatively minor budgetary items in 1977, then extending to a pilot scheme of overall LFM in eight schools in 1982: Downes points out that this was not designed as a cost-cutting measure, but to give increased flexibility to schools in managing their resources (1988, p. 4). Downes goes on to list the principal objectives of LFM as a whole (1988, pp. 5–7):

1. increasing the school's 'sense of autonomy and institutional pride';
2. increasing the 'scope' of management at school level (e.g. virement of funds, delegation of essentially administrative tasks to administrative staff);
3. creating more flexible management, quicker to respond;
4. extending the understanding of educational matters, and extending participation (e.g. to governors, parents);
5. providing greater incentives for economy, as the school itself benefits from any saving; and

    'less widely proclaimed but sometimes heard' (Downes, 1988, p. 7)

6. placing the onus on the 'point of delivery' (here, the school) in the overall reduction of public spending;
7. increasing the entrepreneurial element, the notion of enterprise.

This outline of the objectives of LFM (as it then was) is interesting for its diversity. The emphasis upon delegation, and upon passing-down budgetary responsibility to cost-centres, are not the sole property of the New Right. The decentralizing Left, and traditional Liberalism, can also find elements here of which to approve: participation, flexibility. As LFM became LMS, however, it more clearly came to resemble a product of Conservative policy on education and on competition.

The local management of schools: LFM becomes LMS

The Education Act 1988 took the development of delegation much further by prescribing a statutory framework: a general compulsion upon local education authorities to delegate budgets and decision-making to individual schools. LFM became LMS – a change in terminology which occurred between the 1988 Act and the subsequent Circular 7/88, a change Gilbert traces to the work of management consultants Coopers and Lybrand in making 'more explicit the shift in managerial responsibilities involved' (Gilbert, 1990, p. 15). The limited delegation of budgets gave way to an overall delegation of responsibilities, including staffing. The newly defined LMS had several elements of relevance to our overall discussion, as follows.

1. The link to a particular view of the objectives of LMS, deriving from Conservative policy, in contrast to the more pluralistic nature of LFM.
2. The compulsion upon all local authorities to participate, and to adhere to the prescribed timetable for its introduction.

3. The introduction of LMS alongside other key educational 'reforms', deriving also from the Education Act 1988, especially:

   (a) the National Curriculum, defined by central government and
   (b) the introduction of Grant Maintained status for schools which 'opt-out' of LEA control following a ballot of parents, henceforth to be funded directly by central government.

4. The increased role of school governing bodies in the management of individual schools.

It is the **total** effect of these various provisions plus the effect of separate legislation (including the ways in which schools have to take account of CCT in awarding contracts) which creates the impact of LMS upon local authority management.

What is LMS?

The Education Act 1988 placed an obligation upon Local Education Authorities to introduce a scheme of financial delegation for all its maintained schools, and for the devolved management of budgets by the governing bodies of the schools concerned. The actual scheme of delegation had to be submitted to the Secretary of State by the end of September 1989, with a phased introduction of school-based budgets by 1993, with all transitional arrangements ended by 1994. Even where full delegation did not initially apply – for instance, the smaller primary schools –the allocation of budgets to schools was formula-based, so formula-funding was and remains a central feature of LMS. Naturally the formula itself is a prime concern of schools, for it determines the total allocation of funds to the individual school. In sum, LMS is about **formula funding plus managerial devolution**.

> Clearly, under local management, formula funding and delegated budgets become the bases of the finance of schools. As such, the formula or budget become the instrument of control as well as of planning (Parry, 1990, p. 84).

Athough LMS delegates extensive managerial responsibilities to governing bodies and of course in practice to the head teacher, it does this within the parameters of a formula devised by the LEA. Any formula will produce winners and losers, as it involves a redistribution of resources in real terms between schools. In a period of overall budgetary standstill or contraction, formula-funding may of course only delegate the misery. Intentionally or otherwise, hard decisions about – for instance – charging for school-related activities are passed down to the school instead of being dealt with at a politically exposed level within the LEA.

The formula itself is not drawn-up by central government. The formula, and the scheme of which it is a part, are drawn up locally, with the statutory expectation of consultation with governing bodies and others. Thus it is not possible to describe the typical formula. However, it would include a method of allocating the **aggregated budget** (the budget for delegation to schools after deducting mandatory and discretionary exceptions, i.e. budget items retained by the LEA), a calculation of **pupil numbers** as the basis of allocating at least 75% of the aggregated budget: perhaps a form of weighting pupil numbers according to **age**; an explanation of any **social factors** included in the formula, for instance where free school meals uptake is used as a proxy for social need; **building** related costs; other **school-running** costs; a breakdown of how **teaching and non-teaching staff** allocations are derived; and any **transitional** arrangements for the early stages of LMS, now phased out.

CASE STUDY 2.4 Competition and the local management of schools

The local management of schools (LMS) is essentially concerned with

- formula funding;
- devolved budgeting;
- devolved management;
- reduction of direct service powers and responsibilities of the LEA;
- increase in direct service powers and responsibilities of school governing bodies.

LMS is also a case study in competition, in senses less obvious than the direct public/private distinction associated with Compulsory Competitive Tendering. LMS is about **competition** in the sense of:

1. **Marketing** In the potential competition for pupil numbers associated with greater parental choice, the school begins to 'market' its activities, its 'achievements' as conventionally measured, to attract the parents of potential entrants. 'Sadly, the theme has been taken up within the profession and terms like merchandise, product, marketing and customer are bandied without a clear analysis of their possible meaning within education' (Cave and Demick, 1990, p. 71).
2. **Virement: the freedom to move resources between budget heads at the school level** Although formula funding determines allocations of funds to schools, it does not determine how individual schools choose to spend money. There is competition between conflicting demands for spending at the level of the school.
3. **The adoption of market mechanisms** The school as a 'cost-centre', managerial devolution as a whole, 'income-generation', and cash limits are all features of a competitive free market – LMS is concerned with the growth of such market mechanisms within individual schools.
4. **The end of monopolistic control** Educational policies of the late 1980s and 1990s have undoubtedly meant an increase in **central** government influence, not least through the National Curriculum. LMS and related

changes have, however, meant a reduction in the monopolistic influence of the LEA **and** of the individual school. This is illustrated by the following extract from the draft scheme of delegation of one LEA.

The LEA will survive and develop in any significant sense if, and only if, it offers a service to schools, which the schools want and cannot get better anywhere else. Correspondingly, schools will survive and develop only if they offer a service to pupils, parents and the community which those pupils, those parents and that community want and cannot obtain better elsewhere (Newcastle upon Tyne City Council, 1989a, p. 15).

This final element is perhaps the most fundamental aspect of the competition associated with LMS: even without considering the separate development of grant-aided status ('opting-out') which takes the competitive process so much further for some schools.

Formula-funding determines the total share of the aggregated budget distributed to the school, but once allocated to the school, governing bodies have freedom and discretion to decide how the budget should be spent. Their **spending decisions** are not formula-based. Such **managerial discretion**, rather than formula funding itself, is the real innovation of LMS – its opportunity or its danger, depending on circumstances or individual viewpoint.

To quote from Newcastle upon Tyne's scheme of delegation:

It should be noted that although an individual school's entitlement will be calculated from a number of sub-formulae for different elements of expenditure, it will be entitled to organize its budget as its governors determine within the total amount of cash available (Newcastle upon Tyne City Council, 1989b, p. 44).

Looking at the implications of LMS for management it is not necessarily very useful to focus upon the minutae of the formula. A formula is not inflexible. Leonard makes the following statement:

A formula is by definition, specific and admitting of no exceptions or pragmatic variations; by contrast, schools are full of people and systems whose needs are not determined by simple rules (1988, p. 62).

This is to miss the point slightly. It is easy enough to introduce weighted calculations into formulae, to quantify social need however imperfectly, and to introduce compensatory items into the formula. The key points about LMS are:

- the LEA's determination of the general school's budget to start with – is it more, less, or the same?
- the school governing body's devolved and discretionary powers to organize spending as it sees fit from the total allocated.

Both these aspects of LMS imply new managerial demands – at the LEA level, and at the school level. A little more can be said here of the overall context of local authority management under LMS.

The implications of LMS for local authority management

Arguably the LEA retains considerable strategic input under conditions of LMS. Parry sums this up.

> The introduction of local management schemes will alter the role of LEAs. They will not be able to exercise detailed control over the bulk of spending in schools with delegated budgets. Their role will become more strategic and they will have important responsibilities for monitoring and evaluating the schemes (Parry, 1990, pp. 82–3).

This suggests that the specific skills of the **strategic** manager in the LEA become ever more important under LMS. These mirror the kinds of skills required of the **corporate** manager under CCT, discussed above, including:

● resource **co-ordination** at a high level;
● proximity to **decision-makers**;
● **drawing together** disparate staff;

plus, one could now suggest:

● high-quality **information** provision and collation, essential for LMS;
● a participative and **open** management style, e.g. in contacts with schools.

Additionally, it should be remembered that the LEA is not synonymous with the local authority in formal terms. The traditionally separate nature and status of the LEA may still affect authority relations, especially at senior level.

The government itself also envisaged, or said it envisaged, a greater strategic role for LEAs within the LMS regime.

> Under schemes of local management LEAs will take on a more strategic role. They will be free from the need to exercise direct, detailed control over the bulk of spending in schools with delegated budgets, but will have a vital overall responsibility for ensuring that local management is effective in delivering better education (Department of Education and Science, 1988, Para 18).

Under LMS, then, strategic management may flourish within the local authority in setting the framework, 'enabling', monitoring, evaluation, and supporting what remain its employees in the schools. This requires particular skills, in changed circumstances. But the point should not be taken too far. It would be disingenuous to suggest that LMS represents a new strategic dawn for local government if it is accompanied by budgetary cutbacks, by large numbers of other schools in the authority moving to grant-maintained status, or by highly centralized curricula schemes and testing requirements.

LMS and CCT

Both LMS and CCT derive from legislation enacted during the third successive Conservative government, and reflect the political and ideological imperatives of those years, particularly in the shifting boundary between public and private sectors. Both policies have also sought to challenge the power of professional (and public-sector trade union) interests, and both policies have significant implications for the management of people.

Under CCT, monopoly provision still obtains at the point of use. It is impossible to sustain an argument that CCT creates a market choice at the level of the individual customer. The 'market' argument for CCT must rely on the assumed benefits of introducing a quasi-market mechanism at the point of allocating monopoly contracts among rival bidders. Central government has of course prescribed the rules under which the process of tendering is conducted.

The implications of LMS are somewhat different. Central government influence is similarly increased through its role in stipulating the rules of the game, its power to approve or vary schemes of delegation, and its powers in the area of the National Curriculum. The role of the LEA as direct 'provider' has dimished, although arguably a significant strategic function exists. The power of governing bodies has increased, but it is important to note that the composition of governing bodies –parents, teachers, the LEA, others including employers – may tend to favour certain interests over others.

Perhaps LMS, like CCT, generates a greater need for effective strategic management at the corporate level: but takes away some of the means of achieving this.

Managing competition: concluding comments

Competition in local government is not new. However, the **growth** of competition, and the **compulsion** upon the local authority to participate, are new. This chapter has reviewed the increased scale of competition, and has used the key illustrations of CCT and LMS to draw conclusions about the response of local government to the 'competitive environment'.

The growth of competition has led to a **diversification** of management styles and skills. In the case of CCT, the distinct skills of client department manager, corporate manager and in-house contractor were identified. It is to be expected that the further extension of CCT to a range of white-collar services and to housing management will reinforce this trend toward distinct forms of management **within a single local authority**.

It would be far too simple to equate the management of competition with an overall commercialization of management or a general adoption of private sector values or techniques. Certainly, such a move toward commercialization and the private-sector model is **part** of the current story of competition in local government. Equally, however, it is clear that (depending on the manager's specific role within the structure of the authority) competition may be driving client departments closer to the public. Additionally, strategic management seeks to preserve and extend the corporate interests of the authority as a whole, based in the values of local government. This greater diversity of management structures and objectives under conditions of competition alters the relative priorities between line-management, contract management and the expanding area of a more widely defined resource management.

The case study illustrations of CCT and of LMS alike demonstrate the growing diversity of required managerial skills in the competitive local authority. A final problem remains. Diversity and functional specialization within management may be desirable. However, a point is reached within local government where **diversity becomes fragmentation**, where (for instance) the particular role occupied by the in-house contractor raises doubts about whether that contractor is still part of the local authority in any real sense. In short, competition may ultimately undermine the structural and managerial **integrity** of the local authority.

Summary

This chapter has examined aspects of competition within contemporary local government, with particular emphasis upon Compulsory Competitive Tendering and the local management of schools. It can now be assumed that local government managers work within a fundamentally **competitive environment**, irrespective of particular policy developments in the future. It has been argued in this chapter that competition has led to a **diversification** or even fragmentation of local government organization, around client-purchaser, contractor-provider, and central-corporate roles. This fragmentation has in turn led to changes in the **managerial skills** required of officers, depending upon their particular jobs: line-management, resource co-ordination and project management now assume differing degrees of priority for different officers. Although public management now more closely resembles private-sector management, it would be a gross oversimplification to regard the two as synonymous. Local authorities still operate within a normative framework, **determined politically**, which directly impacts upon the management of public services.

Discussion questions and guidance

1. *'Local government should be business-like, of course, but it is not a business. It embodies a completely different set of ethics altogether' (Jack Straw, Labour, Environment, 1993). Which 'set of ethics' is being referred to here, and in what ways do such ethics differ from those of a 'business'?*

It is being asserted in the quotation above that local government is characterized by a distinctive set of values and, further, that such values are different from those of private industry. An exploration is required here of the public/private distinction, and the alleged normative and cultural gap between the two. It could be argued that the gap is not as significant as implied above. Alternatively it could be argued that such a gap formerly existed, but has been eroded by the exposure of public services to private competition, for good or ill. Much of Chapter 2 relates directly to this question, which could be illustrated by reference to CCT or LMS, but a more general issue of the values of local government is implied too. Whiteoak (1992) discusses Cheshire County Council's internal market and the possible bringing together of public- and private-sector ethics. The quotation which closes Case study 2.1 is also of relevance:

'we have to seek the best of commercialism, but at the same time retain traditional local government values'. In your view, what exactly does this mean?

2. *Identify the principal managerial skills required of the in-house contractor, the client-side manager and the central corporate manager under conditions of Compulsory Competitive Tendering.*

The task here is to specify the **particular** management skills demanded by an environment where the local authority has – to a greater or lesser extent – become split along client and contractor lines, and where there is still a central corporate or strategic focus of management at the heart of the authority. It was suggested in the discussion of the 'three Cs' in Chapter 2 that this relatively fragmented environment required **different** skills of managers according to their location. You may or may not agree. Try to elaborate and extend the discussion of the particular skills required or, alternatively, say why the competitive council still requires a set of common skills among its managers.

3. *'Commercial management implies less interest in social goals such as equal opportunities policies. The need to compete implies a move away from centralized bargaining on wages and conditions towards local labour market rates.' Discuss.*

This statement is from Parker and Hartley (1990, p. 13) and contains a number of terms which might be examined further in any attempt to 'discuss': for instance, 'commercial management', 'social goals'. Having defined the necessary terms, the task becomes one of assessing whether the statement appears to be plausible, and, if so, moving on to examine its consequences for (e.g.) the public, employees, managers and the local authority as a whole.

4. *If the Local Management of Schools is about formula funding, managerial devolution, and decentralization of power to the school level, how can it also be conducive to a 'more strategic role' for the local education authority?*

The 'more strategic role' for the LEA was envisaged by the Department of Education and Science, as it then was (1988, para 18). This ostensibly greater strategic role for the LEA was held to arise because the LEA would be 'free' from the need to exert direct everyday control over its schools. On one level, then, the question requires a consideration of competing philosophies: has the LEA been pushed out of day-to-day schooling, or has it had a freedom bestowed upon it? These considerations have a clearly ideological element too. The question also implies a more concrete and detailed review of the specific implications of LMS. There are tensions between centralization and decentralization. These are usefully explored by considering detailed practical aspects: what does LMS actually involve? Case study 2.4 is of some relevance here, together with the sources for LMS cited within Chapter 2.

5. *Identify and discuss the managerial skills required by LMS at (a) the school level and (b) the LEA level.*

The question is specific in seeking a concise statement **and** discussion of the management skills implied by LMS. At the school level, it must be remembered that governors, head teachers and other teachers have distinct roles in 'management': formally laid down in the case of the governing body, but arising from the structure of the school itself in the case of teaching staff generally. These demands also imply the need for training, among both lay governors and professional teachers, which might repay some further consideration: what kind of training? provided by whom? funded by whom? In this setting, it is then necessary to consider the LEA level. The growth of LMS and, to a lesser extent, grant-aided status, moves the LEA manager much further to a position of co-ordinator and resource manager rather than line-manager. Is the LEA manager equipped to carry out this role?

6. *What do you consider to be the natural limits of CCT, beyond which 'local government' would be redundant?*

A wide-ranging discussion is implied here. The question is speculative, but the answer should be based in an appraisal of relevant source material: discussed in Chapter 2, with relevant discussion also in Chapters 1 and 7. The 'defined activities' subject to Compulsory Competitive Tendering under the Local Government Act 1988 have been extended to an increasing range of services: leisure management was added at an early stage, and thereafter followed by a lengthy lead-in to 'white collar' CCT, and housing management CCT. Is the extension of CCT a process which can continue incrementally without fundamentally undermining local government? Or does the competitive process lead to a desirable and overdue change to the fundamental nature of local government? Alternative developments may also be considered in response to this question. Some Labour thinking is toward integration of NHS and local authority functions. How would **this** affect the nature of local government? It may be, of course, that local authority management is not defined by the **quantity** of services delivered at all.

7. *The senior council officer increasingly 'has to manage within a competitive environment'. Identify and evaluate the principal threats and opportunities presented by greater competition within local government.*

The quotation above is taken from the beginning of Chapter 2. A general evaluation of increased competition in local government is required, illustrated by reference to CCT or to LMS or other specific examples but aiming for an **overall** identification of 'threats and opportunities'.

Suggested further reading

Walsh, K. (1995) Competition and Public Service Delivery, in J. Stewart and G. Stoker (eds) *Local Government in the 1990s*, Macmillan, London, pp 28–48. Walsh considers the experience of CCT as part of a wider assessment of competition in local government.

Taylor-Gooby, P. and Lawson R. (eds) (1993) *Markets and Managers: New Issues in the Delivery of Welfare*, Open University Press, Buckingham. A book of readings which considers the management of competition across a range of organizations.

Fenwick, J. (1995) Compulsory Competitive Tendering in Local Government: Selected Themes and Sources. *Management Bibliographies and Reviews* **21** (4) (June). Provides a summary and review of research studies and practical reports published specifically in the area of CCT.

Hender, D. (1993) *Managing Local Government Services*, ICSA Publishing/Local Government

Chronicle, Hemel Hempstead. Focusses particularly upon running the DSO and some of the practicalities of managing competition.

Deakin, N. and Gaster, L. (1995) Local Impact of Contracts for Service Delivery on Social Cohesion. *Local Government Policy Making*, **21** (4) (March) pp 21–32. Some implications of the growth of contract management.

Jackson, P. and Price, C.M. (eds) (1994) *Privatisation and Regulation*, Longman, London. Includes an interesting chapter (pp 120–148) by Peter Jackson on competition and contracting.

MANAGEMENT AND THE PUBLIC 3

There has been in the 1980s and 1990s a 'rediscovery' of the public in local government, in the form of a consumer perspective, a 'closeness' to the public, or a responsiveness to the 'customer'. It may be argued that these perspectives represent a dramatic contrast to traditional modes of service delivery based on the paternalism of the local council; or, alternatively, that the growth of 'consumerism' is a relatively superficial trend with no lasting significance for the way local services are defined and provided. This chapter explores the different meanings of the consumer perspective and its practical implications for the manager of local services. It examines the problem of collecting consumer information, and the greater difficulty of subsequently acting upon that information. The question is then posed of whether the rediscovery of the public implies a new model – a paradigm – of public management overall.

Introduction

The relationship between the local authority and the public is changing. In particular, there has been a rapid growth of interest in the public as consumers or customers. Indeed, it is possible to speak of a consumer 'perspective' in local government, variously known as a public-service orientation (PSO), a concern with the 'customer', a process of 'listening to the public', or an emphasis upon the user of public services: in short, a 'closeness' to the public.

The initial attractions of a consumer orientation are self-evident.

> Its immediate appeal lies in its apparent simplicity; local authorities are being asked to identify the 'customers' for the services which they provide and communicate with those customers in order to provide services which are of value to them (Hague, 1989, pp. 1–2).

The terms of debate are imprecise and perhaps – as discussed below – attractive for that very reason (Fenwick, 1989). The 'consumer' may for instance denote only the user of a certain service, and thus be distinct from the 'public' generally, but if so there is a problem of how to regard former, or potential, users. Furthermore, it has now become possible to look beyond the consumer perspective in isolation, to incorporate – as Stewart (1994) suggests – more substantive elements of citizenship and empowerment.

> An emphasis on the public as customers has helped to build more responsive organizations, but by itself it is not enough. There is a need to go beyond consumerism, to encompass empowerment through choice and to strengthen citizenship (Stewart, 1994, p. 28).

Whatever view is taken of the consumer perspective, and recognizing its ambiguity, it does imply a changed relationship with the public. This chapter explores some of the difficulties and tensions of the consumer concept, and considers whether the consequent changes in local government have been superficial or more fundamental. The relevance of the elusive concept of the consumer to current public-service provision and public management **practice** is then explored.

The consumer concept in local government

The consumer concept tends to be linked to the notion of an enabling authority. Drawing from the work of Clarke and Stewart (1988), the Association of District Councils summarizes the enabling council in terms of five possible roles:

- direct service provision – the traditional model;
- the regulatory authority – monitoring and enforcing the rules of service provision;
- the contract authority – containing distinct provider and client elements (e.g. under CCT or community care);
- community government – local councils as the grassroots unit of government;
- representation – the local democratic political function (Association of District Councils, 1990, pp. 7–8).

This elaboration of the enabling authority helps us to understand that consumerism is not something grafted on to traditional patterns of local government where the producer was assumed to know best. Instead, consumerism has arisen alongside changes in the nature of local government itself, in particular changes associated with 'enabling', contracting, competing, and winning the confidence of the public.

The consumer perspective began to gain attention in the mid-1980s, based on an unusual unanimity among academic commentators (e.g. Clarke and Stewart, 1985), the political Right (e.g. Ridley's discussion (1988) of the enabling authority) and the political Left (e.g. Labour Party, 1988) that a fundamental reorientation of the relationship between public services and the public was underway. Old forms of paternalistic management had, it seemed, gone: the emphasis had moved from service producer to service consumer. However, the seeming unanimity between different commentators was relatively superficial. It rapidly became clear that there are various ways of listening to the public, and various publics to be listened to. Although the consumer orientation is now very much a part of the discourse of the contemporary local authority – and of other public services such as health authorities, trusts, and central government executive agencies – it continues to be open to multiple, perhaps conflicting, interpretations.

> The nature of consumerism has been extensively debated, both in terms of consumer identification and in establishing the ideology that flows from a consumer-based perspective. Rhetoric may be more apparent than reality (Harrow and Shaw, 1992, p. 115).

These 'extensive debates' include the question of whether the development of a consumer perspective denotes a serious change in the respective power of public-service provider and public, or a merely ephemeral change to a more 'user-friendly' style (Fenwick, 1989, p. 45).

The consumer perspective has been taken to have several possible meanings in local government, for instance the direct polling of public opinion, marketing, public relations, 'user friendly' reception areas, or involving the public in decentralized decision-making (Fenwick and Harrop, 1990). Such interpretations are not necessarily thought through in any systematic way, and different 'publics' may well have contrasting views. It is a particular difficulty of the manager here to respond to councillor-driven exhortations to be closer to the customer, while trying to clarify just what this means, as well as reconciling the consumer perspective with other objectives such as cost savings. The consumer concept is fluid and imprecise. This is not to say that it is without practical value. Indeed, the very imprecision of concepts may assist their usage, the differing interpretations helping to manage conflicts.

This ambiguity of meaning is evident in considering the distinct groups of local government actors to which consumerism may be of interest: elected councillors, the public(s), and council officers (Fenwick, 1989, pp. 45–50). Councillors may favour consumerism because of its compatibility with their political priorities and the hoped-for electoral benefits. The public may favour a consumerism not for its own sake, but in terms of its meanings for service quality, responsiveness of officers, and availability. Council managers can find in consumerism a positive component of service evaluation, review and even self-appraisal: what might have seemed a threat can become an opportunity.

> Consumerism is as much a spur to critical self-examination by local government officers as it is to blanket service expansion ... Managers and other officers may derive benefits from consumerism not by its reassurance that they are doing a marvellous job (although, when they are, a little recognition is no doubt welcome), but by an unsentimental review of officers' style, activity, and relationship with the public (Fenwick, 1989, p. 46).

But what exactly **is** the consumer concept? Pollitt chooses to distinguish the public service orientation from consumerism as a whole, arguing that the PSO represented (or was thought to represent) a distinctive core of public-service values (citizenship, participation, a public-service ethic) and not merely a customer orientation (1990, pp. 149–51). Pollitt indicates the difficulties of the PSO so conceived: the possible clash of different public 'values' (e.g. between participation and overall equity), the threat posed by a thoroughgoing PSO to some of the established interests in local government which have claimed to be its advocates, and the considerable implications for resources (1990, pp. 152–3). The perceived threat of a PSO to vested interests is a key point.

In effect the PSO proposes a major programme of cultural change, one which appears to threaten the power base of both professional service deliverers and elected councillors. It would undermine both departmentalism and profession-alism by increasing the power of customers relative to providers (Pollitt, 1990, p. 152).

When the consumer orientation is taken seriously, it may thus be seen as a threat to traditional practice. Yet – as suggested above – this possible threat can be turned around into something more positive. Undesirable threats can be regarded as desirable risks, notwithstanding the difficulties of applying private-sector risk analysis to public-sector management (e.g. Harrow and Willcocks, 1990). The central factors in determining the consumer concept's status as problem or as opportunity are factors such as internal management structure, training and preparation for change, the culture of the local council, the political lead, channels of communication with the public, and relations with central government. Not all such factors are within the control of individual managers, and there has to be a balance with other day-to-day pressures:

Juggling the interests of consumers, employees and the public to achieve an acceptable balance of objectives is a paramount task for the public services manager (Harrow and Shaw, 1992, p. 131).

Despite conceptual problems, it is recognized that the rediscovery of the public, and a distinctive set of public service values, represents a real alternative to existing management approaches. It is particularly important to note that a developed consumer orientation changes internal management practice as well as external relations. Specifically, a consumer perspective tends not to be compatible with a rigid line-management regime dominated by reward and sanction as the central motivators. The cultural and behavioural change at management level associated with the consumer orientation can be characterized in a number of ways. Pollitt talks of this as an alternative to neo-Taylorism (1990, p. 151). Hambleton talks of public-service reform (of which 'consumer solutions' are one variant) as an alternative to bureau-cratic paternalism (1992, p. 12). Whatever terminology may be used, it is important to be aware at this point of:

- multiple and contrasting meanings of the consumer orientation in local government;
- the difference between private-sector models of the customer, and public-sector models based upon citizenship and public service, the two models perhaps co-existing harmoniously, perhaps conflicting;
- the relevance of a consumer orientation for internal management processes within the local authority as well as external links to the public.

The consumer approach is not confined to local authorities. It has also had a consid-erable impact within health services and central government agencies. Perhaps the experience of other public-service agencies may illuminate the consumer perspective in local government.

Writing of the health service, Steele links consumer appraisal of services very much to a concept of service **quality**: 'the over-riding criterion for quality is the satisfaction of user requirements' (Steele, 1991, p. 211). Linking consumerism to the concept of quality reminds us that the consumer perspective has at least part of its origin in the private-sector analogy, that 'the customer is right' in appraising the quality of services received. This in turn is linked to a private-sector notion of excellence, derived from the by now familiar work of Peters and Waterman (1982).

Accepting the 'quality' criterion, there may – again – be a radical or superficial interpretation of what the consumer perspective is about.

> At one end of this spectrum, appraisal is simply a process by which the provider can obtain information from an otherwise passive user (survey work, for example). At the other extreme, appraisal becomes an empowering process leading to user participation in the planning and even delivery of services (Steele, 1991, p. 212).

These words neatly summarize the problem of consumerism: whether the consumer perspective has actually led to user participation in 'planning and even delivery of services' in contrast to what Harrow and Shaw (1992) characterized above as mere 'rhetoric'.

The politics of consumerism

The difficulties of the consumer concept, when applied to the public services, have arguably been present all along. In the field of local government studies, the development by Clarke and Stewart (1985) of the public service orientation is now well known. Based upon explicit restatement of the principles that local authorities exist to provide public services, that the standard of those services is primarily to be judged by those receiving them, and that good services suggest a closeness (presumably in the senses of physical access and of responsiveness) to the consumer, the PSO represents, as we have seen, a specific **operationalization** of a consumer perspective (Clarke and Stewart, 1985; see also Clarke and Stewart, 1990).

Academic and conceptual development of the consumer perspective was a product of the 1980s, notably in response to the Thatcherite agenda for change in public-services provision. However, it is frequently overlooked that specific examples of local authorities 'listening to the public' in the contemporary sense date from the early 1970s, for instance in Kershaw's discussion of the 'impact studies' of Sunderland in the 1970s (Kershaw, 1977). The attraction of Clarke and Stewart's particular concept of a PSO was in its apparent simplicity, in its appeal to several different political audiences by seeming apolitical, and, crucially, in its arrival at the right time, when the pace of change in the management of public services was already considerable.

Further, it has been very difficult to argue that public services do **not** exist for the public, or that services should somehow be remote from rather than close to the consumer. Bureaucratic paternalism tends not to have a vocal band of supporters, even when it is practised. However, none of this removes the initial 'problematics' of the consumer concept for those concerned with the organization and administration of local government. These problems are, still,

● does the consumer orientation somehow remove public services from political debate?

- how do we know what 'the public' thinks or wants?
- if we did know, how would we act upon that knowledge?

At a fundamental level, there is the question of who is/who are the public – to whom are we listening? At its most naive, the consumerist concept assumes that public opinion is uniform, to be collected in a straightforward manner. However, it can be argued there are in fact several 'publics'. Partly this is a matter of vocabulary: use of terms such as customer, client, consumer, community, people, or public implies a certain view of the problem, a certain discourse for approaching it, and perhaps a political standpoint relating to the (individual) consumer or the (collective) community. However the question of 'who is the public' is not only about terminology. Some publics are more visible, and more powerful, than others.

Gyford comments:

> both women and blacks shared the critique that they were in some way 'invisible' publics to professional and political decision makers, whose assumptions were predominantly those of white males. This critique was expanded by disabled people and by gays and lesbians who complained that those dominant assumptions were also those of the able-bodied and the heterosexual (Gyford, 1991, p. 7).

This crucial question of 'who is the public' can be either a strength or a weakness of the consumer concept. It may be a strength if any systematic searching-out of consumer perspectives does indeed ensure the inclusion of the various publics; it may be a weakness if the consumer perspective simply means greater attention to the already articulate. And, however this is resolved, once the existence of multiple publics is recognized there can no longer be any simple 'listening to the public'.

In addition to the conceptual difficulties so far outlined, writers have also drawn attention to the theoretical context in which the consumerist idea has grown up, linking the consumer concept to ideological and structural changes in the public sector. It is interesting to note that the Association of District Councils, in summarizing the key themes of local government change, links consumerism very clearly to the Conservative agenda:

> expanding government of the 1970s has been replaced by an era of financial restraint and the emphasis of much recent legislation has been to place responsibility less on collective 'community' provision and more upon the individual or the family. ... Individuals, as parents or council tenants are also being given greater say in the services they receive and they are being presented with alternatives to local authority provision. As a consequence a new customer-orientated approach to the management of local government is developing, stressing closeness and responsiveness to the needs of customers/consumers (Association of District Councils, 1990, p. 5).

Market-based notions of the individual 'customer' of public services have a clear relationship to the post-1979 Conservative critique of public-sector services which focused upon the supposedly over-large unresponsive and inefficient bureaucracy. It can be argued that the consumer concept in local government is thus misconceived: it implies a personal choice of public services in a quasi-market where such a choice does not exist; it neglects the social control nature of a significant proportion of local public services; and it is, as noted already, an essentially individualist rather than collective (or community) concept (Burns, Hambleton and Hoggett, 1994, pp. 44–6).

Yet the critique of monopolistic service provision, and the consumerist 'solution', have by no means been confined to the New Right or to market theorists. Hambleton (1992) also identifies the 'bureaucratic paternalism' of public-service provision 'pre-1980', characterized by 'large hierarchical organizations' within local government, and by

> the remoteness of centralized decision-making, irritation with the insensitivity and lack of accountability of at least some officers, and frustration with the blinkered approach often asociated with highly departmentalized organizations (Hambleton, 1992, p. 11).

Hambleton distinguishes the 'old solutions' of local government ('broadly pre 1980') from the 'new patterns' emerging as alternatives to bureaucratic paternalism (1992, p. 11). In particular, he distinguishes two responses to traditional practice: first, the replacement of public provision with the private market, 'usually associated with the radical right'; secondly, replacing bureaucratic paternalism with non-market based 'public-service reform' (1992, p. 11). The category of public-service reform is important here, for it is subdivided by Hambleton into 'consumerist' and 'community-based' solutions. Consumerist solutions 'give primary emphasis to enhancing the responsiveness of local government services to individual customers' while community-based solutions focus upon 'collective interests' and 'political account-ability' (Hambleton, 1992, p. 12).

> The consumerist approach is essentially concerned with the reform of local government considered as an administrative system, whereas the community-based approach seeks to reform local government considered as a political system (Hambleton, 1992, p. 12).

Thus, the crucial difference between individualist and collectivist modes of public service reform needs to be identified in any particular organization. Hambleton reserves the 'consumerist' label for the former: for **individualist customer-oriented initiatives**.

This is a useful refinement of the concept, which also allows that a consumer initiative should not be thought to be synonymous with a market-based initiative. There are many examples of individualist initiatives in local government which are not market-oriented. Social surveys of consumer opinion for instance (see Case study 3.3) are based upon individuals but may be designed to identify unmet need and social deprivation in, say, particular localities.

However, the distinction between individual and collective action does point to the essential constraints upon the role of the council manager. The local authority manager tends to be limited to an individualist notion of problems and solutions, even in the context of mass service provision. This is primarily because problems are articulated individually. Collective solutions are sidelined into specialist corners of the authority, such as those concerned with community work. Indeed, Hambleton is aware of the implication of this: decentralization 'below the level of the local authority' becomes a main concern of his analysis (1992, p. 9). Thus, the consumer orientation may raise questions about the inherent limitations of local authority management itself.

Before turning to the practice of consumerism, with specific case-study illustrations, some final observations about the political context are appropriate. The consumer concept clearly has some links to the priorities of the Thatcher years. Indeed, consumerism arises from ideological and theoretical developments which predate Thatcherism. As Gyford notes, it has been suggested that from the mid-1970s Britain has experienced a gradual deindustrialization, with a population movement away from the major urban areas (Gyford, 1991, p28). Local government could no longer operate as unreconstructed mass-production (so-called 'Fordist') units for local services.

Thus, 'post-Fordist' methods of production and distribution for public services began to develop, just as they had in areas of private industry: smaller-scale, user-friendly, characterized by new technology and changed labour relations (see Gyford, 1991, p. 29). We might also add that the simple fact of financial limitations was another spur towards change. Gyford – summarizing Stoker (1989) – notes that the 'rigidities' of Fordist local government started to give way under both the Thatcher project and the pressure – e.g. for 'consumer rights' – from consumers themselves (Gyford, 1991, p. 31). Hence, the arrival of consumerism in local government.

The consumer orientation is clearly a potent concept. Yet taking into account the theoretical/ideological context for the emergence of consumerism, the contribution of academic writers who have developed the idea, the growth of practical initiatives within public services, and the different political expectations which have been brought to bear, it is hardly surprising that consumerism is an elusive, as well as a powerful, concept.

The practice of consumerism

Initial experience

It is useful to move now from the idea of the consumer, to the **practice** of a consumer orientation. It may be that the consumer perspective becomes clearer by focussing on the practice of consumerism in local government, for if meaning lies in use, the under-lying concept is illuminated by practice. Alternatively, it may be that an ill-defined concept becomes even more imprecise and contestable in its translation into practical activity. Thus, examples of listening to the public will be considered, in order to draw conclusions for management practice.

CASE STUDY 3.1 Consumerism and local government: initial practice

The National Consumer Council (NCC) made an early attempt to translate a concern with 'consumer assessment' of local authority services into a series of practical measures (National Consumer Council, 1986). The NCC study thus represents an initial illustration of how to move from a general interest in the consumer to the definition of specific indicators, and then to the creation of guidelines for collection of consumer-led data.

Working with Cambridgeshire County Council and Newcastle City Council, the NCC study aimed:

- to identify output measures which would allow consumers to assess the performance of their own local authority (NCC, 1986, p. II) – such output measures would provide consumers with a broader basis than merely financial information upon which to assess services.
- 'to improve decision-making within local government by making it more consumer-oriented' (NCC, 1986, p. III). Thus, for the NCC, notions of greater accountability, and of improved decision-making, were to be the two main **practical** advantages of adopting a consumer orientation.

Within the two contrasting local authorities (urban/rural; metropolitan/non-metropolitan; district/county) specific services were selected for the formulation of consumer-oriented indicators of performance, this selection of services aiming to include 'the relatively simple as well as the more complex, and including at least some services known to cause problems for consumers' (NCC, 1986, p. IV). The concentration on **selected** services, rather than an undifferentiated perception of the local council as a whole, was also a lesson of the Newcastle surveys (Case study 3.3).

The services selected in the NCC study were housing, road lighting, public libraries, street cleaning and refuse collection, trading standards and services for the under-fives (NCC, 1986, p. IV). Notwithstanding the stated reasons for this selection, it is notable that the list **excludes** the bulk of education and social services – the two largest elements of local council expenditure but, arguably, the most difficult in which to identify the 'consumer', or to distinguish consumer-friendly welfare functions from more contentious social control functions of the local authority.

Since the NCC study (1986), there has been a considerable development of subjective performance indicators. These have latterly been refined by the Audit Commission (1993a; 1994a) to produce a greater standardization of user-information under the terms of the Citizens Charter (see Chapter 5).

The challenges posed by the early attempts at the practice of a consumer orientation remain, however:

- **definition of the relevant consumer group – which public?**;
- **formulation of 'output measures' which are relevant to the public (addressing the question of accountability) and also useful to the local authority (addressing the question of decision-making);**

- **quantifying information in order to reach conclusions about essentially qualitative factors**;
- **acting upon the information thus obtained**.

It can be seen from Case study 3.1 that the National Consumer Council, in what was explicitly referred to as a 'guideline study', chose to focus upon **selected** council services in its attempt to put consumer assessment into practice. For each service, it sought to define output measures deriving from consumer evaluation of services. What then were the 'output measures': what did consumerism mean in practice?

> Defining theoretical performance measures was just the first step. **We needed to know that they would work in practice and be of use to members, officers and consumers in general** (NCC, 1986, p. IV: emphasis added).

For housing, practical measures relating to consumer satisfagtion included a housing repairs checklist, complaints, and various descriptive statistical indicators. For road lighting, 'our only "success" was to develop indicators for road lighting maintenance' (NCC, 1986, p. XXII). For libraries, most indicators developed were quantitative – numbers of books, staff, buildings – but with important qualitative measures based on user discussion groups and a new library service checklist. (Library service indicators are considered further in Chapter 5). The other three service areas selected by the NCC produced a similarly mixed picture. The practical work of the NCC and the participating local councils was, in the 1980s, innovative. More detailed guidance, grounded in practice, has since been developed. For instance, the Local Government Management Board has provided a detailed review of the operation and impact of complaint systems (LGMB, 1992), while the Association of County Councils has published a thorough guide to 'customer service' with appropriate case studies (Webster, 1991).

The NCC study suggested strongly that quantitative and qualitative elements need to be present in any consumer research. However, the study did not really clarify what a consumer assesment **means** – i.e. what is being assessed, and by whom? It is necessary to distinguish here between secondary sources of consumer data (e.g. through complaint systems) and primary information gathering (e.g. through 'consumer surveys').

Consumer surveys

A number of local councils carried out general consumer studies in the 1980s, both prior to and following the interest of commentators such as Clarke and Stewart (1985). The social survey method was used to provide an insight into the overall levels of satisfaction with services. If these studies are based around a concept at all, perhaps it is that public opinion data have a self-evident value – that it is worth while in itself to know what the public thinks. Technical questions of whether the results accurately reflected public opinion, or policy questions of whether the results would actually affect service delivery, tended not to be the prime concerns of such studies. Authorities such as Glasgow and Islington carried out early surveys of public opinion.

Cleveland County Council had also, for several successive years, been conducting a poll of public opinion about a range of County Council and District services. Newcastle City Council (see Case study 3.3) carried out three in-depth ward consumer surveys in 1985 and 1986 which themselves have found their way into the subsequent literature (NCC, 1986, p. XVIII; Gyford, 1991, pp. 102–3).

All these surveys share some similarities: they are large scale; they employ general satisfaction – dissatisfaction scales about broad service areas; they combine qualitative and quantitative indicators of public opinion; and, it has to be added, they tend to generate uniformly positive findings. No examples of such surveys producing gross levels of overall consumer **diss**atisfaction come readily to hand. This stems not from deliberate partiality in the design and administration of such research. Rather, it derives from the inevitable way in which broad-brush social surveys will tend to collect broad-brush reassuring and rather anodyne positive feedback. Such information may be of more interest to the local councillor than to the council manager who seeks the specific output measures predicted by studies such as that of the National Consumer Council.

One of the few attempts by a local authority to render explicit the more difficult aspects of the consumer concept was made by Harlow District Council, whose checklist for public consultation includes (1990, p. 22): whose views are being sought? What will happen if public views conflict with established policy? Why is the consumer being consulted? Are some 'publics' more important than others? These sorts of issues are normally left unexamined, but it is in precisely such questions that concepts as well as practice may be clarified.

It is also necessary to consider here the weight to be given to the results: the claims made by local authorities for percentage satisfaction ratings may be highly contentious. Consider, for instance, Cleveland's claims in its unsuccessful submission (1992) to the Local Government Commission dealing with local government reorganization. Citing Harris research for use in the County Council's submission documentation, Cleveland says – in support of its claim to be the sole tier of local government for the area – that the results demonstrate 'the public was more satisfied with the County's services than they were with the boroughs' (Cleveland County Council, 1992, p. 140). Yet this is based on 79% satisfied with the County's services, 73% with the boroughs' services; 16% dissatisfied with the County's services, 24% dissatisfied with the boroughs' services: hardly a clear-cut verdict, and failing to distinguish degrees of satisfaction or public knowledge of which services are provided by which authority.

Harrow and Shaw feel there are many rationales for listening to the public, but that 'pro-user' arguments essentially have two strands: that 'consumer experience' is a crucial part of service evaluation and quality evaluation; and that consumers have rights to influence services (1992, pp. 120–1). It should also be added that **surveys** are not the only method of collecting consumer information, even though they may be the most usual technique. Hague (1989, p. 35) identifies the use of consultative meetings, complaints, suggestion schemes and 'hot lines' to senior managers. Gyford (1993a) discusses the 'public question time' in Braintree District Council. Here, formal provision is made for 15 minutes of questions or statements from the public in advance of meetings of the council's area committees – there are three such areas, each with three service committees.

> It was decided to opt for the most open door arrangements possible. This would allow questions or statements to relate to any matter of council responsibility or of local concern. They could be on policy or on individual problems, whether or not they were on the meeting agenda and regardless of whether they fell directly within the field of the particular committee at whose meeting the representation was made (Gyford, 1993a, p. 18).

Such innovation notwithstanding, it remains true that the social survey is the principal means of collecting primary consumer data in local government. Case study 3.2 outlines some examples of health service practice in using a wider range of consumer-driven research methods.

CASE STUDY 3.2 Consumerism and health: further practice

The multiple methods of collecting consumer information employed by East Cumbria Health Authority (1992) illustrate how practice has developed beyond descriptive statistics and consumer surveys. East Cumbria lists eight methods it uses in the collection of consumer information relating to health needs:

1. street surveys;
2. 'focus groups' of the public, given a topic to discuss in an open ended way (close to the market research interpretation of 'qualitative' research);
3. health forums (public meetings) with the Community Health Council;
4. a public panel, matched to population characteristics as a whole, members of which are sent a number of questionnaires over time, in conjunction with the Family Health Service Authority;
5. a 'delphi' panel – with the FHSA and CHC – focusing on common issues identified by 'key individuals', public or professional;
6. health profiles for the area;
7. GP visits;
8. an overall health strategy.

Health organizations and agencies have tended to use a rather wider range of consumer research methods than has traditionally been the case in local government. Writing of the Health Service generally, Steele (1991) lists surveys, discussion groups (e.g. of carers), depth interviews (e.g. 'critical incident analysis' of the stages of medical intervention), user panels, and 'less conventional' techniques of collecting consumer information. The less conventional category includes: 'councils' – a continuing group of users, meeting to discuss the service and advise management; 'advocates' – although Steele does not use the term – meaning that others involved in the NHS such as the Community Health Council may speak for consumers because they are closer to them than NHS employees can be; 'quality circles' – ad hoc groups summoned together to advise managers about a particular problem; and 'diaries' – the patient's own record of the episode of care (Steele, 1991, p. 214).

Health organizations may of course rely on fairly simple patient surveys or complaint levels in contrast to such multiple methods. Case study 3.2 indicates however that there remains considerable scope for innovation in devising methods of collecting consumer information.

It can be seen from Case study 3.2 that 'listening to the consumer' may be operationalized in a number of ways. It is fairly obvious that some methods of collecting consumer data have a greater validity than others. The task of the responsible officer in a local authority is then to formulate methods which are at once valid, reliable, acceptable to the political leadership, inexpensive, achievable in practice, and ultimately useful to practitioners: a daunting specification perhaps, but consistent with the demands of consumerism. In practice, as noted above, local authorities have tended to adopt survey methods in the collection of consumer data. Case study 3.3 refers to the ward-based consumer surveys conducted in Newcastle upon Tyne.

CASE STUDY 3.3 A local authority consumer survey

The ward-based consumer survey has now become reasonably familiar within local government. The large sample size and the detail collected in this case study, however, are of interest.

A series of detailed consumer surveys was carried out in three wards in Newcastle upon Tyne in the 1980s (City of Newcastle upon Tyne, 1985; 1986). The surveys arose from a request from the Performance Review and Efficiency Sub-Committee (a Sub-Committee of Policy and Resources) for consumer research which would:

1. identify the degree to which particular services are used;
2. collect details of public perceptions of service quality;
3. measure satisfaction and dissatisfaction with services;
4. collect consumer views of future service development.

The surveys were designed and carried out by the in-house Research Section of the City Council. A lengthy interview questionnaire was prepared to include coverage of all City Council services plus key services provided by other public agencies such as policing, health and transport. The relevant council departments and external agencies were closely consulted in preparing the questions. The large scale and cost of such research presupposed strong political support for it taking place at all.

The first survey (in West City ward) selected a 10% sample from the electoral register, in total 753 individuals. The refusal rate was low (48 people or 6.7% of the sample) but a large number (121 or 16.8% of the sample) had moved, even using the new register: a feature of the social and mobility characteristics of the area (itself relevant to the use of services). The following two surveys, in contrasting wards, were on a similar scale.

The survey incorporated both quantitative and qualitative elements. As the meaning of the responses given clearly depended to a considerable extent upon the subjective perceptions of the person interviewed, and an overall framework of meaning then had to be added to responses for the purpose of analysis, it is clear that the research is a departure from the pure positivist, quantitative, approach of most Local Authority social research (City of Newcastle upon Tyne, West City Consumer Survey, First Report, Appendix II, 1985).

Results were disseminated back from Performance, Review and Efficiency Sub-Committee to each service Committee, and the corresponding management groups. The extent to which this information became **useful** to council officers, councillors or indeed the public – in contrast to being merely interesting –remains a central question of such consumer research in local government.

The scale of the Newcastle ward consumer surveys, discussed in Case study 3.3, is unusually large, and the results obtained are unusually extensive and detailed (City of Newcastle upon Tyne, 1985; 1986). The value to senior managers of the information thus obtained is related to how specific such information can be about particular service areas. Consider, for instance, the questions relating to whether the 'consumer' found the council employee, on most recent contact, to be:

helpful or unhelpful;
friendly or unfriendly;
efficient or inefficient;
interested or not interested in the problem;
quick or slow to respond.

It is here that the consumer perspective demonstrates both its strengths and its very considerable weaknesses in relation to the management task. It is without doubt both interesting and useful for a manager to know that 40.9% of those who have recently been in contact with the authority found the officer quick to respond, while 43.8% found the response to be slow (City of Newcastle upon Tyne, 1985). This would at least be useful in initiating further study: for instance, of response times in relation to housing repairs. However, the weaknesses of such data are evident too. It means little to know that 51.8% considered the council employee to be efficient while 29.6% considered that officer inefficient (City of Newcastle upon Tyne, 1985).

For the line manager or resource manager, efficiency is not a matter of public perception, but is (or should be) a measurable element of employee performance. Difficult territory is now encountered, for a subjective perception of efficiency may refer to something quite inefficient objectively – for instance, through spending a disproportionate amount of time on one consumer's problem, to the exclusion, given a finite quantity of time, of other consumers. Something is being measured here, but it is not efficiency.

The limits of consumer research are encountered when attempts are made to objectify essentially subjective feelings. It is appropriate that senior officers neither reject consumer research as fashionable but empty, nor embrace it with wholly unrealistic expections of what it may be able to measure. There should instead be a dispassionate analysis of exactly what it can deliver.

The implications of the consumer perspective for local authority management

It seems that 'subjective indicators' of **overall** performance – e.g. through a general consumer survey – tend not to feed directly into policy and management. The interesting is not necessarily useful. Thus two aspects arise for further discussion. First, is it to specific studies of **particular** services that we need to look to find consumerism being acted upon? Secondly, if the many general population consumer polls are not 'acted upon', then what function do they perform?

Arising from Case study 3.3, referring to the Newcastle ward consumer surveys, existing practice has moved toward specific services. This mirrors the early preference of the NCC study (1986). 'The current position is that surveys of consumers are used on an ad hoc basis by several Departments in the context of studies of specific services' (City of Newcastle upon Tyne, 1987, para 5.4).

Even more significantly, after the conclusion of an in-depth general population consumer survey in three wards with a sample of 1500 or so completed interviews, the recommendation was for the specific not the general.

> The results of the three wards consumer survey do not support the development of a uniform corporate approach to consumer survey based performance review work. The main reason for drawing this conclusion is cost or rather value for money ... there are more effective ways in which surveys could be used to improve the responsiveness of the Authority to users and potential users of services (City of Newcastle upon Tyne, 1987, para 5.6).

The 'more effective ways' are identified as specific consumer research in particular service areas.

Even where consumer research moves from the general to the particular, it is not necessarily acted upon. The problem then shifts from the drawbacks of the data to the organizational problems of implementation: of acting upon (even apparently valuable) consumer data at all. Here, it is necessary to confront some essentially structural problems of local government.

- First, managers in local government are formally part of a bureaucratic line management system. Project management and contract management notwithstanding, this is a vertical system. It does not readily extend out of the organization to incorporate the public.
- Secondly, managers in local government are socialized into regarding the councillor as the appropriate proxy for the public: why look further?
- Thirdly, fundamental reasons for non-implementation of consumer data refer to the values, culture and changing paradigms of the public services. This also helps to address the question posed above of why such research continues to flourish if it is not acted upon: implementation may not be the intended aim at all. The aim may be to demonstrate to internal and external audiences the organization's adherence to 'consumer' values, as an end in itself. This in turn may be related to changes in management and organization of the public services.
- Fourthly, constraints upon resources are a permanent feature of local public services. Even where consumer information is collected systematically, is reliable, and is usable, it may be impossible to act upon in the absence of resources. This leads to an argument that such information may actually have a negative function in 'raising expectations' which cannot be met: or, alternatively, that information of this kind is an effective tool in the political battle for more resources.

It can be suggested that the consumer perspective is but one element of an overall change in the prevailing model – and hence practice – of local authority management. Initial changes to public management – attuned to innovative practice and mindful of private-sector approaches – have arguably been transcended by a new public management paradigm based upon contracting, multi-agency provision, permanent financial constraint **and** taking the consumer seriously. These changes in public-service practice have been driven by explicit central government policies: Thomson lists the key themes of government policy in these areas as privatization, delegation, competition, enterprise, deregulation, service quality and reduced trade union powers (1992, p. 33).

Stewart and Walsh (1992) detail the rise of 'the public as customer' in local government, central government and health, linking this to the growth of internal contracts, competition, flexible pay and conditions, performance measurement, market mechanisms and the broad changes discussed above. The cumulative, and intended, effect of such changes has been to alter the culture of local government management, consistent with central government policy (Stewart and Walsh, 1992, p. 508).

Although public-service reform has ostensibly been introduced in order to improve service quality, efficiency and effectiveness, it may instead have represented the adoption – or imposition – of an inappropriate private-sector model for the public services as a whole. 'There are distinctive tasks in the public domain, but there are also distinctive purposes and conditions. It is for this reason that the private sector model is inadequate as a basis for management' (Stewart and Walsh, 1992, p. 511). Within this changed culture of public service management, Stewart and Walsh find the terminology of consumerism to be of limited value: it may simply be inappropriate.

> The language of consumerism has a contribution to make to the public domain, but a more complex language has to be developed which also recognizes coercion, arbitration, rationing and public purpose (1992, p. 514).

Within a changed context of local authority management, then, consumerism has its value: and its clear limits. This more critical approach to the consumer perspective has been developed by many writers on public management. Harrow and Shaw (1992) suggest that the range of 'consumer guardians' created by Conservative privatization programmes and health service reforms may merely maintain the tradition that professionals know best.

From quite a different direction, but amounting similarly to a cautious view of consumerism, is the argument that listening to consumers may actually disadvantage them, because of consumers' own low expectations of what should be demanded of public services (Steele, 1991, p. 217). More critical still, Pollitt – in comparing the experience of public services in Britain and the USA under the conservatism of Thatcher and Reagan – finds no prospect of greater user involvement via 'the consumerism of the new right', which he contrasts to 'the active participation of users and taxpayers in the running of everyday services' (Pollitt, 1990, p. 183).

Thus, consumerism in the public services has now been researched to an extent where it is possible to locate it within new and still developing patterns of management, and where it is possible to be critical of the concept while drawing what is useful from it. In these senses, consumerism is coming of age.

A new paradigm?

Richards (1992) extends the discussion by moving to the consideration of management paradigms. She poses the central question of 'who defines the public good?', exploring the ways in which the power to make this definition may – perhaps – have moved away from the expert/professional to the consumer. Richards speculates that the traditional paternalist paradigms ('we know best') for managing public services gave way under conditions of financial stringency to pure efficiency paradigms in the late 1970s: and then, in turn, a new consumer paradigm began to emerge.

> The public administration paradigm was challenged by the political and economic circumstances which led to the emergence of the efficiency paradigm, with its emphasis on getting more for less. The efficiency paradigm in turn seems now to be challenged ... by a move to incorporate a consumer focus. The new practice of public management suggests that a consumer orientation is taking hold and is shifting the balance of powers which had previously prevailed (Richards, 1992, p. 29).

Thus, to restate an emerging conclusion of some importance, even when the general emphasis on 'listening to the public' has not had a demonstrable direct impact on the provision of public services, it may have exerted considerable influence upon current styles of public service management. This has contributed to the emergent models of public management discussed above.

The new models of public management incorporate an essential, if critical, consumer element. It is worth noting that this represents an alternative not only to the traditional paternalist models of local government management, but also to the Taylorist notions of management imported from the private sector. Local government is not a site for scientific management and the manager-led planning of production. This is not to suggest that private-sector management models are irrelevant. Taylorist methods of employee selection and job analysis remain common practice (Torrington, Weightman and Johns, 1989, p. 18). Indeed, developments in Total Quality Management (TQM), and in more specific techniques such as quality circles (see Rees, 1991, pp. 58–60) are equally applicable to public and private management, and quite compatible with the developments discussed in this chapter.

However, private-sector management models do not transfer straightforwardly to the management of public services. This is readily supportable by further consideration of the non-market nature of many local government services, even though proponents of the market could continue to argue that efficiency and competition can be introduced into all council services at the purchaser/provider stage of the process. Whatever view is taken of this central question of public and private models of management, there has certainly been increasing overlap of public, private (and voluntary) sectors, and this is likely to increase further.

Finally, it is worth emphasizing the opportunities thus provided for consumers, and the urgency of overcoming any perceived threat. The lesson of the preceding discussion, for anyone with a managerial responsibilty in local government, is to avoid at all costs the danger outlined by Pollitt (1990, p. 151):

> for some of the more traditional minded local government officers real moves towards a more customer-responsive organization may seem just as morale-bruising as the imposition of neo-Taylorist controls by central governments.

The consumer and the manager: problems and opportunities

By now it is clear that the consumer perspective creates both problems and opportunities for the local authority manager, and that consumerism does not stand alone: it is part of a deep-seated process of change in public management. These concluding comments deal with some aspects of likely importance for the future.

Different publics

The problem of defining the consumer still requires resolution in any particular practical setting. To focus, as local government tends to do, on 'users' of services may be insufficient. 'Users' are not synonymous with 'residents' of the local council area, for instance in using roads or leisure facilities. Here, the consumer may live somewhere else, related in the former case to the local authority by some necessary usage of a common public resource, in the latter case by commercial buying of a service at the point of use.

There is a significant conceptual problem for those local authorities who measure the dis/satisfaction of consumers as residents, and seek thereby to derive evidence of public support. The 'consuming' public is much wider, but would be impossible to access comprehensively. The non-resident notion of the consumer also poses problems for a definition of consumers in terms of (rate, poll tax, council tax etc.) **payers**. The consumer may be user, resident, customer, citizen, each term implying a particular view of what is to be done. 'Consuming' may even add a spurious status, as when tenants' views are perceived as more important than those of other publics as a consequence of the landlord role of the council.

It may be that – the limits of the consumer concept being fairly clear at this point – local authorities begin to reject consumer language altogether. The crucial question then becomes one of what is to replace consumerism. The alternative notion of citizenship may be revived as a guiding principle in running the public services, and the 'depoliticization' implied by consumerism is transcended.

Specifically, it is very likely that consumer data will increasingly be incorporated as performance indicators in local authority management: bids for housing investment funds already use such indicators. In the National Health Service indicators of consumer satisfaction may be, and are, written in to contracts, for instance that the provider has to obtain (say) a 60% satisfaction rating to retain the contract. Without doubt there will be ever greater emphasis within local authorities upon measurement of consumer satisfaction: with real consequences.

Further, the growing familiarity with and use of consumer information will imply a differentiation of various publics. General ward surveys will not generate the required information. The comments of Harrow and Shaw are relevant:

> Customers may be patients, clients, customers, claimants, users, participants, residents, community charge payers, taxpayers; . . . Most of these descriptive terms have different cultural connotations – 'clients' and 'claimants' being dependants; customers, direct payers; participants, public spirited volunteers, and so on. An alternative categorization might be, cynically, in terms of the political damage they may do – the unstopppable, the buy-offable, and the neglectable (Harrow and Shaw, 1992, p. 116).

Perhaps senior officers in local government will devise – with consumers – forms of direct public representation in local authority decision making. In some local councils, carers and people with disabilities already participate in the social services or equivalent committee (integrating consumers as **users** into the political structure) and representation of trade unions (a collective 'consumption') may occur at other committees. Such direct representation relates back to citizenship. Perhaps the concept of citizenship (an implicit rejection of the premise of individualist consumerism) stands at one end of a continuum: the concept of a purely contractual relationship (the most commercial interpretation of consumerism) stands at the other.

Local charters

Local authority officials are also likely to be increasingly involved in the production of Citizen and Customer Charters, which may or may not be based on initial research such as consumer surveys. The existence of an effective charter has implications for the way in which local authority management is structured internally as well as externally, for it demands a move away from traditional lines of communication. Case study 3.4 outlines a specific example of a Consumer Charter.

CASE STUDY 3.4   A Customer Charter

The Citizens Charter and the Patients Charter are familiar features of central government policy, but 'charter' initiatives have also been developed independently within local authorities, and not necessarily within the same political parameters.

Leicester City Council's first Customer Charter was produced at the end of 1991; the second Charter was developed during 1993. Between these two dates, opinion research was conducted by the council to identify what the public actually want from the Charter.

> The information people tell us they are most interested in having about services is, first, who to contact at the Council about different issues, with direct line phone numbers; second, the quality of service they can expect from particular services; third, information about how to complain to the Council; and fourth, information about forthcoming developments in the city (Dungey, 1993, p. 8).

It was found that the public is sceptical about the worthy general sentiments of such charters. There was felt to be a preference for concrete practical information. The opinion research is meant to be part of a continuing process of asking the public about their priorities for services. Such charters in other authorities may not, however, have been based on original opinion data of this kind. Paternalism may persist: or simple lack of resources.

> Charter developments are meant to be central to the creation of more customer-centred, rights-based public services. It seems ironic, to say the least, that most of these Charters seem to be based on the old pattern of the organization deciding what the public can have, and then telling them (Dungey, 1993, p. 8).

The Consumer Charter – in central government, health or in local government – may be relatively superficial or more far-reaching in its scope. It may amount to window-dressing, or to a real attempt to identify the public's (or publics') priorities. This mirrors the ambivalence of the consumer orientation itself. Ultimately, both 'consumer' perspectives and Charters may be superseded by more fundamental change, but their present importance should not be undervalued.

Concluding comments

> Consumerism or charterism is an important influence on local government but increasingly it will be seen as an inadequate response. It is a stage to be gone through in the development of management in local government (Stewart, 1994, p. 29).

Conceivably, as suggested at the beginning of this chapter, the consumer perspective has been attractive to public service providers because it has appeared to move difficult questions about quality and cost out of the fractious political arena into an apolitical setting where 'listening to the public' has a self-evident meaning and is of itself desirable: a depoliticization of the role of the public which may, ironically, undermine rather than strengthen public services. The consumer perspective could disadvantage the very consumers it purports to place at the heart of public services. Harrow and Shaw suggest a 'patrician view of consumerism' may have arisen, in which senior managers' or politicians' 'user friendly' style predominates, but with no real input from the consumers themselves (Harrow and Shaw 1992, p. 118). The consumer perspective rules: the consumer does not.

> The managerialist bandwagon has not only rolled through new-right councils but become the stock in trade of most local authorities. Officers' meetings resound with a new language that refers to former clients as customers, produces business plans and seeks training, not so much in public administration but in the techniques of marketing and customer care (Chandler, 1991, p. 173).

Where does this leave the local authority manager? Practice – e.g. designing a consumer survey – may still be at the margins of the real problems and opportunities. Kelly (1992, p. 9) argues that the consumerism debate has moved on from 'changing structures, systems and procedures' to areas of responsiveness, quality and empowerment. Yet it is in precisely these areas that the debate and practice may not have moved on at all.

Finally, Harrow and Shaw remind us that public service managers may – unlike their private sector counterparts – actively attempt to avoid retaining customers (1992, p. 120). This is not merely traditional user-unfriendliness. There may be good reasons for seeking to part company with the customer: the appreciative and very happy recipient of a scarce resource may need to make way for someone with an objectively greater need. These problems are at the limits of consumerism. They are likely to increase, not decrease.

Summary

It has been argued in this chapter that the consumer perspective, notwithstanding its ambiguities, provides an opportunity for the redefinition of the relationship between the local authority and the public. It can and does assist rather than undermine managerial performance within the authority. However, there are problems with consumerism too. A reliance upon 'consumer surveys' as the sole or main vehicle of collecting public views is too narrow. A definition of the consumer solely as individual customer is similarly narrow, and ignores the necessarily collective nature of public provision and consumption. Further, there are several **publics** for which services are provided, not a single undifferentiated public. In terms of shaping models and principles of public management as a whole, the consumer perspective may not always be significant or fundamental in itself, but is important when considered alongside the growth of competition, contracts, decentralization and access to information.

Discussion questions and guidance

1. *'The phrase "bureaucratic paternalism" succinctly describes the old solutions that have become today's problems in local government. Too many local authority departments were built up to become large, hierarchical organizations structured to mass produce services'* (Hambleton, 1992, p. 11). *Is this an accurate description of the way in which local government today is organized and run? Is local authority management one of the 'old solutions that have become today's problems'?*

This question deals not primarily with the consumer perspective itself, but rather with the conditions under which the perspective became significant. The nature of 'bureaucratic paternalism' as a form of organization and management in local government requires elaboration here, illustrated with specific service examples. Bureaucracy and hierarchy require some examination: functions and dysfunctions. An evaluation of whether Hambleton's description fits local government today – and how this is changing – then follows. The consumer orientation is one of the possible changes. Relevant material for this question will be found towards the end of the section of Chapter 3 dealing with the concept of the consumer orientation.

2. *Formulate a systematic programme for the collection of consumer information within your local authority. Specify and justify your timetable and budget, and identify the mechanisms for feeding the results into the management of the authority.*

This exercise involves the consideration of consumer surveys (see Case study 3.3) and of non-survey methods (see Case study 3.2). The strengths and weaknesses of different ways of collecting consumer data should be evaluated. It might be remembered that the authority probably already collects some 'consumer information' which can be used, e.g. complaint levels. The constraints of budget and time must be considered, along with the availability of relevant skills (can the programme be formulated in-house?). Assuming the required information is collected, methods of using it in the management of the authority need to be specified in advance. It may be that corporate and operational managers have different needs here. Can the data be used at all? Gill and Johnson's introduction to research methods in applied management settings (1991) is a useful methods text.

3. *Assess Richards' claim (1992) that consumerism represents a new paradigm of public management.*

Here, the principal interest is not in problems of practice and implementation. Instead, the question concentrates upon the model of public management implied by the consumer orientation. Refer here to academic sources discussed in Chapter 3, including Harrow and Shaw (1992), Stewart and Walsh (1992) and Richards (1992), along with the more general management literature where appropriate (for instance Torrington, Weightman and Johns, 1989, especially chs 2 and 6). Some consideration may need to be given to the distinctive features of public (as opposed to private) management before assessing the possibility of a specific consumer paradigm within public management. Fenwick, Harrop and Elcock (1989) provide a broad review of the changing climate of public management.

4. *Select one broad area of local authority provision (for instance education, social services, housing, environmental health) and then identify:*

- *consumer measures of performance for key aspects of that service;*
- *methods for incorporating consumer performance measures into the process of performance review as a whole;*
- *any areas of the chosen service for which consumer assessment is not appropriate.*

The task here is to transform a concern with the consumer into a specific set of subjective performance measures. Case study 3.1, of the National Consumer Council study (1986), is an essential starting point. Material on performance review in Chapter 5 should also be consulted. It is particularly important to break down the chosen service area into its constituent operational parts: within social services are (e.g.) services for children, families, elderly people, people with disabilities; and there are cross-cutting divisions into residential, day-care, and so on. Contracting-out services (e.g. of residential elderly care) complicates the total picture further, yet makes effective review of performance even more crucial. It will be necessary to be aware of the inherent limitations of performance measurement as well as the particular limitations of seeking to formulate subjective indicators. Consider the respective contributions of qualitative and quantitative measures – are some aspects of provision beyond measurement?

5. *'It is appropriate that senior officers neither reject consumer research as fashionable but empty, nor embrace it with wholly unrealistic expectations of what it may be able to measure. There should instead be a dispassionate analysis of exactly what it can deliver'. What **can** consumer research deliver to senior officers?*

This statement is taken from Chapter 3, at the end of the section entitled 'the practice of consumerism'. It requires an examination of precisely how senior council officers can use the fruits of consumer research: be as specific and practical as possible. This should ideally be applied to knowledge or experience of a particular local authority. Develop your own case study if possible.

6. *'At Leicester City Council, we aim to emphasize publication of information and standards of greatest interest to the public. This is often not the information needed by managers or*

accountants' (Dungey, 1993, p. 8). Does a consumer 'Charter' in particular and the consumer orientation in general mean that managers and the public have different needs: different information needs, different service priorities, different standards?

Consider here Case study 3.4 from this chapter. Particular examples from Leicester City Council are also referred to in the LGMB guide to 'encouraging and managing complaints' (1992). The discussion of information and the public in Chapter 6 may also be of use. The essential problem is that the consumer orientation, if taken seriously, may expose differences of interest between the manager and the public. One response, of course, is **not** to take the consumer orientation seriously: if it is implemented only at the level of a superficial user-friendliness, then few problems (or costs) arise. The challenges arise for those authorities ambitious enough to adopt the consumer orientation in order to effect real organizational change. This question invites an exploration of these problems, together with possible solutions.

Suggested further reading

Gyford, J. (1991) *Citizens, Consumers and Councils: Local Government and the Public*, Macmillan, London. Assesses many of the problems of a consumer orientation, with useful examples.

Prior, D. (1995) Citizen's Charters, in J. Stewart and G. Stoker (eds), *Local Government in the 1990s*, Macmillan, London, pp 86–103. Reviews the growth of charters and their differing links to consumerism and citizenship.

Burns, D., Hambleton, R. and Hoggett, P. (1994) *The Politics of Decentralization: Revitalizing Local Democracy*, Macmillan, London. Considers citizen participation and the regeneration of local accountability. Includes many references to practice.

Barnes, C. and Williams, K. (1993) Education and Consumerism: Managing an Emerging Marketing Culture in Schools, in K. Isaac-Henry, C. Painter and C. Barnes (eds), *Management in the Public Sector: Challenge and Change*, Chapman & Hall, London, pp 115–132. Explores the growth of a consumerist ethos in education. This links to our twin themes of competition and consumerism.

Harrow, J. and Shaw, M. (1992) The Manager Faces the Consumer, in L. Willcocks and J. Harrow (eds), *Rediscovering Public Services Management*, McGraw-Hill, London. pp 113–140. Considers problems as well as opportunities in the practice of a consumer approach.

Richards, S. (1992) *Who Defines the Public Good? The Consumer Paradigm in Public Management*, Public Management Foundation, London. Examines whether the consumer perspective constitutes a new model, or 'paradigm', for public sector management as a whole.

MANAGEMENT IN A COMPARATIVE CONTEXT

4

The management of local authorities in Britain takes place in an international context which is growing in significance. Having considered the competitive environment and the rediscovery of the public within a domestic setting, a context has now been provided for a comparative discussion of local government. The international dimension is important in several senses. Europe provides opportunities for the development of local public services in Britain. Equally, European regulation may provide constraints. Examples from Europe – and beyond – place the management of British local government in a **comparative context**. The serious comparative **analysis** of local public service provision remains an underdeveloped area of study. However, a review of the comparative context in which British local government operates begins to illuminate domestic experience in a practical sense, and also suggests productive areas for comparative research in the future.

Introduction

The study of British local government in a comparative context has been relatively neglected. Only recently (e.g. Chandler, 1993) has any coherent comparative study been attempted. The comparative study of the **management** of local public services has been even further neglected. Yet comparative study of local public service management is of crucial importance, for instance in

- suggesting ways forward for service development in the UK;

- identifying good practice;

- extending the basis for comparative analysis and the building of explanatory models;

- assessing the significance beyond the UK of fundamental changes of orientation in public service management, such as the growth of contract management and the market mechanism.

A number of reasons may be suggested for the underdevelopment of comparative analysis.

First, 'public administration' as a field of study in Britain has tended to be descriptive, insular and relatively parochial in its focus on the development of British institutions.

Secondly, insofar as comparative analysis has been carried out, it has tended to look toward American material (e.g. Pollitt, 1990). This has a value in itself, but leaves out of account non-European societies such as New Zealand which have public service traditions comparable to those of Britain (Wistrich, 1992) or European countries such as the Netherlands which are readily accessible for comparative study in terms of both geography and language.

Thirdly, a degree of ethnocentrism is present in the focus upon local government management in Britain alone.

Fourthly, a genuine concern exists in relation to the nature of comparative analysis. Is comparative study possible at all, given the conceptual and practical contrasts between different countries, the difference between the unitary and the federal state, the profound differences in the degree of centralization and decentralization in Europe alone, the contrasting legal, cultural and political context, and the formal relationships of local governments to central administration in different societies? Even if the considerable problems of comparative **study** are overcome, this does not necessarily generate comparative **analysis**.

> The comparative analysis of social and political systems is fraught with difficulties. A key problem in comparative studies is that of finding the correct balance between description and analysis (Stoker, 1991, p. 4).

Alongside the relative neglect of a comparative dimension within academic studies, British local authorities have increasingly sought to exploit extra-national opportunities, e.g. in the growth of economic development activity; in developing specialist knowledge of European sources of funding among senior officers; and in specific links with particular towns and cities in Europe and beyond. The **economic** thrust of much current international contact in local government reflects the need to compensate for the constraints of domestic funding and the collapse of old industries. To some degree local government has looked outward by necessity.

The following discussion is based upon two assumptions: first, that a comparative dimension is now an essential aspect of any **practical** review of trends, developments and possibilities in running local services; and, secondly, that a comparative dimension is also an essential part of any **analytical** account of overall managerial change, for instance the growth of private-sector models of management. At its least, comparative study provides a context for subsequent understanding of the management of local government. At its best, a comparative account provides an analysis of cross-national changes in the process of management itself, including the balance between public and private provision and the relationship of state and market.

The discussion is structured into two distinct parts. Each provides a comparative perspective.

First, an overall description and discussion is provided of local government and local service provision in selected countries. The societies included here are:

- the Netherlands: a Western European near-neighbour and constitutional monarchy;
- the United States: a Western industrial nation, a federal state, with cultural and political traditions which contrast to those of Britain and some parts of Western Europe;
- New Zealand: a society geographically distant from Britain, but with a set of political parties and a tradition of public services closely akin to the former colonial power;
- Denmark: a Northern European society, member of the EU, but with a distinct tradition of a large public-service sector, high taxation, and high level of local services.

The selection of course could have been made differently. There is no claim to be comprehensive. Instead, the intention here is to point-up **similarities and differences with the local structures and organizational-political arrangements** which apply to Britain. This contributes to a **comparative perspective** in the sense of a comparison with **local government systems and processes** in Britain. Some of the implications are then drawn-out.

Secondly, some key themes are introduced, arising from experience in particular countries but having a potential application to local services as a whole. These themes include:

- market and state;
- control and autonomy;
- central and local;
- public and private;
- elected and appointed.

The development of these and further themes would provide another yardstick for assessing British experience. As well as comparing local government in Britain with other countries, it becomes possible to compare experience in a number of countries against general principles. A **comparative perspective** is sought here in the sense of **a comparative analysis** of managerial change.

Among the reasons identified by Clarke and Stewart for the study of local government in a comparative European context is the following:

> Britain now stands out as exceptional in the extent of its centralization at a time when other countries are decentralizing (1991, p. 13).

If accurate, this view of a relatively (and increasingly) centralized British political system has direct consequences for the place occupied by local authorities in providing local services, and for the particular role of the local authority manager today.

Local government: selected comparisons

The Netherlands

Below the central government level, there are three layers of subnational government in Holland:

1. **Provinces** (a total of 12)   This regional tier of government is responsible for a range of services including the environment, planning, transport and public works.

2. **Municipalities** (a total of 647)   This level of government equates most closely to what is understood as local government in a British context. The municipalities have a wide range of services to deliver, but it should be noted that some services are provided jointly with the provincial tier, or indeed with central government: 'co-governmental' tasks (OEDC, 1993, p. 202). The difficulties of direct comparison with Britain are evident from the start. For instance, the municipalities provide education, but only 28% of children are in this public system, the majority attending denominational schools (OECD, 1993, p. 189).

3. **'Polder' Boards**   This component of local government (perhaps more accurately local administration) is responsible for services and duties related to drainage and waterways, linked to the historial importance of land reclamation in the Netherlands.

The **municipality** is the key element for any analysis of Dutch local government. It is to be noted that one of the elements of Dutch central government's public service reforms has been the 'decentralization impulse' – the devolution of more duties **from central to local government**. This has been particularly prominent since 1991. 'The Government gave fresh impetus to the devolution of responsibilities and resources to lower tiers of government' (OECD, 1992, p. 63). The Dutch municipality, then, has had a greater range of services to manage – in direct contrast to the gradual removal of the responsibilities of British local authorities.

The attempt to transfer duties from central government to local government in the Netherlands is not motivated by a contrasting political approach to that of Britain. Indeed, the main Dutch public-service reforms have been carried through by Right/Centre and coalition government. Such changing coalitions may well be a feature of Dutch central government in the late 1990s and beyond, given the decline of the main parties and the growth of hitherto more marginal political groupings at the election of May 1994.

The relevant contrast between the Netherlands and Britain is not one of party politics. It is the contrast between a relatively decentralized system and a relatively centralized system.

Recent attempts to decentralize services further by transferring more services to the local level are motivated primarily by the desire for cost savings at the centre. A specific aim of the Dutch government's 'great efficiency operation' from 1990 onward has been to slim-down central government to what is deemed necessary, and no more. Once transferred to the more local level, it may indeed be that municipalities contract-out services to the private sector though without the compulsion associated with British experience.

It is possible to argue, then, that the decentralization of the Dutch system is a decentralized service provision rather than a decentralized policy-making. Bekke, for instance, considers that Dutch local authorities 'function to a great extent as offices for central government in the local community' (Bekke, 1991, p. 123). According to this view, Dutch decentralization does not denote autonomy or independence for local government – instead, it means a form of agency status. However, it can certainly be said that, in comparison to **Britain**, the municipalities of the Netherlands **do** enjoy a relative independence of both provision and policy-making.

As in Britain, private-sector involvement in the delivery of local public services has increased in Holland during the 1980s and 1990s. There is no compulsion to submit a set of defined activities to outside tender in Holland. Contracting-out reflects instead a general concern with businesslike government, and a particular form of contract management which has developed in Dutch municipalities since the 1980s.

> Agreements are made between the governing body and officials about the tasks to be executed and the performance to be delivered, leaving management to decide how it will execute the tasks (Bekke, 1991, p. 131).

This **managerial autonomy** is another facet of decentralization. In addition to the decentralized administration of services to the municipalities, there is scope for decentralization of management **within** the municipality. Managerial autonomy implies a reduced role for the local political leadership. Once goals and policies are broadly determined, managers get on with managing. At this state, the private sector may be brought in to deliver specific services according to a set contract. Structures and roles in the Dutch municipalities do vary, but within Dutch local government as a whole there is considerable scope for managerial devolution. A leading example of managerial change in the Netherlands municipality is provided by Case study 4.1, which looks at Tilburg council.

CASE STUDY 4.1 The Netherlands: the Tilburg Model

The general themes of managerial devolution and budgetary decentralization are illustrated in the specific example of Tilburg.

Within Tilburg City Council, elected politicians remain responsible for determination of overall policy, but service managers are given considerable freedom in operational terms and in the implementation of policies.

'Once the strategy has been formed, managers are left to manage in the most efficient way' (Open University, 1992).

This form of contract management represents a move from a hierarchy to a network form of organization: from a bureaucratic structure to a network of profit centres – with managerial devolution and accountability for each profit centre. Managers are contracted to secure a particular service, and to make a return. There is no political dimension at the stage of service delivery in a sense comparable to the British council committee.

The Tilburg system was set up with the intention of profit-centres being open to competition from private contractors too. Such contractors may include the voluntary ('non-profit') sector as well as the private company – the City Council contracts voluntary organizations to provide certain community services on the basis of agreed targets and a business plan. The Tilburg system represents

> a model of a decentralized and relatively deregulated form of managing local government services.
>
> It is thus possible to assess the extent to which changes in UK local government management are conforming to a pattern identifiable in other European countries.

Although the Tilburg council has been regarded as something of a model for other local authorities to learn from, it is important to recognize that managerial innovation in Dutch local government has taken several forms. Not all municipalities have moved in the same direction as Tilburg. The diversity of local organizational arrangements in Holland stands in contrast to the uniformity of the British system of local government and is a further aspect of decentralization.

In the period 1984 to 1988, Delft adopted many of the changes associated with Tilburg – contract management, devolution of responsibility for resources, a relative independence for different service areas – but additionally it developed a high-profile consumer/customer orientation. Delft has organized a large panel of households to provide regular customer feedback on services provided, and those subjective performance indicators are used in the monitoring of services. Capelle aan den Ijssel has followed a similar path. 'In line with the changes at Tilburg and Delft, Capelle's organizational renewal took the form of decentralizing functions to restructured service departments' (Snape, 1994, p. 47). However, Capelle went about the process of change more rapidly and abruptly, leading to some problems of friction and morale which do not seem to have characterized these processes at Delft and Tilburg.

Competitive tendering in Britain (see Chapter 2) has been a matter of compulsion, and has been strongly charged in political and ideological terms. Municipal services in Holland have also been subject to contracting-out. However, the Dutch context has been less obviously ideological than that of Britain. A study of competitive tendering in 15 European countries found that the political complexion of Dutch local authorities did not seem to influence their approach to competitive tendering (Council of Europe, 1993, p. 42). In considering the **extent** of privatization, similar results were obtained. The study suggests that, in the Netherlands,

> privatization at local level is mainly based on rational/pragmatic considerations. After all, 'contracting out' is the most 'non-political' form of privatization, and is therefore the most heavily influenced by pragmatic and commercial arguments (Council of Europe, 1993, p. 46).

It is inconceivable that the view put forward in the Council of Europe study would be expressed in relation to Britain. This illustrates once more the contrasts and insights produced by comparative study. Contracting-out in the Netherlands – as one element of managerial change – does not seem to have been ideologically driven from the centre. Perhaps as a consequence, it is treated relatively pragmatically at the local level.

In the Netherlands, local government has faced an agenda which will be familiar to all those with a knowledge of British local government: a 'businesslike' approach, a slimming-down of overall public expenditure, a resource-led approach to local management, increased private provision, an emphasis on the 'customer'. Although the agenda may be similar in the Netherlands and Britain, responses have differed. The differences in the way public-service reform has been tackled in the two countries are differences in local–central relations and in particular the extent of centralization. The greater managerial autonomy and devolution in Holland arise from a fundamentally decentralized system. The differences between the two countries are not primarily political: it would be more accurate to call the differences cultural.

The United States of America

In Britain and other European countries there are considerable differences in local service provision, but there have also been some common themes: a social-democratic welfare ethos to a greater or lesser degree; common historical experience; and, increasingly, a context of regulation and statutory provision arising from the Treaties of Rome and Maastricht and from membership of what has become the European Union. A comparison with local government in the United States, however, poses certain problems.

Historical expectations of **public** provision in the United States differ from those of Europe. The strong recovery of the Republicans in the mid-term elections of November 1994 was based in part on an appeal for 'less government' which, for historical and ideological reasons, carries considerable weight. Government spending in the USA tends to be less than the Western European norm. Public spending and public receipts, as a proportion of Gross Domestic Product (GDP), are smaller in the United States than in all Western European countries except Switzerland: see Figures 4.1 and 4.2, derived from OECD profiles (1993). More recent figures, although using different definitions, indicate a similar relative position. Current general government **revenue** as a percentage of GDP is lower for the USA than for any of the Western European countries, and current general government **expenditure** as as percentage of GDP is lower for the USA than for any Western European countries apart from Switzerland and Iceland (OECD, 1994, pp. 40–1).

Local politics are constituted differently in the USA and Europe. The federal nature of the United States makes a comparison of 'central' and 'local' difficult, and central–local relations are themselves considerably less clear-cut than in the UK. 'Intergovernmental relations in the United States are more a tangled web than a layered structure' (Norton, 1994, p. 406). Nonetheless, as we will see below, certain parallels with British public service reforms may yet be identified.

Lavery (1992) notes that British and United States local government contrast significantly in terms of size, range of functions, types of authority (e.g. city, county, district), method of raising income, and degree of party political involvement. Lavery identifies three forms of local government in the United States (1992, p. 9):

1. **The Commission** Composed of a small number of elected members, the Commission is responsible for the range of local government services. Each commissioner heads a specific department. Lavery indicates that this form of organization in local government is in decline.

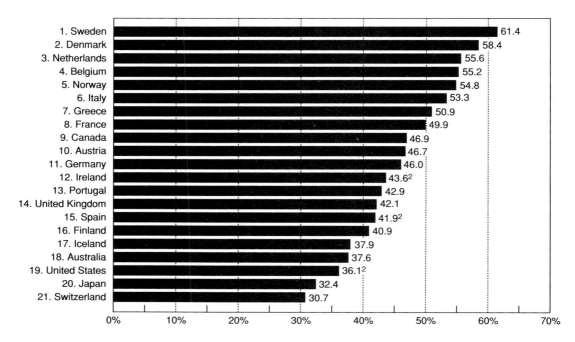

Figure 4.1 Current weight of the government sector: public expenditure and GDP
Figures refer to 1990 (except (2) 1989).
Source: © OECD, 1993, *Public Management: OECD Country Profiles*. Reproduced by permission of the OECD.

2. **The council manager** A small elected council 'appoints a professional manager
   to be responsible for running the authority' (Lavery, 1992, p. 9). The Council
   manager has a considerable operational autonomy – a freedom to manage.
3. **The mayor/council**. Here, an elected mayor is also the council's chief executive.
   Lavery identifies 'weak' and 'strong' mayoral systems, where the mayor may either
   co-exist with other directly elected senior officers, or, alternatively, where the mayor
   'shares responsibility for policy-making with the council, but is totally responsible
   for administration' (Lavery, 1992, p. 9).

All types of local government in the United States are 'creatures of the state': they exist
to perform only those functions given to them by the legislature of their particular state
(Keller and Perry, 1991, p. 34; Chandler, 1993, p. 140; Norton, 1994, p. 395). It should be
noted that this legal phrase refers to **the state**, not the federal government. 'Not even
mentioned in the federal constitution, local governments are creatures of the states and
their powers and authorities are derived entirely from the states' (OECD, 1993, p. 327).
Beneath the level of the state, the next layer of local government is the **county**, of which
there are over 3000 in the United States, and which have traditionally (though not exclusively) been run by a Commission (Keller and Perry, 1991, pp. 35–6).

   The municipal authorities, the general-service **cities**, may be run in a number of
ways, as indicated above. Originally the mayor/council system dominated. This
system reflected the "separation of powers" conception embodied in state and national

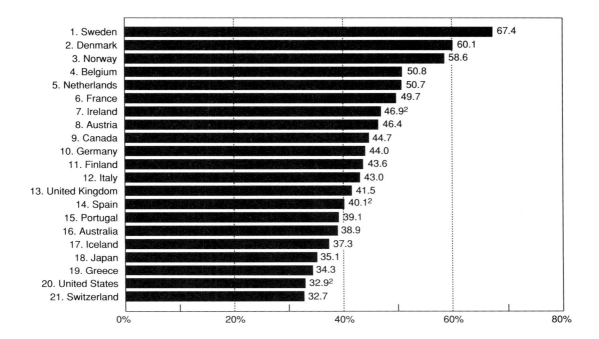

Figure 4.2 Current weight of the government sector: public receipts and GDP
Figures refer to 1990 (except ([2]) 1989).
Source: © OECD, 1993, *Public Management: OECD Country Profiles*. Reproduced by permission of the OECD.

governments' (Keller and Perry, 1991, p. 40). The Commission, and then more significantly the Council Manager system, came to be seen as more streamlined, perhaps
more attuned to a managerial approach to running the main urban areas. The 'ideal-
type' city manager is responsible to a small elected council, can be dismissed at any
time by that council, and has wide 'hire and fire' powers of his or her own.

The systems of United States local government described here are not exhaustive,
nor exclusive. Indeed, an elected mayoral post may be bolted on to the basic council
manager system (Keller and Perry, 1991, p. 42; Hambleton, 1991, p. 4). Variations exist
within these basic models. However, it is possible to identify **distinguishing characteristics** within the various United States systems of local government, and to analyse
these comparatively.

The council manager system, or equivalent form of organisation, seems to have a
particular relevance beyond the United States. As will be seen below, there is a resem-
blance to the very considerable autonomy given to the restyled New Zealand chief
executive. The council manager mode of local government organization also has
parallels with the managerial devolution of the Tilburg model in Holland. In both
systems, managers-are-there-to-manage under a general and strategic policy framework provided by a steamlined elective tier.

The prospect of a council manager free from day-to-day political supervision has
appealed to elements of the British Conservative Party. There are indeed British local
authorities where the chief executive officer has taken the title of manager although

this may not imply wholesale adoption of a managerialist ethos. The council manager model may also be considered more closely in Britain as the client-contractor form of organization comes to dominate local government as a whole (see Chapter 2). The 'council manager' is now a term with an international currency. Case study 4.2 presents the developed council manager system in Phoenix, Arizona.

CASE STUDY 4.2 The United States: the Phoenix Model

Phoenix has adopted and developed a council manager system of local government. The elective tier is small: eight councillors plus an elected mayor. The elected group gives managerial authority and operational freedom to an appointed council manager. This elected council – small by British standards –has overall responsibility for policy and can remove the council manager at any time. There is thus a concentration of power in two senses:

1. a concentration of power in a small elected group;
2. a concentration of power in the office and post of council manager.

It could be argued that the check against abuse of the former is the electorate, and against abuse of the latter is the absolute accountability of the manager to the council. These checks are important insofar as this model is the main alternative to the council/mayor model with its in built 'constitutional' system of checks and balances.

Does the system work? Phoenix attracts considerable favourable attention. Lavery notes: 'Phoenix is seen as a national leader on competitive tendering and efficiency improvements. It is the only local government case study in the forthcoming Tom Peters' book on excellence in the public sector' (1992, p. 10).

The Phoenix city manager system has internal and external management implications. Externally, there is an emphasis on public consultation – on being responsive to the public – which is particularly important given the small number of elected members. Internally, the council manager system is non-bureaucratic, relatively 'results oriented' (Hambleton, 1993, p. 17). A customer- friendly, broadly private-sector inspired, entrepreneurial model seems to be the motivating force. It is to be remembered too that **party** political affiliation is not a feature of this system: indeed, it is prohibited (Lavery, 1992, p. 10).

'Phoenix has sophisticated management systems with business planning, internal trading accounts and merit pay for senior staff. It is widely regarded as the best managed big city in the US' (Hambleton, 1993, p. 17).

Following the decline of the traditional Commission, the mayor/council system represents the alternative to council manager models. The mayor/council is still significant in the larger cities. Stoker and Wolman point out that nearly 60% of cities over 250 000 in population use a mayor/council mode of organization (1992, p. 242). The **strong** mayor system involves a leadership role which is currently unknown in British local government.

> In the strong mayor form, the directly elected mayor thus serves as the chief executive in a structure which closely resembles the separation of powers on which the American national government is based. As a result, the mayor is highly visible and frequently is the source of political leadership for the city (Stoker and Wolman, 1992, p. 243).

What are the characteristics of the United States mayoral system? Clearly the **elective** nature of what in its 'strong' form amounts to a chief executive officer provides a larger degree of managerial authority – just like the appointed city manager. However, an elected post is bound to stand in a different relationship to both council and public when contrasted with an appointee. The difference may be problematic. A report of a speech by the mayor of Indianapolis suggests that he may derive authority from an appeal 'over the heads of the council to the voters' (reported in Local Government Chronicle, 23 April 1993).

The style and programme of this Republican mayor emphasized competition, performance measurement, tendering-out and the link between services and costs. Perhaps the 'strong mayor' is characterized by an activism: defining problems, picking-up current issues in the city, leading a coalition of what Stoker and Wolman describe as 'local business elites, labour and municipal bureaucrats' (1992, p. 245). The strong mayor is in a position of significant political **leadership** and influence, but not political **control** in the sense of party formations in British local authorities. The mayoral system also places managerial and political roles together in a relationship unfamiliar within British experience.

The strong mayoral model is managerial freedom plus political clout. The weak mayoral model is more akin to the separation of influence and the balance of powers in Britain, with the important difference of a greater elective element among senior officials in the United States example. Increasingly, both city manager and elected mayor models are cross-cut by themes such as these, identified by Hambleton (1993, pp. 16–17):

- **private sector contracting**, with an established history in the United States (albeit, Hambleton suggests, not as extensive as sometimes thought);
- **municipal enterprise**, for instance Baltimore and Seattle as examples of cities developing their own utilities and forms of local revenue for local provision;
- **developing the voluntary sector**, in contractual arrangements for delivery of local services;
- **internal management** changes, towards non-bureaucratic business planning, and managerial flexibility;
- **partnerships within the local community** which redraw the boundaries between local state and community groups – Hambleton gives the example of neighbourhood initiatives in Baltimore.

It can readily be seen that such **themes** are recognisable in both Dutch and British experience. It also seems that, in the United States, the differences between the city manager and elected mayor models are narrowing, as more council-manager cities introduce the elected mayor alongside the manager: 'the distinction in form is starting to become blurred' (Hambleton, 1991, p. 4). The view can tentatively be advanced that structural/organizational adaptations in different societies are tending to converge in the face of a common agenda for change. Managerial devolution, a new public–private mix, a critique of the assumed dysfunctions of public-service bureaucracy are encountered, it seems, everywhere. However, comparisons are still at an early stage of development. It is appropriate at this point to consider another example, from the Southern hemisphere, but with historical and cultural links to Britain.

New Zealand

New Zealand presents an interesting comparison with European and North American examples of local government reform. Culturally linked to European, and in particular British, history, with political parties more closely resembling their British than their American counterparts, and geographically distant from both Europe and North America, New Zealand has carried through a major programme of public-service reorganization. Both local and central government underwent a substantial change during Labour Party administration in the latter half of the 1980s.

The changes which took place in New Zealand between 1984 and 1990 involved the reorganization of local government, elements of privatization, reshaping central government departments as quasi-commercial agencies, subjecting nationalized industries to market systems of management and operation, increasing efficiency and user-influence in public service provision, and lowering the tax burden. New Zealand experienced an overall public-sector 'reorientation', of which the significant changes to local government were a part. New Zealand's reforms began later than those of Britain but have gone further and deeper.

> Renewed belief in the market as the best determinant of allocative efficiency has been the spur to the changes (Wistrich, 1992, p. 119).

The central principles of New Zealand public service reform are to be found in its Treasury's reports on 'economic management', produced in 1984, and 'government management', produced in 1987. The latter report – produced for the incoming Labour Government, about to start its second three-year term of office in 1987 –represents an intellectually coherent set of ideas on the role of the state and role of the market alongside specific proposals. Wistrich (1992, pp. 121–2) summarizes the principles of New Zealand public service reform as follows:

- executive agencies to be run by senior managers, with time-limited contracts, appointed by ministers;
- managers to act as employers, with devolved authority over wages and conditions;
- public funding to be linked to specified outputs, using full-cost calculations;
- performance to be assessed formally;
- improved reporting of agencies and their managers to the political level;

- policy advice and delivery of services to be separated out (in the context of a belief in 'agency theory' present also in the reform of British central government departments);
- central controls to be at the minimum level necessary.

The principles of reform have been enacted in various ways throughout the New Zealand public sector. 'State-owned enterprises' became managed on commercial lines while remaining in public ownership – a reform process still continuing, although many such industries have now been sold off to the private sector altogether. Central government agencies became subject to a commercial regime of financial management under the State Sector Act 1988 and the Public Finance Act 1989. Local government was reformed under the terms of the Local Government Amendment Act 1988. The Audit Commission writes of New Zealand local government reorganization in the following terms.

> The New Zealand reorganization is akin to the British reorganization of 1974 when a pattern of very modest urban and rural district councils was amalgamated into the present district council pattern to create units with improved professionalism, ability and resource base. New Zealand local government is fairly 'small beer' given its limited range of functions compared with the UK pattern. As it does not locally administer national services it is relatively 'at ease' with New Zealand central government. And its ability to fund its services from locally raised revenues underpins its independence (Audit Commission, 1993, p. 4).

By 1989 the new local government system of New Zealand was in place. The previous system had comprised almost 500 separate authorities: 21 regional authorities, 231 territorial councils (counties, municipalities, towns and districts) and 242 'special purpose' authorities concerned with hospitals, rivers, pest control and many other single service functions. The pre-1989 system had grown-up directly from the British-inspired local government system set up in the nineteenth century. From 1989, the local government system in New Zealand existed on a much smaller scale: 14 regional authorities, 74 districts or cities, and 7 special purpose authorities, i.e. less than 100 local authorities in total.

The considerable reduction in the total number of New Zealand local authorities does not, of course, bear any **necessary** relation to increased efficiency, effectiveness or other generally desirable goals. Indeed, reducing the number of elected members and number of elected authorities might have negative consequences, e.g. for local accountability. Partly to deal with this possibility, the reorganized local government system in New Zealand includes a community/neighbourhood level too which has a defined role in, for instance, providing a public input into the annual plans of the municipal authorities.

Social and educational services are not local authority responsibilities in New Zealand. There is a regional tier of government in New Zealand which is absent in England and Wales. However, there are common elements too. Culturally and politically there has been a recognisably similar debate in New Zealand and in Britain. To some degree there is a common discourse. Chapman (1989) suggests that the public-sector reform process in the two societies was – in the 1980s – comparable.

Also – notwithstanding the Audit Commission's identification of an independence in New Zealand local government – there is a shared tradition of **centralism** in the two countries. Reforms are centrally driven in both societies. Local independence in New Zealand is more to do with lack of responsibility for major services than to any culture of decentralization along Dutch, or even American, lines.

The centrally driven reform processes in New Zealand and Britain have been implemented in different ways. In Britain, central government policy towards local government has not only been centrally determined, but has also been directive and punitive. This has been clear in the penalties imposed for 'overspending' by British local authorities and, especially, in the statutory prescriptions of British CCT. In New Zealand, there has been more emphasis upon incentives within a more devolved structure, as the best way of implementing market reforms (Chapman, 1989, p. 44).

The Treasury has had a very significant role in shaping the direction of public service management in New Zealand. Chapman points to the central involvement of the New Zealand Treasury in 'policy advice on public-sector reform' (1989, p. 47). Within this process, micro reforms and financial incentives have had more significance in New Zealand than in Britain. The differences between the two societies are not differences of centralism: the differences lie in the **instruments** of centrally driven public-service reform. An example of this is to be found in the work of the Local Authority Trading Enterprise (LATE), i.e. the New Zealand equivalent of the British DSO. The LATE has far more commercial freedom than the DSO to raise money, enter contracts, and participate in the marketplace, yet the operation of competitive tendering in New Zealand local government is largely non-compulsory. Competition **without** compulsion may ironically be more thorough-going than statutory prescription (Fenwick, Ranade, Snape and Harrop, 1994). Equally ironic, these far-reaching reforms in New Zealand were implemented by Labour governments prior to the Conservative victory in 1990.

The system of local government which has been created by the New Zealand market reforms is presented in Case study 4.3.

CASE STUDY 4.3 New Zealand local government

In 1984 there was a total of almost 500 regional, municipal and special purpose local authorities in New Zealand. The officer-member (managerial-political) model was derived from British practice. Almost all finance for New Zealand services, however, was raised locally.

From 1989 there has been a simplified system of around 95 local authorities. However, structural reorganization in itself is only a framework. Management is a process which takes place within the formal structure. The essential point about New Zealand reorganization of local government is that it was a vehicle for the implementation of fundamental market-based reforms of public-service management.

Local government reorganization was not an end in itself. It was a means of empowering councils with the critical mass of ability and resources to implement other reforms leading to greater accountability, transparency and contestability in local government services (Audit Commission, 1993, p. 5).

'Contestability' refers to competition between local service providers, including contracting-out.

Characteristics of the reformed model of managing local government in New Zealand are:

- reduced but more specific role for elected members in policy determination and monitoring;
- the chief executive as sole employee of the council: fixed-term contract, performance-related pay, and managerial authority and autonomy;
- responsibility of all employees through direct line- management to the chief executive who effectively functions as the employer;
- competitive tendering, largely not compulsory;
- access to information (comparable to British provision);
- public consultation on annual and other plans.

The current New Zealand ethos of local authority management is based on a private-sector model, and is market-led. This has been achieved without some of the legal compulsion of the British system. The reforms of local government in New Zealand started later than in Britain, but have gone further. The mechanisms of reform differ between the two societies: 'the emphasis in New Zealand is away from direct central control to regulation through established self- governing systems' (Wistrich, 1992, p. 132).

It is clear that parallels exist between the New Zealand Chief Executive and the United States City Manager. Managerial devolution, a 'freedom to manage', a private-sector model (fixed-term, performance related), and a results-oriented regime are features of United States and New Zealand local government. The Dutch reforms are similarly managerialist in nature, even though they do not concentrate upon the empowerment of one senior manager alone. In all three systems, there is an increased emphasis on performance, and a reduced role for elected councillors. Have the changes in New Zealand been successful?

The Audit Commission (1993) finds both strengths and weaknesses in the New Zealand reforms of local government. The original impetus for reform, deriving from ideas developed within the New Zealand Treasury, was characterized by an emphasis on accountability and the monitoring of performance; a stress on incentives and the separation of principals from agencies; a focus on consumer preferences and a revision of public sector employment contracts; an emphasis on management rather than policy; the disaggregation of large bureaucratic structures and a strong inclination to competitive tendering (Audit Commission, 1993, p. 2).

Structural reorganization of New Zealand's system of local government seems to have been a necessary condition for implementation of such principles. However, structural reorganization was not a sufficient condition for complete managerial change: this also depended upon the culture of change associated with political developments in the early 1980s, and the perceived inadequacies of traditional public service management. Without doubt, the post-1989 chief executive in New Zealand local government is in a position to succeed in strict managerial terms of cutting costs and increasing efficiency. Such managerial autonomy, authority and discretion certainly feature in any comparative analysis of the societies selected for study in this chapter. However, there are drawbacks.

Given the new role of the New Zealand Chief Executive, there is a question over whether the elected members 'have enough to do' (Audit Commission, 1993, p. 6). There has been some lack of clarity about the respective roles of Chief Executive and (salaried) members. The Audit Commission study also refers to

evidence of 'last will and testament' deals by terminating councils; of 'sweetheart' deals with redundant officers; of problems of reconciling operational and information systems between amalgamating councils; and of the complication of revising land use development plans to new boundaries. In particular, the unpopularity of changes in local tax burdens consequent on reorganization has been a continuing destabilizing influence (1993, p. 1).

Perhaps such drawbacks are the temporary effect of change **per se**. It would hardly be expected that the very considerable changes implemented in the way local and central government are run in New Zealand would be without transitional problems. Supporters of change would point to the undoubted economies of scale and efficiencies of management which now characterize New Zealand local government. Others might feel that the ambiguity surrounding the new role of the elected council member is a symptom of an underlying ambiguity about accountability and public input into the new arrangements. In either event, the managerialist, performance-related, fixed-term and resource-led Chief Executive in New Zealand local government is a key aspect for further study. It would be fruitful to compare and evaluate the United States City Manager and the New Zealand Chief Executive. The result of such an evaluation would tell us a great deal about the future of managing local government in Britain.

The key changes to local government in New Zealand arise from the period of Labour governments between 1984 and 1990. However, in 1990 the National Party – the conservatives – was elected to government with a large majority and in 1993 narrowly re-elected. This change has placed the process of public-sector reform in a qualitatively different context. It is no longer a matter of using the market mechanism for quasi-social welfare objectives as Labour would have claimed to have done during its tenure.

Instead, the structure of public provision has been rapidly changed toward a private-sector model which is seen as desirable in itself. The state-owned enterprise has increasingly become a private enterprise *per se*. The Employment Contracts Act 1991 is amongst legislation which tends to 'individualize' the employee–employer relationship, along the lines of accumulated British trade union legislation. Health care is no longer universally available free of charge. The equivalent of British child benefit has been abolished. New Zealand, which developed a comprehensive publicly provided social welfare system ahead of all other industrial societies, including Britain, has arguably become the first society to dismantle that system.

The political changes in New Zealand render any prospective analysis difficult. The 1993 general election was accompanied by a popular vote to change the British style electoral system to one based upon a form of proportional representation. Subsequent elections will thus be less likely to produce overwhelming majorities for any party. However, it is very clear that market-based models for delivery services will continue to characterize both Labour and National Party thinking, albeit with a different emphasis in either case.

Writing of the period 1984 to 1990, the Audit Commission drew the following conclusion:

> Overriding all of the detailed reports of the experience of individual councils, one dominant message emerges. New Zealand was clear about its objectives, and swift about their implementation (Audit Commission, 1993, p. 17).

Such ideological single-mindedness seems to have characterized developments since 1990 too.

Denmark

Local public service provision in Denmark differs from that of Britain, the United States, the Netherlands and New Zealand in one important respect. The public sector is larger in Denmark than in almost all other major industrial countries, whether measured as government employment as a proportion of total employment, public expenditure per capita, public expenditure as proportion of GDP, or public receipts as proportion of GDP (OECD, 1993, pp. 351–2). This is illustrated in Figures 4.1 and 4.2 above. For the past 50 years or so, Denmark has been characterized by high public service spending, and high taxation, arising from the political dominance of the Social Democrats' welfare and interventionist culture.

The Danish Social Democrats were in power until 1982. A conservative-led coalition took over in 1982, although the Social Democrats remained the largest party. Different Conservative-led coalitions followed. The Social Democrats subsequently narrowly regained power, leading a centre-Left coalition with a single-seat majority up to the 1994 election. A further narrow Left-wing coalition emerged after the election of September 1994. During the 1980s and 1990s many familiar themes came to dominate Danish thinking about public services: lowering the tax burden, increasing private-sector activity in service provision, creating greater efficiency. However, these pressures have not had the dramatic impact of (for instance) New Zealand's Labour-inspired market reforms of the late 1980s, or the even more free-market inspired policies of New Zealand's conservative governments of the 1990s.

There are two reasons why the pace of market-led reform in Denmark has been relatively gradual. First, the political and cultural dominance of a public-welfare orientation is deeply embedded. Secondly, the decentralist political system, with its relatively independent local authorities, is structurally resistant to any sudden programme of change being imposed from the centre. Consequently, an **agenda** for reform of local public services in Denmark has emerged with similarities to many other countries, but implementation through specific policies has taken a rather different course.

Local government in Denmark is based upon:

* predominantly local means of taxation for local services;
* multifunctional local councils, tending to provide a greater range of services than in Britain, including social security and some medical services;
* party political organization.

There are three levels of government in Denmark: central government, the 14 county authorities, and the 275 municipalities (Nissen, 1991, p. 190). In direct contrast to experience in Britain, the trend in 1980s Denmark was towards a transfer of tasks from central government downward. This has parallels with Dutch experience. In Denmark, Nissen talks of:

> the massive decentralization of tasks from central government to municipalities and, more often, to counties (1991, pp. 192–3).

Alongside the local control of local services, and a cultural tradition of independence from central government, local government in Denmark has a tradition of independent financial decision-making.

> Local authorities [in Denmark] are free to decide the standard of their services and to fix a tax level to cover the costs ... The underlying philosophy is that financial responsibility depends on local taxation rights. It is believed that if equity is ensured by measures of equalization according to needs and resources, then decentralization will lead to higher efficiency through voter control (Norton, 1994, p. 337).

Local government has nevertheless faced constraints from the specific approach of centre/Right (and subsequently centre/Left) national governments and the changing national economy. Penalties were introduced in 1986 to keep local government within defined spending limits, with the sanction of an effective 'fine' to the Treasury for transgression (Bogason, 1991, p. 283; Nissen, 1991, p. 194).

The management of the Danish municipal authorities differs from the committee structure and administrative hierarchy of the British model. Municipalities in Denmark do not appoint a separate executive to implement council decisions. Instead, sub-committees act as executive bodies. Some sub-committees are required by law (e.g. finance and social services) but others are set up on the basis of local decision and preference (Kolam, 1991, p. 15).

The mayor is a key figure, in a role reflecting the party political make-up of the council. The mayor serves for the full electoral period of the council, four years, and has 'daily administrative responsibility for the affairs of the council' (Bogason, 1991, p. 271).

> The mayor is chairman of the local council and leader of the administration. The chief executive officer acts as adviser to the finance committee and the council and is often the chief personnel officer as well. The head of the other sectors of administration are subordinate to the chief executive in matters of management, but are subordinate to a committee and its chairman for the tasks of the sector (OECD, 1993, p. 73).

The mayor is a full-time elected member of the council, with influence over its finances and overall policy. Local income tax is the main source of local finance in Denmark.

There has been debate surrounding the future of the county council tier in Danish subnational government (Bogason, 1991, p. 269; Nissen, 1991, p. 195). As the local municipality is already responsible for a large number of services, and as the central government of the day will always be responsible for certain core responsibilities, the rationale for the county authority, especially in a context of increased private provision, has perhaps become less clear. It should also be noted that there is considerable formal co-operation between local authorities in Denmark. The OECD refers to an increasing number of 'inter-municipal enterprises and institutions' dealing with services such as insurance, research, waste and auditing (OECD, 1993, p. 73). There are formal limits to such joint ventures in Britain.

In more general terms, party politics are an essential part of Danish local government, as they are in Britain. (This contrasts to the ostensibly non-political nature of, say, United States managerialism). Many of the 'officer–member' relationships in Denmark seem familiar because of this party political context. Bogason (1991, p. 275) suggests that 'there is frequent and consensual interaction between chief officers and their committee chairman' in Denmark. Officers may be concerned with practical administrative questions, but these practical matters have been defined initially within the local political system.

Danish local government has always had a 'strong ethos of autonomy' (Norton, 1994, p. 331) and – like Sweden and Norway – has also been an active participant in the 'free local government' initiative, which Bogason describes in the following terms.

> The general idea is to permit local governments to disregard certain state regulations in order to promote localized solutions to local problems, in particular in order to use local resources more efficiently (Bogason, 1991, p. 285).

The free local government initiative is summarized in Case study 4.4.

CASE STUDY 4.4 'Free local government' in Scandinavia

In Denmark, Sweden and Norway local authorities may apply to take part in the 'free' local government programme. This began in Sweden and, applied to a Swedish context, 'sets aside mandatory application of uniform national legislation and regulations affecting the structures, organization and operation of local authorities' (OECD, 1991, p. 56). In other words, it gives local councils a freer hand, and was taken up by Denmark and Norway in the same terms. As well as **deregulation**, it involves **innovation** in responding to local need.

The Danish initiative began in 1984. By 1989, there were 268 such experiments in operation in Denmark within 30 municipalities and 6 counties (Bogason, 1991, p. 285). It is interesting to note –in comparison to Britain's centrally determined process of Local Management of Schools (see Chapter 2) – that some Danish local authorities have exercised their 'freedom' to delegate managerial authority to individual schools as a local choice.

The free local government experiment is consistent with the strong historical tradition of relatively **autonomous** local government in Denmark. Local councils may thus provide local solutions to local problems providing these are not specifically prohibited in law (Lauritzen and Hague, 1993, p. 12). This contrasts to the position in Britain where local authorities have the power to provide services lawfully only within strictly defined limits.

Norway, similarly inspired by the Swedish example, introduced a free local government programme in 1986. The projects approved (on application to central government) are intended to achieve:

- better adaptation of local government to local conditions
- improved service for the general public
- better and more efficient use of the available resources (Lodden, 1991, p. 200).

These objectives are shared by the Danish scheme. It is notable that the **objectives** are recognisable as those of British public service reform from 1979 onward too. However, crucially, the Scandinavian model of implementation has been co-operative, permissive and based on the theme of **decentralization**, while the British model has been prescriptive and centralist.

The free local government scheme is not intended to be an open-ended deregulation. It is meant as a programme of experimental pilot schemes – monitored to identify any wider lessons to be learned.

It can readily be appreciated that the 'free local government' approach has political, administrative and managerial elements.

Politically, the notion of a local government free from central government constraint is powerful in Denmark, and is consistent with the historical and constitutional position of local councils. Rose, for instance, talks of the initiative being consistent with 'values which lie at the heart of local government in the Nordic area – autonomy, democracy and efficiency' (1990, p. 217).

Administratively, the initiative may not always have delivered the intended freedom of action immediately. Negotiations between local and central government

> create an apparent paradox; on the one hand ostensibly liberating local authorities from rules and procedures, on the other enmeshing them in a complex procedure of proposals, negotiation and agreement with Central Government Agencies (Etherington and Paddon, 1991, p. 8).

Managerially, the programme can nevertheless provide a local autonomy, deregulation, a freedom to manage resources and services imaginatively: **a 'freedom to manage' but not an apolitical managerialism.**

Although the use of contracting-out now seems to be almost universal, the degree of **compulsion** placed on local councils to contract-out services to the private sector is, as we have seen, subject to wide international variation. In Denmark, the processes of competitive tendering and subsequent contracting-out are not compulsory. Circulars from the Ministry of the Interior in 1984 and 1992 recommend the increased use of competitive tendering, especially for current expenditure services: in terms of capital expenditure items, there is already considerable contracting-out in Denmark (Council of Europe, 1993, p. 23).

Smaller municipalities generally contract-out to a greater extent than the larger municipal authorities, although all councils tend to contract-out the big capital projects. The 1992 regulations were intended to encourage further contracting-out, but it is to be emphasized that there is no list of defined activities and no proscription of anti-competitive behaviour as defined by central government. The **cultural** climate in which local authorities go about competitive tendering in Britain and in Denmark is quite dissimilar. The Council of Europe study of competitive tendering writes of Denmark in the following terms.

> The use of competitive tendering is . . . still a matter of local decision. The government has not wished to take steps towards rules making competitive tendering obligatory' (Council of Europe, 1993, p. 23).

A 'restructuring' of the methods and scope of local public service provision has occurred in Denmark, Britain, and other Western societies. The post-war expansion of public services has halted. New forms of management are emerging. Structural factors (largely economic) seem to provide a common framework in which reform of public management is taking place internationally, yet the nature of reforms may vary considerably from one county to another. Lauritzen and Hague argue that 'the reconstruction of the public sector has followed different trajectories in Britain and Denmark respectively' (1993, p. 2). Structural forces provide the context and impetus for change in public-service provision, but in seeking to account for differences between societies 'we have to look at other factors such as institutional differences and political ideologies and cultures' (Lauritzen and Hague, 1993, p. 2).

The specific public-service reforms of Denmark have a party political dimension, but have not been determined by party political factors alone. As noted above, conservative-led government in Denmark dates from 1982, in the shape of a right-wing coalition led by Poul Schluter. This government introduced its 'Modernization Programme' in 1983, the key elements of which were:

- decentralization;
- increased use of market mechanism;
- deregulation;
- customer service;
- emphasis on personnel;
- development of information technology (OECD, 1990).

The Modernization Programme has formed the basis of Danish public service policy ever since, and has been extended and developed within the shifting coalitions. In 1991, the Danish government stated that 'modernization' in the 1990s means a central role for the **citizen**, through 'better and cheaper solutions enabling a lower burden of taxation', and also means an **international** dimension to public service provision as a whole (OECD, 1992, p. 32). It is reasonable to characterize the 'modernization' initiative as the emphasis upon better quality of service without increased public expenditure.

Denmark, since 1982, has exhibited a concern with the same objectives of public-sector reform as many other societies in Europe and beyond. The methods of reform in Denmark have, in contrast to Britain but with some similarities to the Netherlands, respected the relative degree of independence of local authorities. Once again, it seems that a **cultural**, rather than party political, difference separates British public service reform from that of other countries. There is not a culture of central prescription in Denmark.

> The main reason for the limited state intervention in the reconstruction of local government in Denmark must be found in the strong Scandinavian, and especially Danish, notion of 'local self government' (Lauritzen and Hague, 1993, p. 12).

This cultural difference transcends party political differences. In the United States, an historically conservative political culture emphasizes local **self**-government as strongly as it is emphasized in the historically social democratic countries of Scandinavia. The Netherlands is characterized by a similar presumption toward local judgement and preferences. It is the centralist culture of Britain which is different. The experience of New Zealand also draws in part from this centralist tradition, for historical reasons.

The **cultural context** as identified here is of considerable importance in the understanding of local authority management in Britain today. The cultural context defines the central/local relationships **within which** central government exercises authority, prescribes a further set of regulations, introduces another piece of legislation about local government, or whatever. The cultural context in Britain is centralist, and since 1979 has become increasingly so in terms of the duties, permitted activities, and financial independence of local councils. As Wilson and Game succinctly put it, 'there are no longer many countries in which local government has apparently less financial discretion' (1994, pp. 162–3).

Consideration of competitive tendering and the wider changes to local government in Denmark reinforces an emerging conclusion from such comparative study that all major industrial societies are addressing a recognizably similar agenda of public service reform. This agenda includes direct tax restraint, increased competition, 'quality' initiatives, a private-sector model of the customer, and performance measurement. However, the agenda is being addressed differently in different societies, irrespective of local party political similarities. The culture of local–central government relations, however, seems crucial.

Having examined features of local government organization in a number of different societies, some general themes may now be suggested to assist in drawing overall conclusions.

Toward a comparative analysis: key themes

As noted at the beginning of this chapter, it is prudent to be cautious in comparing local government systems and practice across different societies. Comparative descriptions are illuminating, but comparative **analysis** presupposes an account of the political systems of each country, the national history and constitution, the functions of each public organization, financial relationships, taxation, public spending, the legal context, the extent to which duties are delegated to subnational government – and much more besides. Such factors would have to be linked to models of public-sector management, and to theoretical accounts of the changing nature of the local state, for truly comparative analysis to begin. No such analysis yet exists.

The comparisons above begin to suggest, however, certain common themes, applicable across several societies. Such comparisons could readily be extended to other countries as a basis for further study. For instance, in Japan the powers of competence of local authorities are wide, contracting-out is common and is encouraged by central government, private contractors may compete for services and, in addition, services may be provided by 'local public enterprises': public bodies set up by the local authority, but self-funding (Yokota, Leggett and Kasatani, 1992). The Japanese Local Public Enterprise and the New Zealand Local Authority Trading Enterprise provide an interesting specific opportunity for further comparative analysis. Practical considerations limit the number of such examples in any comparative study, but the potential for comparative analysis is clear enough.

The following discussion considers some of the variables which would need to be present in developing a comparative framework.

Market and state

The tension between the market mechanism and state-led planning in the provision of public services is, seemingly, universal. Local public service management in the United States has been, for historical and ideological reasons, market-led. The structures of United States local government – non-party, managerial, individualist – are consistent with an overall market orientation. In the Nordic countries, by contrast, the market has historically been subordinate to a social-democratic welfare consensus: a leading role for public provision, based on high taxation and high public spending. The Right-wing governments of Denmark in the 1980s did not replace the ideology of 'welfare capitalism' with the 'free market' in the fundamental sense that the British conservatives might claim to have done. The United States and Scandanavia represent fairly clear-cut examples of 'market'- and 'state'-led models of public provision, but generally societies will exhibit a rather more complex mix of guiding principles or ideologies. Britain is a case in point.

In Britain, a public service consensus gave way in the late 1970s to a sustained effort to impose a market discipline upon the services and management methods of local government. The 'marketization' of British local public services has been tempered by a considerable measure of central control – 'hierarchy' as much as 'market'. The mix of market and state in British local government is also associated with the rise of a 'new' public management: small-scale, ostensibly consumer-led, responsive, innovative. These developments may be viewed as an attempt to reconcile market and state in British public service management. The British Labour Party has similarly attempted to reformulate the state/market relationship in its rejection of 'old' socialism based on a state-led model (e.g. Meacher 1993).

The critical discussion of a consumer perspective in Chapter 3 has an international application too. The concern with the 'customer' could itself be examined cross-culturally. For instance, Andreassen (1994) has considered public-sector consumer satisfaction in Norway, through an essentially quantitative analysis of possible indicators of such satisfaction. The many possible ways of 'listening to the public', and the problems, are not confined to the United Kingdom.

The development of CCT in British local government (see Chapter 2) similarly has implications for comparative study. CCT may involve the rhetoric of the market, but it also represents the centralist and prescriptive traditions of British government so evident in any international comparison. It is a 'market' and a 'competition' **imposed**, rather than being the product of a freely operating market mechanism. Thus – particularly in Britain – market and state may come together in a number of contrasting ways. It can be argued that state regulation itself may **promote** the market.

> In the traditional caretaker model of the state a public sector of a certain size has been a necessary condition for the existence of a market mechanism. Government regulation may benefit rather than oppose the workings of the market mechanism (Lane, 1993, p. 20).

To develop this a little, it could be argued that markets do not and cannot determine the allocation of significant statutory and collective services of local government, e.g. aspects of the social service or environmental functions. Cochrane points out that 'quasi-markets' – using market terminology and procedures but 'frequently bureaucratically managed' – are a more significant feature of British local government than the market proper (Cochrane, 1993, pp. 53–4).

Quasi-markets do not deliver some automatic consumer empowerment.

> There is certainly important evidence that market theories have influenced the direction of change at local level. But the influence has had ambiguous results. Much of the evidence suggests a stronger role for core elites within local government, both officer and councillors, rather than their replacement by an effective system of consumer choice (Cochrane, 1993, p. 67).

Thus the balance of, and relationship between, market and state is the first key theme or variable in the building-up of comparative analysis of local government practice.

Control and autonomy

British local government is formally subordinate to central government. The constraints and regulations placed upon local authorities by successive government legislation are politically but not constitutionally questionable. The formal position of British local government contrasts to the constitutional independence of Danish subnational government, the decentralization of the Dutch system, or the federalism of the United States.

Within the British framework, however, local authorities may still be afforded greater or lesser degrees of **relative** autonomy. The trend is toward a lesser degree. There is little doubt that the extent to which governmental power is centralized in Britain goes against the European move to greater decentralization (Clarke and Stewart, 1991, p. 13). In the mid 1990s, the trend in Britain is towards a greater central control of local public service provision. Such control is exercised either by central government compulsion upon local government as in CCT or LMS, or by central government appointed agencies or government directed QUANGOs taking over functions from elected local Councils (see Chapters 1 and 7). This transfer of power may take the form of Urban Development Corporations, Training and Enterprise Councils, or other agencies. The task of management within local government may at best become one of co-ordinating the efforts of a range of local agencies (see the discussion of multi-agency local provision in Chapter 7) or, at worst, one of acting as agent for some minor duties passed down from the centre.

There is no way of knowing how the tension between control and autonomy may ultimately shape the future of local government in Britain. It is, however, a theme which constitutes another necessary dimension of comparative analysis. In developing this theme, it would be essential to recognize that there are different forms of control, and different forms of autonomy. We could begin to formulate this as shown in Figure 4.3.

Further development of the control/autonomy typology might include degrees of autonomy **within** the local authority for managers at different levels compared to the local political level; controls exercised at **intermediate** levels of government such as

Control typology

(a) Direct compulsion, e.g. statutory prescription of how local government must conduct its affairs as in British CCT.

(b) Control through the market, regulation, incentives and competition, as in the radical reforms of local government in New Zealand between 1986 and 1990.

Autonomy typology

(a) Managerial autonomy, e.g. a relatively individualist 'freedom to manage' as in the Tilburg model of the Netherlands, or the City Manager of the United States.

(b) Political autonomy, e.g. a significant degree of independence of sub-national government from the central authorities as in Denmark

Figure 4.3   A typology of control and autonomy

regional authorities, where those exist; and the differences of **cultural** context in which control is exercised at either local or central level. It is in the conflicts and tensions associated with control and autonomy that the relationship between local and central government is most clearly defined.

Central and local

The degree to which services are managed and delivered locally is a further important comparative theme. The 'decentralization impulse' of the Netherlands has been discussed. It is to be emphasized that a number of 'local' levels exist. Within subnational government, services may be retained at a regional level rather than delivered at the most local level possible. Even within local government proper – that is, the most local level on which public services are organized and delivered – there are differences of emphasis. New Zealand, for instance, retained and extended its network of **community boards** as part of its overall reorganization (Audit Commission, 1993, p. 4).

Throughout the Nordic countries, municipalities may set up **neighbourhood councils**, frequently linked politically to the ruling groups at municipal level (Kolam, 1991). Some British local authorities have experimented with a neighbourhood level of consultation, such as Middlesbrough, or have gone further with formally localized organization and decision making, such as Tower Hamlets. In Sweden, Norway, and Finland there is a more toward creating **citizens' offices** – which give access to the range of public services, irrespective of which agency provides them.

> In Sweden there are four main arguments for establishing citizens' offices: better access to service; a more efficient organization; maintaining service in rural areas; and support for democratic goals (for example informing people about their rights and duties as citizens). (Segerlund, 1994, p. 58).

The central/local distinction thus applies on a number of levels. It may be a predominantly political distinction, or it may signify a largely administrative process. It may be relatively superficial, or be fundamental. It may be concerned with removing power, or with empowerment. It varies. In all countries, however, the extent to which public-service provision is being localized is another important variable in comparative analysis. The undoubtedly different **meanings** associated with the 'local' would be a significant element of that analysis.

Decentralization initiatives directly affect the nature of day-to-day service management. In a Nordic context, Segerlund suggests one aim of the citizens' office 'is to develop a more generalist front-line official who can take decisions, and give a more advanced administrative service on behalf of state and municipal authorities' (1994, p. 57). Yet again, a certain managerial devolution is implied: a recurring theme in comparative study.

Public and private

The changed relationship between **public and private provision** has affected the nature of local government in Britain and almost every other country. Yet the distinction between public and private is not synonymous with that between state and market. The state may closely oversee a thriving private economy (as in the former Yugoslavia), while the market may include a large public sector (as in Britain). In comparative study, the theme of state and market refers to the **allocation** of services above all else. The theme of public and private refers to the ownership, objectives and nature of services, together with their costs.

In Chapter 2, it was suggested that competition between public and private providers of local services is changing the nature of local authority management. Part of this change was said to be the adoption of private-sector models for the management of particular services, whether the contractor was in fact private or not. Moreover, competition between public and private was seen to lead to diversification of management structures, and differentiation of managerial skills, around the differences between client, contractor and corporate management. A comparative perspective would consider the applicability of these managerial changes to other countries.

Contracting-out of hitherto publicly-provided services in the Netherlands has been discussed. Denmark too has reassessed the balance of public and private provision, from a starting-point of much more extensive public provision than Britain or the Netherlands. There were specific privatizations in 1991 in Denmark (e.g. Girobank, Tele-Danmark) as well as new rules in 1992 to encourage local authority contracting-out (OECD, 1992, p. 32). The British Labour Party in February 1994 announced that private and public co-funding of major services was here to stay, and at its party conference of that year began the process of amending Clause Four (a commitment to public ownership) of its constitution. The formerly Communist countries of Eastern Europe have abandoned monopoly public provision.

It would seem that a re-evaluation of the balance between public and private local service provision is underway across the industrialized world. This new balance brings with it managerial change. Comparative study may identify differences, similarities, and common practice, and it may draw out overall implications. As the changed relationship between public and private develops, the difference between public and private may become less clear.

> There has been a marked blurring of the distinction between the public and the private, in terms of policy responsibility as much as in the form of service provision (Cochrane, 1993, p. 99).

Under CCT, for instance, a notionally public-sector tender may be characterized by staff levels, cost, working conditions and service characteristics which are indistinguishable from the private sector. This may be the future, internationally.

Elected and appointed

The formal relationship of local government and central government has been discussed. It has been seen that New Zealand local government is constitutionally subordinate to central government (OECD, 1993, p. 217). The same is true in Britain. In Denmark, local government has a formal right to manage its own affairs, subject to ultimate Parliamentary authority. The United States is of course a federal system, the nearest equivalent in Europe being the German system of government.

Having established the **formal** place accorded to subnational government in a particular country, comparative analysis may then turn to the increasingly important distinction between **elected and appointed** agencies at the local level.

The growth of a 'non-elected local state' is particularly contentious in Britain in the 1990s. The Labour Party, in the House of Commons on 24 February 1994, claimed that QUANGOs were spending £24 billion of public money currently, projected to rise to £54 billion by 1996. Jack Straw (Labour, Environment) characterized the QUANGO as follows:

- **power without responsibility** through lack of accountability;
- **high payments** for part-time appointees, in contrast to the allowances paid to non-salaried elected councillors in local government;
- **honours** available for leading political appointees;
- **bypassing local democracy**, for instance when Urban Development Corporations override the local planning authorities (LGIU, 1993b, p. 1).

The general point to be derived from study of the British QUANGO is that comparative analysis must address the question of accountability. This is partly a matter of the accountability of individual managers to the political level of the organization. It also refers to the overall accountability of the organization, for instance, the accountability of the QUANGO in the local community.

In Britain, even the most senior council official – the Chief Executive – is responsible to the elected level. This is not merely a 'constitutional' issue – it affects the day-to-day nature of local authority management. The characteristics of council management in Britain, whether judged negatively (too cautious, reluctant to innovate, beholded to ill-trained political masters) or positively (consensual, service-oriented, responsive to public needs), derive from existing patterns of accountability. The growth of appointed local agencies changes all this.

Changes in public accountability are occurring in other countries too, but largely **within** the structures of local government. In New Zealand and parts of the Netherlands alike, an increased 'freedom to manage' for senior council officers has been associated with a reduced, albeit more 'strategic', role for elected members. This is comparable with experience of the United States' Council Manager system, with its very small, policy-making, elected group. However, British experience increasingly seems to be different in kind, as the democratic local level is bypassed altogether by the growth of the appointed agency.

The balance between the elected and the appointed layers, and the replacement of local government by appointed organizations in some areas of its work, constitute another central theme in the development of comparative analysis.

Concluding comments: living in an international community

It was suggested at the beginning of this chapter that local government itself has been more ready to look out to the international community than academic studies have been to incorporate a comparative perspective. Practice has preceded theory. What does the comparative context mean for managers within British local government at present? Terry (1993) has suggested that British membership of the European

Community – now, the European Union – has moved from acceptance of obligations to a more active stance in seeking to influence events.

In the late 1970s, local authorities began, through economic development and other initiatives, to seek the advantages associated with economic aid from the European Social Fund and the European Regional Development Fund (Terry, 1993, p. 156).

> The growing awareness among local authorities in the 1980s of the importance of promoting economic development seems to have been a strong incentive to seek EC funds (Terry, 1993, p. 157).

Interest in the international dimension began, then, with a desire to maximize the inward flow of resources: either direct funds for local authority expenditure, or inward investment for projects within the local authority's area. Arguments about Britain's contributions to, and receipts from, the EU can easily turn into a crude tally of winners and losers or simplistic political sloganizing. However, it is possible to go beyond this rhetoric to establish an 'account' of financial relations with Europe with more precision.

> It was clear when Great Britain joined the EC in 1973 that it would be a large contributor and a small beneficiary because of its relatively large external trade and its small agricultural base ... An interim settlement in 1980 provided for compensation on the expenditure side ... This was followed by the corrective mechanism agreed in 1984 and extended in 1988. The UK has a rebate of 66% of the net difference between the UK's contributions and receipts; this was estimated at 2.27 billion ECU in 1992 (McCarthy, 1993, p. 45).

It has now perhaps become more generally understood that Britain receives from, as well as contributes to, overall EU funds. Moreover, local government is no longer restricted in its international contacts to town-twinning, economic development, or, indeed, to Europe. It is clear that local government in Britain can learn from good practice elsewhere – in particular, how other societies are responding to a common agenda of financial restriction in different ways.

The practical interest shown in United States' forms of local government (e.g. Lavery 1992, Hambleton 1991) is an example of the value of learning from experience in other countries. Equally – to continue the example of the United States – more detailed analysis of practice can point to differences as well as to common experience. Pollitt (1990) comments on the 'broadly similar' ideology of the Reagan and Thatcher years, but adds that differences of emphasis have always characterized the British and American approaches. Local service provision in the United States was already less politically driven and more 'technicist' than in Britain (Pollitt, 1990, p. 181).

> At the level of practice many more differences became visible. These were inevitable, given that the two countries started from very different positions in terms of their constitutional structures, patterns of party political activity and public service cultures. Indeed, perhaps the more surprising phenomenon was the extent to which similarities did appear (Pollitt, 1990, p. 181).

This passage from a comparative study of public management in Britain and the United States neatly points up some key aspects of our discussion. Without doubt, different countries can learn from each other, and apply common aspects of good practice. However, as soon as a more analytical approach to comparative study and interpretation begins, the variables to be considered become innumerable, and the differences between countries more evident than the similarities. Perhaps, because of this, comparative analysis is impossible. However, the view taken in the present study is that comparative analysis can proceed through the development of interpretive and explanatory themes derived from close study of practice in different countries. Comparative analysis is possible: indeed, it is crucial in the development of the theory and practice of British local government today.

Summary

This chapter began with a discussion of local public service provision and management in selected countries. The identification of differences and similarities in the experience of other societies provides an initial comparative **context**. The further elaboration and development of a comparative discussion of British public service management is in itself valuable in the identification of good practice, and the sharing of experience. Comparative **analysis** implies more than a comparative discussion, however. Comparative analysis includes a review of political and cultural factors in each society, possible theoretical explanations of changes in public service provision, the formal legal/constitutional position of local government in each country, and the development of key themes which assist the understanding of contemporary local government. Possible themes have been introduced and discussed as a move **toward** the development of a comparative perspective. These themes have been presented as a series of dichotomous variables:

- market − state
- control − autonomy
- central − local
- public − private
- elected − appointed.

This allows us to locate particular societies toward one end of the scale or the other for each of the variables. This forms the framework for beginning truly comparative **analysis** of managerial change in local government in different countries.

Discussion questions and guidance

1. *To what extent would an American-style 'city manager' improve strategic management in British local government?*

In considering this question, bear in mind that the City Manager (or 'council manager') system in the United States implies a greater concentration of power than is normal in British experience. There is, for instance, a much smaller elective group in United States local government than in British councils; the City Manager has a great deal of delegated authority and autonomy; and there is a straightforward line management responsibility vertically to and from the City Manager (compare the New Zealand

Chief Executive here too). Thus a city manager could not be imposed on a British local council as it exists now: other parts of the structure would also need to change. 'In theory, a centralized power structure should make it easier for a local authority to act as one organization and this is critical to good strategic management. Does it work in practice?' (Lavery, 1992, p. 11).

Following from Lavery's question, we would need to decide if the city manager system does work in the United States, before considering its application to Britain. There is also, of course, a variety of criteria against which to judge 'success'.

2. *'Renewed belief in the market as the best determinant of allocative efficiency has been the spur to the changes' (Wistrich, 1992, p. 119). How far is this statement true of public service reforms (a) in New Zealand and (b) in any other country with which you are familiar?*

The 'market' is invoked as guiding principle – or as malign influence – in many areas of public policy, not always with any clear idea of its meaning. It is necessary here to examine the nature of the market principles and policies introduced by the New Zealand Labour Governments 1984 to 1990. Wistrich (1992) summarizes the background reports of the New Zealand Treasury. Arguably, the market mechanism ultimately produces a dismantling of the same public services it may initially have distributed 'efficiently'. For a bleak account of New Zealand public provision since 1990 see Walker (1994). Equally, adherence to some form of market mechanism for the distribution of public service seems near-universal, across different political parties and different countries. Consider one other country – perhaps Great Britain – in addition to New Zealand.

3. *'Local government reorganization was not an end in itself. It was a means of empowering councils with the critical mass of ability and resources to implement other reforms leading to greater accountability, transparency and contestability in local government services' (Audit Commission, 1993, p. 5). Discuss.*

The Audit Commission statement is intended to refer to New Zealand. You may wish to 'discuss' in that context, or with reference to Britain's local government reorganization 1995/96, or both. The important aspect is to link structural reorganization to supposed objectives, and to examine the link between these two elements critically. Case study 4.3 provides further discussion of the same quotation. The reorganization of British local government is also discussed in Chapter 7. The question may be taken further into other public service areas if this helps to illuminate the underlying principles. For instance, the British National Health Service implies questions about the objectives of structural reorganization and also about adaptations to market forces.

4. *Michael Heseltine has suggested that Britain consider adopting an elected mayor system (Stoker and Wolman, 1992, p. 242). Assess the possible advantages and disadvantages of such a change.*

In their paper on United States' experience, Stoker and Wolman describe the mayor in this sense as 'an individual, elected separately from the council' who would 'take over the councils executive responsibilities' (1992, p. 242). Consider the impact of such a system on the operation of local government in Britain, including the impact on elected members as well as senior managers. The mayoral system in the United States – in both 'strong' and 'weak' forms – is discussed above in Chapter 4 Stoker and Wolman provide a more detailed account of the US mayor in their paper for the Local Government Management Board (1991).

5. *Evaluate the extent to which the international dimension is (a) a constraint and (b) an opportunity for the local authority manager in Britain.*

This general question permits a number of approaches depending upon your own interests and experience. On one level, British local authorities are provided with tangible opportunities for resources from European funds, and officers may be designated specifically to maximize this income. Equally, constraints arise from Europe regulation, e.g. in relation to foodstuffs, or vehicle specifications and so on. Where constraints do exist, additional arguments are required to establish the likely desirable or undesirable consequences for domestic service provision. On another level altogether, 'opportunities' for British local authority management may be presented by examples of good practice, alternative forms of organization or structural reorganization in other countries in Europe and beyond. In this more fundamental sense, the question refers to what can be **learned from** comparative examples.

6. *Provide a comparative analysis of local authority management in Britain and **one** other country with which you are familiar. Identify common or contrasting practice through relevant illustrations.*

Two elements should be present in responding to this question. First, it is necessary to provide a thorough account of 'running local government' in Britain and in another country of your choice. Although source material tends particularly to be available for European countries (e.g. OECD 1990, 1991, 1992, 1993), there are many other countries of interest – Chapter 4 has included a review of the United States and New Zealand. Secondly, it is necessary to move from description toward comparative **analysis** wherein difference and similarities between countries are developed according to overall **themes**, such as those introduced in Chapter 4. The themes included in Chapter Four are by no means exhaustive. An effective answer to this question might begin to suggest **new** directions for the comparative analysis of local service management. This remains, in the published literature, an underdeveloped area of enquiry.

7. *'. . . it is only in the United Kingdom that a legal duty has been imposed on local authorities to engage in competitive tendering . . . In most countries local authorities can choose freely whether to provide a service directly by means of their own labour force or by contracting out' (Council of Europe, 1993, pp. 4–5). Is competition possible without compulsion?*

It seems clear that competition is indeed possible without compulsion, given the experience of European countries other than the UK. The question thus seeks a discussion of underlying themes such as: the **extent** of competition for local service provision in the absence of central compulsion; the possibility that (given New

Zealand experience 1984–90) the market mechanism may be **more** fully developed **without** compulsion; and the relevance of centralist political culture (in contrast to moves toward decentralization). The report from which the quotation is taken (Council of Europe, 1993) points out that in the absence of compulsion, government may still **encourage** local competitive tendering rather than remaining agnostic. 'This is the case in Denmark, while in the Netherlands, a Committee for the Promotion of Privatization in Local Government was set up at national level' (Council of Europe, 1993, p. 5). Thus there are varieties of 'non compulsion'. In addition to the references made to competitive tendering in different countries in Chapter 4, there is a detailed account of CCT in Britain in Chapter 2.

Suggested further reading

Norton, A. (1994) *International Handbook of Local and Regional Government: A Comparative Analysis of Advanced Democracies*, Edward Elgar, Aldershot. A comprehensive reference source.

Braunig, D. (1992) Management of Local Authorities in Germany and the Netherlands. *Local Government Policy Making*, **19** (3) (December), pp 29–35. A more specific comparative study within Europe.

Chandler, J.A. (ed) (1993) *Local Government in Liberal Democracies*, Routledge, London. Comparative readings, Europe and beyond, country-by-country.

Council of Europe (1993) *The Role of Competitive Tendering in the Efficient Provision of Local Services*, Report no. 49 of Steering Committee on Local and Regional Authorities (CDLR), Council of Europe Press, Strasbourg. Compares the experience of competitive tendering within local government in selected European countries.

Lavery, K. (1992) The 'Council Manager' and 'Strong Mayor' Forms of Government in the USA. *Public Money and Management*, **12** (2) (April–June), pp 9–14. Succinct account of the US system(s) of local government, the principles of which influence current debates within the UK.

Audit Commission (1993) *Phoenix Rising: A Study of New Zealand Local Government Following Reorganization*, Occasional Paper 19 (June), HMSO, London. A detailed study of the old and new systems of local government in New Zealand, again with implications for debates about reorganization in the UK.

MANAGING SERVICES AND MEASURING PERFORMANCE

5

Local government has been encouraged (and to an increasing extent required by statute) to formulate performance indicators for its key activities, to measure its performance, and to review its work in the context of economy, efficiency and effectiveness. In this chapter, the growth of performance indicators and the overall principles of performance measurement are discussed, before looking in detail at practice. The problems are identified, but it is suggested that both managers and local councillors have positive roles to play in performance measurement, provided the local authority has the right structural arrangements, is committed to the process, and has effective mechanisms for feeding the results back into operational and strategic management.

Introduction

It is impossible to define clear-cut and simple reasons for the growth of performance measurement in local government. Referring to the government's Financial Management Initiative of the 1980s, and to the growth of performance measurement across the government sector as a whole, Carter, Klein and Day have suggested that:

> the Government's objectives in launching performance indicators turn out to be both multiple and ambiguous, with some evidence that they have shifted over time (1992, p. 165).

More generally, an implicit comparison between the private and public sectors seems to inform or perhaps misinform performance management in local government. The simple image of the private-sector organization is one of straightforward indicators of performance such as goods sold, customers supplied, delivery times or profits obtained. This tends to be contrasted to an image of public-service organizations with their complex goals, conflicting 'welfare' and 'control' functions, and a disputed legitimacy as the boundaries of the public sector gradually recede.

Such a crudely drawn difference between public and private, however, decreasingly reflects reality. Private sector companies too pursue multiple objectives, require relatively sophisticated means of measuring consumer preference, and need to consider external constraints such as those provided by the national economic environment or European regulation. Further, as Jackson (1993) points out, the more successful private-sector organizations monitor their performance by systems linked to strategic decision-making as a whole.

> Simple input/output measures or profitability and liquidity measures are of very limited value. They provide managers in private sector organizations with little relevant information (Jackson, 1993, p. 10).

Public-sector organizations, furthermore, are not as inexperienced in defining goals and monitoring performance as a simplistic private/public comparison suggests. Twenty years of experience of local authority performance management exists. Furthermore, of course, key public utilities have become private companies, and the boundaries have become blurred between public and private as a whole. Local government services face a permanently changed agenda, and are required to provide direct information about their performance under the Local Government Act 1992, and less directly in their monitoring of public and private contracts awarded under CCT requirements. Central government too has an active interest in local government indicators of need, and of performance, in constructing Standard Spending Assessments and allocating resources. Henderson-Stewart (1990, p. 114) finds 'only very limited truth' in the alleged simplicity of private-sector performance review based on profit, and the alleged difficulty of public-sector performance review based on quality.

Performance management in local government, then, takes place in the context of an increasingly close relationship with the private sector, but where there is no simple private-sector model to which to aspire. The management of performance is now a deeply entrenched feature of local government, a daily feature of both strategic and operational management levels. Performance management links to our recurring themes: competition, listening to the public, accessing information, and managing change. In this chapter, performance management will be examined as follows.

First, the development of interest in the measurement and management of performance in local government will be charted. Reasons for the growth of performance measurement will be considered, alongside any lessons to be learned from earlier attempts to create rational models of budgeting and policy review. The central importance of the 3 Es – economy, efficiency and effectiveness – will be examined, critically, in the context of management as a whole.

Secondly, practical aspects of measuring performance will be discussed, including case studies of specific services from local authorities, problems of using performance indicators, and the extent to which local government managers actually have control over the process of measurement and its constituent parts.

Thirdly, the place of the elected councillor in performance measurement will be considered, including the question of how appropriate structures are created within which politicians can define and monitor policy. What is the manager's role in a process which is essentially political in its objectives?

Finally, there will be a general assessment of performance management in local government, particularly addressing current developments, future prospects, and some continuing problems.

The development of performance measurement in local government

The growth of performance measurement has in fact been the growth of several, related, processes. As the terminology used to describe these processes has been ambiguous, it will be useful to begin with some discussion of terms.

Performance review

Performance review is any systematic attempt to specify what the organization is trying to achieve, how it aims to achieve it, and whether it has succeeded. It is a part of the wider field of policy-making and policy-analysis which also deals with how policy goals are specified and changed, and how policies reach the political/managerial agenda (see Hogwood and Gunn, 1984; Ham and Hill, 1993). Performance review **may** refer to individual performance, staff appraisal, or debates about performance-related pay. Such individualist interpretations of performance are largely beyond the scope of this discussion, but they do help to account for a lingering suspicion of what 'performance review' is really all about. It is used here to refer to **organizational** activity directed toward policy goals.

> In essence, performance review is any process utilized for monitoring and evaluating organizational performance (Monaghan and Ball, 1993, p. 11).

The structures and mechanisms for carrying out performance review vary from one local authority to another. There may be a sub-committee of elected councillors concerned specifically with performance review, as discussed later in this chapter and also in Chapter 6. Officers and members may work closely together on performance review as part of the central policy function (Fenwick, 1992). Equally, performance review work may largely be a subsidiary aspect of the annual budget cycle.

Performance measurement

Performance measurement is a prerequisite of performance review. Performance measurement includes all available methods of measuring achievement of the organization's goals and, especially, of quantifying performance against an absolute standard or against comparative information from another time or another place.

Performance measures are used alongside rather less direct performance **indicators**: the difference between the two is discussed in the next section of this chapter. The difficulties of formulating and using performance measures are numerous. At this stage, some key problems of local government performance measures are that:

- not all aspects of performance can be quantified;
- standards and targets against which to measure performance may be contested;
- information may not exist, or it may be too costly to collect, or it may inherently be unreliable;
- performance measures may not be measures of local authority performance at all: they may instead be measures of socio-economic deprivation, or of central government grant allocations, or some other external factor.

Performance management

Performance management describes the overall process of collecting performance indicators and measures, designing and implementing appropriate management systems, carrying out performance review, and evaluating and acting upon the results of these processes. Performance management is the **practice** of performance review and measurement and, like any other sort of managerial practice, it demands a particular set of **skills**. The goal of performance management is to improve services.

> The term performance management is used to describe the range of processes, techniques and methods to achieve such an improvement, or 'value for money' in terms of managing public services towards achieving defined results (Rouse, 1993, pp. 59–60).

A difficulty with performance management may be that the central interest in service quality is subverted by secondary goals such as achieving a certain budgetary target or having a desired political effect. Another difficulty with the term is one touched on above: it also denotes the whole apparatus of individual appraisal and incentive processes. This suspicion is hard to shake off. Klein and Carter (1988) point out that performance indicators may be used to evaluate organizational **or** individual performance.

> A top-down scheme imposed on the workforce may be treated with great suspicion by staff. It may understandably provoke a response similar to the dreaded factory time and motion study, being perceived as a means of cutting wages or making redundancies. Staff often see it as an instrument for increasing management control over the organization (Klein and Carter, 1988, p. 10).

There are several available reviews of performance management in this individualist sense (e.g. Neale (ed.) 1991) but in the discussions to follow the emphasis is upon the local authority's performance as an organization. The initial lesson for the management of this process is to reassure staff, and perhaps elected councillors, that performance measurement is not a 'dreaded factory time and motion study' introduced through the back door.

The growth of interest in performance

Rouse (1993) identifies three kinds of pressure towards the growth of performance measurement and management.

First, the market orientation of Conservative governments from 1979 onward – strongly influenced by New Right economic ideology – identified an essential inefficiency in the publicly owned monopolistic service-provider.

> Inefficiency manifested itself in a variety of ways: allocatively, in that the things produced were not the ones most wanted by customers; technically, in that production costs were higher than necessary; and dynamically, in that the organizations failed to be flexible, enterprising and responsive to new opportunities (Rouse, 1993, p. 60).

Secondly, the Left-of-centre and New Left critics of paternalistic public-service bureaucracy pushed for an empowerment of service-users, for responsive services and for public services to be effective as well as efficient. This perspective implies a measurement of service effectiveness from the perspective of the public (see Chapter 3).

Thirdly, the gurus of the new style of private-sector management such as Peters and Waterman (1982) and Sir John Harvey-Jones (1988) provided a context in which measuring the organization's performance came to be seen as not only necessary, but also somehow liberating – a way forward for public and private organizations alike (see also Huczynski, 1993). There was an even more direct influence for private-sector management methods when Sir Derek Rayner of Marks and Spencer, and Sir Roy Griffiths of Sainsburys, were brought in by Margaret Thatcher to inject private-sector knowhow into the management of public services (see Rogers, 1990, p. 7).

As in other areas of local authority management – the growth of competition, the rise of the 'consumer' – there have been several pressures toward the growth of performance measurement, and these pressures have not always been consistent. As always, distinct audiences (local authority officers, members, central government, other agencies) will tend to pursue their particular agenda. Performance measurement in local government has expanded for several different reasons.

Carter, Klein and Day (1992) trace the origins of central government's active interest in performance outputs to developments in the Treasury in 1982. The Financial Management Initiative (FMI) which began at that time was ultimately to lead to the restructuring of government departments into 'next steps' agencies, and the general devolution of both financial and managerial decision-making. The emphasis upon performance, the specification of aims, and above all the identification of costs, were to have a major impact upon the way both local and central government went about their business.

The FMI had not arisen in a vacuum. It developed from some of the work previously carried out by the Central Policy Review Staff (CPRS) – the 'think tank' – which from its inception in 1971 under Heath to its demise in 1983 under Thatcher made a considerable contribution to policy review as a whole (see Blackstone and Plowden, 1988). The emphasis upon performance measurement in both local and central government in the 1980s also had identifiable roots in specific existing methodologies.

The Planning, Programming and Budgeting (PPB) system developed in the USA in the early 1960s sought to identify objectives, outputs and costs within a rigorous system of information management (Carter, Klein and Day, 1992, p. 7). Although PPB was never a common feature of local authority policy planning in Britain, its rationale came to be seen as more relevant as local government grew in size and complexity after 1974. In central government, PPB influenced the formulation of Programme Analysis and Review (PAR) under Heath in the early 1970s, consistent with the creation of the CPRS itself at that time.

A further strand in the early development of performance-related thinking was the system known as Zero-Based Budgeting (ZBB), again arriving from the USA in the 1970s. In essence, ZBB is a form of output budgeting and planning, but it goes further than PPB. Zero-Based Budgeting removes **all** assumptions about appropriate spending or about uncritically accepted incremental additions to service budgets. The principal characteristic of ZBB is that it starts with a budgetary blank sheet.

> The distinctive element arrives when the managers of decision units are required to justify in some detail not only what **existing** levels of spending should be maintained and, no doubt, incrementally added to in the next financial year, but why **any** spending on particular 'packages' (services, programmes or objectives) should be continued for a further year (Hogwood and Gunn, 1984, p. 189 – emphasis in original).

In British local government, ZBB did begin to have an impact – not **literally** in producing an initial political or managerial blank sheet of paper, but in encouraging the review of why services, objectives, costs and activities in particular areas exist at all, i.e., an examination of first assumptions and values. In the following discussion of the performance management process, it is as well to remember that initial values and desirable objectives are just as important as performance measurement procedures.

As time went by, ZBB and other specific techniques came, in Britain, to be seen as consistent with the Conservative government's agenda for public service reform (and the particular values of that government) but the principles of ZBB could just as well apply under a government of a wholly different political complexion.

It was noted in Chapter 3 that the 'consumer perspective' in local government arose from a perception of public service bureaucracies as large and unresponsive organizations, devoted to producer rather than consumer needs. Exactly the same perception constitutes a further pressure toward the development of performance measurement.

> The popular view or image of the public sector was that of an inert, unresponsive, bureaucratic giant: a monopoly which, in the absence of the profit motive and the threat of competition was inefficient in its use of resources and an organization which had been captured by the special interests of professional supplier groups.. who served in their own interests rather than those of their clients or the general public (Jackson and Palmer, 1992, p. i).

Indeed, such a view of the unreconstructed public-service sector underlies not only the growth of the consumer perspective and the development of performance management, it has also played a considerable role in the growth of competition (see Chapter 2) and the issue of public access to information (see Chapter 6). The **image** of a public-service sector in urgent need of reform, despite the elements of caricature it may contain, has been a potent symbol in the hands of an ideologically-led central government. This image lies behind the development of performance management. It is another aspect of change in local government – nothing is static.

> The thrust of these changes involved setting clear objectives, thinking strategically, generating management information and measuring . . . performance in terms of what had actually been achieved. In other words, there was a need for a system that would develop performance measures and indicators that would become an integral part of public sector management (Jackson and Palmer, 1992, p. v).

In sum, the interest in and practice of performance management in local government has developed through the uneasy but powerful combination of:

- compulsion from central government;
- a critique from Left and Right alike of traditional patterns of service provision;
- economic constraint and the need to focus resources more exactly;
- the influence of private-sector management models;
- existing, piecemeal, performance programmes and methods;
- a changed political climate overall – a cultural change in local government itself, including value-for-money and quality initiatives.

Having identified key factors in the growth of performance management, the process itself may now be summarized within the familiar terms of the '3 Es'. This provides the basis for consideration of current practice and procedures.

The 3 Es are general accepted to be:

- **economy**
- **efficiency**
- **effectiveness**.

Economy

Economy may be defined as:

> the level of resources (e.g. staff, property) applied to an activity (ADC/PPRN, 1991, p. 6).

However, a minimal definition of economy provides no clues about performance. There needs to be a link to quality of service. A further definition of economy is:

> the purchase and provision of services at the lowest possible cost consistent with a specified quality; something which in principle should be an objective of any public sector service (Carter, Klein and Day, 1992, p. 37).

Similarly, economy:

> entails the purchasing of inputs, defined as the resources used to produce a service or execute a policy of a given quality specification at the lowest possible cost (Rouse, 1993, p. 61).

These more substantial definitions of economy have their problems too. The quality specification may not be 'given': it may be disputed. In practice, 'economy' may be a rather more messy tradeoff between cost and quality than any formal definition can allow. As illustrated in Figure 5.1 (p. 125), economy refers both to cost and to resources: it denotes the real cost of the resources (such as staff or premises) which then become the inputs to the process of measuring performance (Henderson-Stewart, 1990, p. 108).

Thus a seemingly simple concept such as 'economy', familiar as part of everyday language, is fraught with possible complications. It derives some of its ambiguity from the commonsense usage of economy as 'good value' – interestingly, a practical definition which **does** link cost and quality implicitly. Economy can also carry varying political implications, but it is not about cost alone, even when government has wrongly equated 'economical' with 'cheap'. '. . . the tendency for the current government to interpret economy as "cost-cutting" has often transformed economy into an emotive, political term' (Klein and Carter, 1988, p. 6).

The local government manager, in setting up a system of performance measurement, obviously requires clarity of concepts and objectives prior to formulating particular measures. There is no general agreement about precisely what economy **must** mean. However, a basis on which to proceed is that economy denotes the link between **cost** and **quality** in a manner consistent with the particular local authority's priorities and objectives.

Efficiency

Efficiency may be defined as:

> the ratio of inputs to outputs, or the rate at which inputs are converted into outputs (Carter, Klein and Day, 1992, p. 37).

Although efficiency *per se* is not a political concept, the search for **improvements** in efficiency inevitably involves choices – and those choices belong, as Carter, Klein and Day point out, in the political arena. This is potentially a serious difficulty for the local authority officer. Even where there is political consensus in relation to efficiency improvements, this does not render the process of improvement apolitical.

In Figure 5.1 (p. 125), efficiency derives from the relationship between resources and outputs, consistent with the definition above. Put another way:

> **Efficiency measures** show the outputs achieved in relation to the resource inputs, for example the cost per residential place. Where the service facility can be measured, it is also possible to measure its utilization, for example the occupancy of residential homes, or the utilization of recreation facilities (Henderson-Stewart, 1990, p. 108).

Efficiency, then, is a **relationship** – between what has been put in, and what has been produced. Again, the concept is open to misuse. Efficiency may wrongly be equated with cost, although it is not a measure of cost at all. Worse still, both economy and efficiency may be identified with cheapness. In reality, an efficient service may be very expensive, and a cheap service may be using its meagre resources inefficiently.

Local authority managers may be under quite **distinct** pressures under the common guise of efficiency. The need, for instance, to keep the authority within government spending guidelines in order to avoid central government penalty amounts to the need to limit **spending** and has nothing whatsoever to do with efficiency. A high-spending, penalized, authority may be highly efficient.

Quite separately, of course, central government is **also** interested in efficiency, which it pursues principally through the Audit Commission, thereby generating a further set of demands and opportunities.

As Jackson and Palmer point out (1992, p. 16) too much emphasis on efficiency may mean that resources are under-utilized, and, one might add, such an under-utilization would itself be inefficient.

Thus the use of efficiency as a necessary element in the performance measurement equation must, once again, seek to transcend the ambiguities caused by commonsense and ideological uses of the term. The local authority manager may regard efficiency as the link between inputs and outputs, the precise nature of the link depending, once again, on the specific needs and conditions of the particular council.

A final difficulty remains, however.

> Efficiency is frequently employed both as a measure and an objective of programmes (Klein and Carter, 1988, p. 6).

To elaborate, efficiency – as the ratio between inputs and outputs – is a **measure**. However, this measure tends to evolve into an objective in its own right. Efficiency then becomes a measure of . . . efficiency. Thus it is crucially important to be clear about the meaning of such terms in designing performance measurement systems. The goal of an 'efficient local authority' would meet with universal approval, but the performance manager must first ask (and answer) the sceptical question 'what do you mean by efficient?'

Effectiveness

Effectiveness may be defined as:

> the extent to which policy impacts meet policy aims, normally measured by the relationship between outputs and outcomes (Klein and Carter, 1988, p. 7).

Consistent with this, the **measures** of effectiveness:

> show the final outcome of the service in relation to its output, for example the number of pupils passing an examination as a percentage of all the pupils in the age group (Henderson-Stewart, 1990, p. 109).

In Figure 5.1 (p. 125), effectiveness describes the link between output and outcome. Again, there are problems both of concept and of measurement.

First, the meaning of 'output' and 'outcome' is disputed. In Henderson-Stewart's example above, the main point is undermined by an illustration of an outcome (numbers of pupils passing an examination) which could be better considered as an output; and an output (% of pupils in the age group) which could be viewed as an input. The **outcome** of educational experience is perhaps not quantifiable at all.

Secondly, outcomes may, generally, not readily be measurable. To some degree this may apply to inputs and output too, but outcomes, in denoting the ultimate desired state of affairs which it is hoped to achieve, are necessarily less tangible. The difficulty of measuring outcomes is a difficulty in measuring effectiveness.

Thirdly, it is very difficult to establish the **causal** link between measurable output and the outcome to which we have to assume it contributes.

For all these reasons, effectiveness is difficult to measure. This does not mean that it cannot be measured, or that we should abandon the attempt to do so. It may be useful to turn to **qualitative** indicators (rather than quantitative measures) in any review of effectiveness. An example of the use of qualitative indicators of effectiveness is the 'consumer survey' (see Case study 3.3), where public perceptions of effectiveness are given prominence. As noted later in this chapter, the Audit Commission (1993a; 1994a) has moved toward a recommended format for the collection of such consumer-driven indicators.

Even where acceptable methods of judging effectiveness exist, the relationship to the two previous 'Es' may be contentious. A service judged highly **effective** by its users may, on other measures, be grossly **inefficient**. A natural limitation exists here: the answer to this dilemma could only provided by the performance management process; it could not be provided by the techniques of performance measurement alone.

Rouse (1993) offers a definition of effectiveness which is looser than some, but which captures the feel of what effectiveness in a public-service organization is about:

> Effectiveness is concerned with outcomes or impacts, the results obtained or the effects of the service upon clients, and is achieved when the impacts of a policy are meeting its policy aims (Rouse, 1993, p. 62).

The problem of 'effectiveness', however, is that the closer we move to a definition which sits more happily with the service ethos of local government and the importance of public satisfaction, the harder it becomes to measure. There seems to be a choice between a satisfactory but operationally weak definition of effectiveness, and an imperfect but more measurable concept. This is an inherent limitation. The local authority officer involved in design of such processes needs, explicitly, to acknowledge the limits of the effectiveness measures chosen, in the light of local circumstances.

Finally, effectiveness must also refer to the multiple **audiences** for local authority activity (which group of users for instance should judge the effectiveness of statutory mental health services, or environmental control functions?) and to the gap between intended and unintended consequences of providing a particular service.

> **Effectiveness** is usually defined as the relationship between outputs and outcomes and, more precisely, as the extent to which policy objectives are achieved. The limitation of this definition is that it is concerned primarily with the intended effects of a policy, whereas it may be argued that unintended effects can be of equal importance (Rogers, 1990, p. 15).

Indeed, a service may be effective in spite of rather than because of the efforts of the local authority.

Ultimately, despite the measurement problems, effectiveness is **the most important** element of measuring and managing performance. Effectiveness is about 'the quality of the outcome' (ADC/PPRN, 1991, p. 6). Discussions of performance measures and indicators which lose sight of the importance of effectiveness have lost sight of the purpose of local government services.

So far, the '3 Es':

- **economy**
- **efficiency**
- **effectiveness**

have been explored, somewhat critically, fully recognizing their difficulties. All three embody **relationships** between costs, resources, inputs, outputs and outcomes; all three are **processes**, not events; and all three contain **assumptions** about values, about desired states of affairs. The process of performance measurement cannot be a technical exercise which loses sight of its normative base.

Before finally leaving aside the complexities of such concepts to look at the practice of performance management, it may be of interest to note some further 'Es'.

The '3 Es' of economy, efficiency and effectiveness are of course merely a shorthand, a way of assisting our understanding of complex processes. Rouse discusses the role of additional 'Es' such as equity, excellence and enterprise (1993, p. 61). Jackson and Palmer, who have contributed so much to the development of these concepts, offer us (1992, pp. 19–20):

- **equity**
- **excellence**
- **entrepreneurship**
- **expertise**
- **electability**.

to which we might justifiably add, at this point, a further 'E':

- **enough!**

The practice of performance management

Common principles and good practice

A considerable body of information now exists to guide the practical business of implementing and managing the process of performance measurement. In the following review of practice, it should not be assumed that conceptual problems have been overcome. Practice, on the contrary, gains strength from a critical awareness of the problems involved in measuring performance.

Jackson and Palmer (1989; 1992) have set out a number of guidelines relating to performance measurement. Without the information provided by performance measures, they remind us, 'public sector managers are in danger of allocating resources in the dark. They will have little or no idea about how their activities are contributing to economy, efficiency or effectiveness' (Jackson and Palmer, 1989, p. 1).

The preparation of specific performance measures should seek to conform to general principles of good practice. Table 5.1 summarizes some overall principles of performance monitoring, derived from Boyle (1989).

Table 5.1 Principles and practice in performance monitoring

Overall principles

- formulate processes that demonstrate and support high-level commitment
- adopt an approach that emphasizes staff participation
- take into account the relevance of specific tasks performed
- emphasize that responsibility for performance exists at all levels in the organization

Setting objectives and targets

- focus on key user-related and 'climate-setting' objectives
- formulate a plan for the medium-term
- work to an 'annual operational plan with challenging targets'

Collection of information

- collect quantitative data on different elements of performance
- obtain qualitative information to balance raw statistical data
- collect relevant information on the environment/context
- evaluate the reliability of information
- use information technology where appropriate

Feedback on performance

- link feedback to targets
- involve senior management
- involve peers and users in the feedback process

Source: derived from Boyle, 1989, p. 105.

The first section of Table 5.1 identifies principles – participation, delegated responsibility – which will be emphasized repeatedly in any discussion of what performance measurement **ought** to be about. How, though, is the transition made from statements of principle to practical design of performance measurement systems?

The initial design step is to **define the objectives** of the service or activity. Such a definition of objectives must be in a form which allows achievement of those objectives to be measured.

The second design step is to **formulate indicators or measures** to be employed in the measurement of performance. Such measures should not be plucked from the air: comparability, consistency and coherence should be features of any such measures. Jackson and Palmer (1989) illustrate, with examples, how specific measures can be linked to each of the three 'Es' – summarized at Table 5.2.

Jackson and Palmer point out that measures of outcome are much simpler to formulate for 'service' led departments (where presence or absence of a service, or response times, are fairly clear-cut) than for 'policy' led departments where outcomes are less tangible and less quantifiable (1989, pp. 6–7). For instance, in their own example of reduction of unemployment through operating a training scheme, Jackson and Palmer say quantification is unrealistic given all the other possible influences on employment levels (1989, p. 7).

Thus, even where objectives are clearly stated and indicators carefully formulated, considerable caution must be exercised in assuming a **causal** relationship between input (council activity) and output. There may be a value in the use of **intermediate** outputs as concrete, if incomplete and tentative, measures of eventual outcome.

Table 5.2 Performance indicators and the '3 Es'

Indicator	Corresponding 'E'	Example
Cost indicators	Economy	Annual cost per aged person in residential accommodation
Productivity indicators	Efficiency	Number of library books issued per staff member per hour
Time targets	Efficiency and effectiveness	Response time for dealing with grant application
Volumes of service	'Crude measure' of efficiency	Number of housing repairs
Quality of service indicators	Effectiveness	% satisfied with particular service; number of complaints
Demand (or take-up rate) for service indicators	Effectiveness	Numbers using particular facility
Availability of services	Effectiveness and equity	Access to library service in different areas
Outcome (or impact) of policy indicators		Reduction of unemployment through operation of training scheme

Source: derived from Jackson and Palmer, 1989, pp. 5–6.

The third broad design step is to ensure that performance measures are **comparable** – measuring like-with-like, not producing a spurious quantification, and allowing legitimate comparisons over time or between different authorities. The Audit Commission (1992a; 1992b; 1993a; 1994a) is aiming for exactly such comparability in its standard performance measures for the Citizens' Charter, as discussed below.

Finally, design of performance measurement systems needs to incorporate a mechanism for **using** the information once it has been collected. This is partly a matter of information dissemination throughout the organization, and partly a matter of linking the performance measurement process to management structures.

> The question of **who receives the information** is crucial. It is important that performance measures are matched to policy objectives, targets and activities for which specific managers have been allocated clear responsibility (Jackson and Palmer, 1989, p. 13 – emphasis in original).

So far, then, it can be said that performance measurement systems need to:

- clearly state service objectives;
- incorporate coherent and preferably quantitative indicators;
- ensure comparability of data;
- build-in mechanisms for dissemination of results.

At this point a detailed case study will serve to illustrate some practical design issues. Case study 5.1 explores the complexities of measuring the performance of the local authority education service.

CASE STUDY 5.1 Performance measurement and education

Performance measurement in education has become increasingly important alongside:

- the growth in Local Management of Schools (LMS);
- the publication from 1993 onward of 'league tables' of examination performance;
- the changing strategic role of the LEA.

Thus performance measurement has become more important at both the LEA level and at the devolved level. What are the elements of educational performance measurement?

- **Outcomes** The ultimate outcomes of education – eg, an 'educated society', an informed citizen – are not directly measurable, and in any case the meaning of such outcomes is contested. Such outcomes are socio-economic rather than purely educational (Jackson and Palmer, 1992, p. 135). An early discussion of educational performance by CIPFA (1984) regarded 'readiness to be active as a citizen' as an **output** (p. 5) yet this is more properly regarded as an eventual outcome. The outcomes of education may remain intangible, and not subject to measurement or analysis.
- **The mission statement** may set out the policies and goals of the LEA (and perhaps the individual school) and performance indicators reveal the extent to which these are being achieved – Jackson and Palmer (1992, p. 136) divide such indicators into 'quality pointers' and 'scanning indicators':

  - **quality pointers** are qualitative indicators such as level of parent consultation;
  - **scanning indicators** are quantitative indicators such as pupil/teacher ratio, % staff on in-service training (Jackson and Palmer, 1992, p. 144).

- **Indicators of output** provide data relating to teaching outputs, such as qualifications and subsequent employment/training.
- **Non-teaching indicators** provide data about, for instance, use of buildings and energy resources.

South (1986, pp. 12–14) provides the following structure for educational performance measurement – the **types** of indicator identified above can be incorporated within this:

- **The context**: e.g. % receiving free school meals, % statements of special needs;
- **The cost**: e.g. pupil/teacher ratio, gross cost per pupil;
- **The process**: separate indicators relating to teaching staff (e.g. % qualified in their subject), advisory staff (e.g. number of advisers per x number of pupils), ancillary staff (e.g. ratio ancillary/teaching staff), central staff (e.g. ratio of professional education officers to teachers) and parents (e.g. numbers attending open days);
- **The outcome**: separate indicators relating to the curriculum (e.g. % pupils learning musical instrument); assessment (e.g. exam achievements as % age group) and other outcomes, e.g. consumer surveys of parents/pupils/teachers.

There remain some fundamental problems of measuring educational performance, however.

1. **Confusing output and outcome** Specific outputs can be measured. Ultimate outcomes of educational experience are not readily quantifiable. This increases the danger that policy-makers and managers may focus more on the easily measured and unimportant, than on the diffuse but important factors.
2. **Linking input to output** Crude league tables of (e.g.) examination results encourage spurious linkage to (e.g.) teaching methods. Establishing the causal link between LEA and school input, and educational output, is extremely difficult. Jesson and Mayston (1989) attempt a sophisticated statistical analysis of how a certain output (e.g. % pupils achieving at least one graded pass) is linked to a defined level of input. Their 'data envelope analysis' is akin to multivariate analysis in linking change in the dependent variable (output) to manipulation of independent variables (input) but as a technique is beyond the reach of non-statisticians.
3. **Producing comparable data** Comparing like with like across different LEAs (or, increasingly, between different schools) is fraught with problems given different assumptions about resources, policies, objectives, teaching practices or class sizes. This applies to all local authority services to some extent – but applies to education particularly.

Any system of educational performance measurement also needs to reproduce its categories/indicators for each stage – nursery, primary, middle where applicable, secondary. The prevailing LMS formula may in any case contain different weightings for costs and pupil numbers at each stage. The **starting point** for educational performance measurement is thus likely to be the same data as used for LMS calculations – a very useful stock of existing data.

Education is of course a topic of political dispute: the national curriculum, overall 'standards', the alleged advantages of one sort of teaching regime over another, the battle for resources and the lack of jobs for a substantial proportion of school leavers combine to render education a live political issue. This is not surprising, given that education is about the values of society, and those very values are a topic of disagreement. Designing a system for the measurement of educational performance is thus not only a technical question of formulating measures and methods – although the methodological challenge is a formidable one in its own right (e.g. in finding a suitable proxy measure for social disadvantage). The task of **managing** the performance measurement process in education is a quasi-political task involving human resources and power relations in addition to the considerable statistical data required.

Education is the most challenging area for anyone seeking to introduce a performance measurement system. The measurement and management of performance in other service areas creates problems (and opportunities) different from those of the education service. Case study 5.2 considers performance measures for the library service.

CASE STUDY 5.2 Performance measurement and the library service

Jackson and Palmer (1992, pp. 91–5) summarize key indicators in the library service of a Scottish District Council as follows:

1. **Customer demand**, e.g. between 1985 and 1989, 29% decline in both issues, compared to UK decline of 9%;
2. **Customer profile**, e.g. the 15–29 year age group is under-represented: 25% of local population, only 14% of library users;
3. **Take-up of library services**, e.g. 73% of library visitors in the authority were returning/renewing/borrowing books; 8% using other services;
4. **Service provision**: no council policy on size of library catchment areas; consequently some libraries could not become cost-efficient within normal opening hours;

5. **Service costs**: e.g. a no-fine policy; expenditure 1982/83 to 1989/90 rose but membership and book issues fell;
6. **Further issues**: there was no correlation between book expenditure and book issues in this or other Scottish authorities; an increase in expenditure does not in itself prevent a decline in usage;
7. **Recommendations**, e.g. formulate a marketing strategy to stem the decline in usage; review charging policies; survey of users; clarify council policies.

The London Borough of Bexley began at an early stage to incorporate performance monitoring within its overall cycle of business planning. Policy objectives and performance targets were compared and presented as in the following example:

Performance Standards and Targets: Libraries Department

	Estimated workload/planned provision	Target performance
1. Service availability	100%	99.5%
2. Average book issues per library per hour	86	100%
3. Issues per head of population	12	100%
4. Book stock additions – volumes	51 620	100%
5. Computerized catalogue of stock: number of volumes to be processed to complete project	90 000	100%
6. Borrowers' request service: percentage of reservations supplied within 28 days	25 000	70%
7. Sound recordings cost recovery	£19 000	100%
8. Photocopying service cost recovery	£6000	£2000 over expenditure
9. Publication programme cost recovery	£7500	100%

Source: from Audit Commission/LGTB/INLOGOV, 1985, p. 64.

The Bexley example, from a relatively early stage in the development of library service performance measures, demonstrates that important measures for this service can nonetheless be very simple. The Bexley example also illustrates the general importance of measuring performance against a target, thus leading to conclusions that 70% or 100% of the target has been achieved. Targets do allow evaluation against descriptive indicators – but raise obvious questions of who is responsible for target-setting, and whether targets are realistic or desirable ones. The respective roles of manager and councillor in setting targets would require particular clarification.

The Scottish example of library performance measures goes a little further than Bexley. It points-up the value of **comparative** data (over time; between other Scottish authorities; between libraries within the district) and also implies the need for explicit council **policy** against which to measure performance.

The library service example is developed further in the text of Chapter 5, in relation to Audit Commission standard library indicators (Audit Commission 1992a; 1992b; 1993a; 1994a).

It can be seen from Case study 5.2 that relatively simple indicators of library service performance, such as the time taken to supply reserved items, or even just the number of book or other issues, can be extremely informative. It may also be noted that the technology for collecting such indicators is already present in the technology of service provision through computerized issue systems. The presence of such technology means that the cost of collecting routine indicators for some aspects of the library service is minimal. The scale and complexity of educational indicators, as discussed in Case study 5.1, mean that the process of performance measurement is itself a measurable cost to be calculated, not least in managers' time.

Case studies 5.1 and 5.2 also illustrate aspects of overall good practice (see Table 5.1) and the specific indicators examined for education and libraries can be linked up to the '3 Es' as a whole (see Table 5.2). The difficulty of identifying or measuring ultimate **outcomes**, especially for education, is really the same problem as measuring **effectiveness** – which we already know to be the most important 'E' of all, if the most difficult to pin down.

Having considered the detail of some design problems, it is useful to consider other ways of approaching the design of performance measurement systems. Rogers, for instance, has examined experience in a number of local authorities, from which he derives six dichotomies as follows (1990, pp. 25–8):

- **total systems vs partial systems**: a council may opt for an authority-wide approach, involving members and officers, all services defined horizontally, and all levels of the hierarchy defined vertically – or a partial approach, building performance measurement piecemeal;
- **top-down vs bottom-up approaches**: effective review of performance needs commitment at the top, but clearly should not be imposed from the top – 'bottom up' measures have credibility, but also require authority;
- **action vs analysis**: Rogers identifies a difference between action-oriented councils where reference tends to be to 'action plans', 'key results areas' and 'goals', and analysis-oriented councils where the terms 'review', 'evaluation' and 'appraisal' are more in evidence (1990, p. 27);
- **direction and control by councillors vs direction and control by officers**: a familiar difference in emphasis, which is manifest in performance measurement as in other areas of activity;
- **continuity vs change in systems, personnel and political control**: stable staffing structures and political control, with established reviews of performance, help to

establish continuity and the culture of confidence needed for dealing with performance – but a change of key personnel may equally be an effective catalyst for performance measurement (Rogers, 1990, p. 28);

- **internal vs external focus**: the extent to which councils may be inward or outward looking is familiar enough, but Rogers goes further in suggesting that the 'internally focused' council tends to be concerned with **efficiency**, the 'externally focused' council with **effectiveness** (1990, p. 28).

What is the value of such a series of dichotomies in assisting the design of systems of performance measurement? Clearly, as ideal types, the dichotomies do not stand as literal descriptions of particular councils, and are not meant to. The value of ideal types is that they reflect to a greater or lesser extent real experience, and then become a tool for understanding future practice. Thus, alongside the review of conceptual problems, the statement of general principles and the details of some particular indicators from selected services, we can now start to place performance measurement within different types of council – the inward or outward looking, the officer-led or member-led, and so on.

At this point, it may be helpful to consider a further example of practice. Case study 5.3 summarizes the system of performance measurement introduced in Ireland for Social Services.

CASE STUDY 5.3 Performance measurement and social services in Ireland

The Social Welfare Services Office (SWSO) is the executive branch of the Irish Department of Social Welfare. The Aireacht is the other branch of the Department, responsible for policy advice to the Minister. The SWSO runs the Department's long-term services for families and elderly people, and short-term services for the sick and unemployed (Boyle, 1989, p. 145). This model of social services delivery contrasts to that provided by local authorities in the UK, and provides an interesting supplement to the discussion of comparative public service management provided in Chapter 4.

The SWSO established a system in the 1980s for monitoring and management of its performance. This system comprised the following.

- **Six objectives**:
  1. delivering services with minimal delay;
  2. promoting client-oriented services and attitudes;
  3. keeping clients informed;
  4. developing management systems;
  5. developing flexible and cost-effective systems;
  6. controlling abuse of the services provided.

- **A corporate plan** based upon the objectives. Targets are formulated, and an annual plan devised, within the corporate context. Branch managers contribute to setting local targets, with the participation of staff.

  'Individual managers are given a large amount of flexibility in the choice and development of targets, provided they are oriented towards action, reasonably quantifiable, and are given a date to achieve them' (Boyle, 1989, p. 147).

- **Collection of performance information** A Management Services Unit collects monthly data on branch performance. This includes, for instance, the time taken to process new claims, or the number of claims paid. These data are quantitative, and the resulting stock of information provides comparative data (between branches and over time) for use by managers at central and local level. This is supplemented by more *ad hoc* qualitative surveys of clients.

- **Feedback of performance information** A quarterly report summarizes branch achievement of targets. This report is made widely available.

The system set up in the Irish SWSO in the 1980s seems to be characterized by:

- a high level of 'ownership' amongst managers at a number of levels in the formulation of targets and the collection of information;
- a wide dissemination of information obtained;
- an effective complementary management information system (see Chapter 6).

The case study of the SWSO thus provides an illustration of how good practice links up to general principles of performance measurement.
(*Source*: Boyle, 1989, pp. 145–50)

Case study 5.3 further illustrates the way in which general principles of performance measurement may be implemented. A particular feature of this case study is the active involvement of local branch offices and lower-scale managers in design and use of performance data. The 'bottom-up' nature of the performance information of Case study 5.3 reflects universal good practice, although it may not reflect the dominant reality of performance measurement in the UK. Case study 5.3 also reinforces aspects of good practice which have already been discussed including clear objectives, the use of quantitative and qualitative indicators, and dissemination of findings. Perhaps the main difficulty arising from Case study 5.3 would be how to ensure **comparability** of data when there is a high degree of local 'ownership' – reconciling the necessary standardization of performance data with the necessary local flexibility remains a challenge for any system of performance measurement.

Controlling the elements of performance measurement

The principles and practice so far described contain within them one major problem, which will be familiar to everyone in local government. It is the problem of control. Managers in local councils do not control the parameters of their work, the 'factors of production' of the day-to-day managerial process. Junior and middle managers are obviously constrained by vertical authority. However, even the most senior manager, the Chief Executive, is constrained by three factors: the local political leadership, central government, and resources. Additionally, officers at all levels are limited by what kind of information is available, or at what cost it could be made available.

Real-world performance management deals with imperfect – perhaps highly imperfect – data. The matter can be stated in terms of methodology. Unlike the experimental method, based in the laboratory, performance measurement cannot control the variables which we would seek to analyse: whether this is the dependent variable (the output or the ultimate outcome we hope to achieve) or the range of independent variables (the numerous inputs into the process).

The problem of control is not a terminal problem. It does not mean that any attempt at performance measurement is doomed to failure, nor does it mean that intuition is just as reliable a guide. However, the problem of control does (or at any rate should) moderate the claims which are made for the performance measurement process. It is still possible to **measure** processes even where elements of the process are not within the council's control – for instance, measuring the impact of central government funding decisions, or of demographic changes. We might also be faced with an indicator of, say, the socio-economic structure of the local population which has nothing to do with 'performance', individual or organizational. Thus, demand for free school meals is not a measure of performance – but demand for housing repairs might be.

Henderson-Stewart (1990) points out that, as an increasing number of council services are contracted-out, so performance review becomes ever more necessary. Yet, more responsibility is being delegated from the local authority itself to, for instance, individual schools: 'with less central control over "inputs", or over the manner in which services are delivered, councils must now shift their emphasis to monitoring and reviewing the "outputs" achieved' (Henderson-Stewart, 1990, p. 107).

In considering the links between inputs, outputs, the '3 Es', and the problem of control of the elements of this process, Henderson-Stewart's diagrammatic summary is useful (Figure 5.1).

Figure 5.1 is a succinct summary of the performance measurement process overall. Further, it demonstrates the links with the guiding principles of the '3 Es' – a representation of how abstractions such as economy, efficiency and effectiveness do refer to practical procedures. Even though the local authority cannot control all elements of this process, even to **chart** the extent of and impact of particular inputs is a considerable achievement. Figure 5.1 also alerts us to some, by now familiar, dangers. As Henderson-Stewart points out, it is easier to measure output than it is to measure

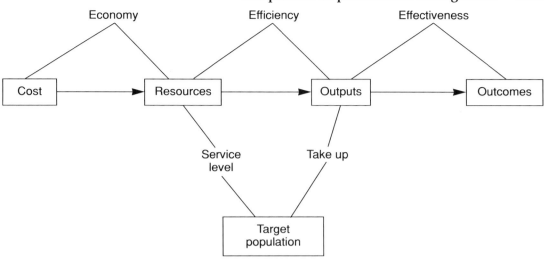

(*Source*: Henderson-Stewart, 1990, p. 108.)

Figure 5.1   The performance measurement process

outcome, and the danger thus arises that performance measurement comes simply to concentrate upon the **measurable** (1990, p. 109). The measurable, as we have seen in considering qualitative indicators, may drive out the important.

Indicators and measures

Are performance indicators and performance measures the same thing? The language of performance tends to slip rather easily between 'measure' and 'indicator'. Any student of public policy would routinely be advised not to confuse these, but there is no consensus in the academic or practitioner literature on the **precise** difference. Caution is therefore advised in deciding how to refer to measures/indicators in the design of performance systems. Rogers suggests that **measures** tend to be seen as 'precise and direct assessments of performance', and **indicators** as 'more indirect assessments' (1990, p. 16). Although this essential distinction between direct and indirect is intelligible enough, the reference to measures as 'assessments' is unfortunate. Indicators and measures describe. They do not assess – people do that, assisted by the available information.

Jackson and Palmer (1992) offer a differentiation between measures and indicators which is akin to, though not synonymous with, the direct/indirect distinction. Performance measures denote a 'clear unambiguous reading' of the link between performance and output; indicators are merely 'signals' referring to a possible link in a necessarily ambiguous context (Jackson and Palmer, 1992, p. 17).

> Where economy, efficiency and effectiveness can be measured precisely and unambiguously it is usual to talk about performance measures. However, when as is most usually the case it is not possible to obtain a precise measure, it is usual to refer to performance indicators (Jackson and Palmer, 1989, p. 2).

In reality, economy, efficiency and effectiveness cannot be measured unambiguously. In this sense it would strictly be appropriate to talk only of performance indicators, not of measures. However, most academic and practitioner discussions of performance do not hold to such a rigid distinction, nor should they. Although the terminology of the performance process is something of a minefield, it can be negotiated by using terms **consistently**, and spelling out **explicitly** any problems with those terms.

The organizational framework

It is self-evident that performance measurement requires a suitable organizational framework. The local authority needs, for instance: the right channels of communication to generate the required performance data; line management systems which ensure the production of reports at the right time for the right audience; a committee cycle and structure which assist rather than undermine the performance process. In the absence of these elements, the individual council officer is struggling against elements of the organizational framework in trying to implement a system of performance management. This does **not** mean that effective performance management must be accompanied by structural reorganization. However, local authorities have tended to make particular progress with performance management when they are already making changes within their organization or reviewing their overall activity.

In Arun District Council in the 1980s, a new political leadership and a new Chief Executive created conditions for change incorporating three elements (Rogers, 1990, p. 36):

● **policy development**: services were grouped into eight programme areas, each with stated aims and priorities for the following four years; external links with public and private agencies were extended; resource management based on economy and efficiency was developed;
● **organizational development**: officer and member structures within Arun D.C. were changed to increase corporate control;
● **systems and process development**: an annual business system was created, based on the new corporate structures, and with clear objectives and procedures for review.

Thus, the 'business system' created in Arun DC incorporates a system of performance measurement. There is no reason to regard these particular organizational changes as being a necessary counterpart of performance measurement generally. However, the example is interesting, for it locates performance measurement formally within processes and systems, **and** it identifies explicit roles for managers and members alike. Rogers (1990, pp. 36–8) describes the six stages of Arun's business system as follows:

● **direction**: the 'direction' of the business system (aims, strategy, policy objectives) is set by the four-year horizon of the local electoral process;
● **planning**: the four-year strategy is matched to the annual resource cycle, including service plans for consideration at particular committees;
● **authorization**: service plans generate specific budgets to 'authorize' spending, alongside plans of work brought together in the Annual Action Plan; performance measures are central here;

- **execution and control**: the execution of work programmes, within budget guidelines, includes an automatic review of progress/performance; a corporate information system is used to provide data for programme committees; additionally, a Performance Review Sub-Committee has a corporate role;
- **completion**: performance against targets is reviewed annually at departmental level (management), at programme committee level (members) and at corporate level via Policy and Resources Committee;
- **assessment**: a permanent programme of performance review takes place via Performance Review Sub-Committee.

The business system described here is one way of building performance measurement into the permanent structures and management processes of the local authority. This example also incorporates the primacy of political goals and objectives through its linkage to the timescale of the local electoral process. In other authorities the role occupied by the central policy function (see Chapter 6) may be particularly significant, without the necessity for a specific business system. More generally, the Performance Review Sub-Committee, or equivalent, has a leading role in oversight and co-ordination of performance measurement. Organizational frameworks for effective management of performance-related review vary considerably. In **all** authorities, however, the **organizational framework** (structure and process, officer and member, departmental and corporate) should be examined and if necessary changed before performance management is implemented.

Designing the system

Through the case studies, examples and discussion already presented, it will have become clear that designing a system of performance measurement includes:

- issues of overall principles, objectives and values;
- issues of technical design, methodology and procedure;
- issues of organizational context, including management systems, information flow and feedback

while recognizing that not all factors are within the control of officers responsible for performance management, and that external (especially central government) constraints may limit the design choices from the start.

Are there any general lessons to be learned from the experience of local councils so far? Likierman (1993) has conducted a study of how performance indicators are used in the public sector. After feedback from over 500 managers, he proposed a list of twenty 'lessons', grouped under four headings. These are taken to describe good practice in the use of performance indicators in public and private organizations alike and are summarized in Table 5.3. The focus, explicitly, is upon managerial use (Likierman, 1993, p. 15).

The information summarized in Table 5.3 necessarily simplifies a more complex series of lessons, and in this form cannot deal with some of the subleties of Likierman's classification. For instance, the question of proxy indicators (Table 5.3, point 14) is a topic in itself. It refers to the use of an alternative indicator in place of something

Table 5.3 Performance indicators: 20 lessons

Concept

1. Include all relevant elements: ensure choice of indicators is comprehensive
2. Choose the right number of indicators for your particular organization
3. Provide for qualitative indicators
4. Reflect the political context, and patterns of accountability

Preparation

5. Formulate indicators in conjunction with those affected
6. Guard against short-term indicators alone
7. Ensure indicators reflect the work of managers in the organization
8. Include mechanisms for reflecting external or uncontrollable changes
9. Use the experience of others
10. Ensure standards are realistic before setting targets

Implementation

11. Be prepared to revise newly established indicators
12. Link indicators to existing systems (e.g. budgetary/management systems)
13. Ensure indicators are understandable to and accepted by those affected
14. Choose proxy indicators carefully
15. Review internal and external relationships (e.g. to customers) alongside introduction of indicators

Use

16. Ensure the information is trusted
17. Use the results to inform discussion, not to provide all the answers
18. Ensure there is feedback, and dissemination of findings
19. Make appropriate judgements about different indicators – they are not all equal
20. Present results in a 'user-friendly' format, at the right time, in the right way.

Source: derived from Likierman, 1993, pp. 15–21.

which cannot itself be directly, or readily, measured. Different levels of free school meal take-up in different parts of a city, for instance, might serve as a proxy for the different socio-economic characteristics of those areas. This of course would be a fairly crude proxy, but proxies are inherently rather blunt instruments.

The enduring value of the lessons summarized in Table 5.3 is that they derive from the experience of performance measurement in a large number of public-sector organizations. This brings us full circle from our initial discussion of the desirable features of performance measurement in the abstract. A similar characterization of good practice can now be seen to derive from experience.

Having explored the principles and the practice of performance measurement, it is necessary to give some separate attention to the local political level. Thus the next section considers the role of the elected member in performance measurement.

The role of the councillor

The elected member may stand in an uneasy relationship to officers concerned with organizational performance. The boundaries between the policy-making role of the councillor, and the managerial role of the officer, while never wholly separate, are particularly blurred in the area of performance management.

Officers closely involved in the work of a Performance, Review and Efficiency Sub-Committee are working close to the political core of the authority. In contrast, some members may turn away from performance-related work altogether, leaving it to a core of particularly interested members who may have a particular agenda to pursue. Alternatively – and equally to be avoided – councillors may interpret the results of performance-related analysis inappropriately, perhaps by focusing upon individual rather than organizational performance. Instead of this range of problems associated with the elected member, however, there may be very positive relationships with officers. Certainly, support for systematic performance measurement systems from senior councillors can drive through such changes when it really matters.

In all councils, elected members increasingly require a knowledge of the techniques of performance measurement in order, for instance, to review the achievement of the council's corporate policies or monitor the contracts awarded under CCT. The Association of District Councils (ADC), in conjunction with the Policy and Performance Review Network (PPRN), describes how performance review can improve or achieve:

- elected members' use of their time;
- monitoring of success in achieving policy objectives;
- communication of 'requirements and achievements';
- measurable gains in efficiency and effectiveness;
- customer service;
- teamwork around common objectives;
- staff motivation;
- identification of reasons for poor performance (ADC/PPRN, 1991, p. 6).

As pointed out by the ADC/PPRN, elected members themselves need to decide on their performance review needs, bearing in mind their varying roles as local policy-makers, committee member, and ward councillor (1991, p. 8). To this list of councillor roles, it would now be important to add the crucial distinction between client and contractor, and purchaser and provider, on the member side of the authority. The theme of the **competitive** local authority (see Chapter 2) is important in understanding the role of the member in performance review today.

We have already considered the 'organizational framework' of performance-related activity, largely on the officer side of the authority. Councillors too need to work within appropriate frameworks and structures. There is little value in *ad hoc* reviews by individual councillors – a permanent framework is needed. The ADC/PPRN guide considers three vehicles for councillors' participation in a system of performance review (1991, p. 8):

- creation of a specific Performance Review Sub-Committee;
- allocation (or extension) of performance review functions to existing service committees;
- creation of more informal officer/member groups to review policy and performance.

The three possibilities are not, of course, mutually exclusive. Councils can, and do, adopt all three. However, the Performance Review-type Sub-Committee is particularly influential in linking performance measurement to wider strategic and corporate management.

The Performance Review and Efficiency Sub-Committee

A Performance Review and/or Efficiency Sub-Committee may be known by rather different names in different authorities. It is normally a sub-committee of the main Policy and Resources or equivalent committee. It is a common feature of the metropolitan authorities outside the remit of the ADC but is by no means confined to the larger urban areas. A Performance Review and Efficiency Sub-Committee has the **time** and space to consider performance activity across the authority. It may initiate and monitor specific policy initiatives, look in detail at particular services, assess the achievement of corporate policy, and collate the more routine (but important) indicators already available.

It is possible to see the Performance Review and Efficiency Sub-Committee as a sign of the maturity of an authority's approach to performance activity, and it gives that activity a permanent structural role on the member side, but dangers arise too. The most common negative perception of a standing Performance Review and Efficiency Sub-Committee is that it has a 'policing' role – a centralist brief to monitor and thus control all aspects of policy-making and implementation. A related danger is that the Performance Review and Efficiency Sub-Committee separates performance activity from the day-to-day work of committees – thus councillors not directly involved in the Sub-Committee can afford to forget about performance issues. Both dangers imply a third problem – that of an elite group of members, with more information, and more influence, than their colleagues. Perhaps it is not surprising that Monaghan and Ball suggest

> it is not unusual for members to be indifferent to performance review and very occasionally hostile (1993, p. 13).

Although, as Monaghan and Ball add, a complete technical mastery of performance measurement is not needed by even the most convinced councillor, there are problems when the member commitment is not there.

> In the absence of member commitment, the system may fall apart when difficult political questions and choices are forced, or members may support dissident officers in rubbishing the process (Monaghan and Ball, 1993, p. 14).

An effective Performance Review and Efficiency Sub-Committee, or equivalent member group, provides the **structure** to help prevent such fragmentation. Additionally, an Action Plan or comparable document may help to codify the respective role of officers and members. The Action Plan is discussed in Case study 5.4.

In addition to the corporate Performance Review-type Sub-Committee, and the associated Action Plan and management systems, the committee structure as a whole may be reshaped to assist the discharge of members' responsibilities for performance issues. Citing Avon County Council's restructuring of the late 1980s, Rogers (1990) identifies an organizational framework which seems to support the elected member. Rogers notes that the background analysis in Avon

CASE STUDY 5.4 The action plan for performance measurement

Plans are not merely documents: the important part of the plan tends to be the planning process which preceded it. For instance, the strategic planning process in local government generally is more valuable than the eventual strategic plan itself. Case study 5.1 refers to the Mission Statement in helping to set performance indicators against a statement of policy objectives/targets. However, councils also need a plan of how to achieve such targets, and how to know when they have been achieved. The Action Plan serves to bring together:

- council policy;
- action required;
- measures of output;
- evaluation of action.

The Action Plan thus assists:

- departmental managers in seeing the 'total picture' within which particular indicators are to be used;
- elected members in seeing their own role as political representatives within the performance management process.

The ADC/PPRN guide to performance review for members sets out an action plan for the Health and Public Protection Committee of an anonymous local authority (1991, p. 7). Its elements are:

1. **policy objectives**, e.g. prevention of coastal erosion;
2. **proposed action**, e.g. inspection of coast at defined intervals; provision of sandbags at least 12 hours before threat from rising tide;
3. **budget** specified for each item listed under 'proposed action';
4. **output measures**, e.g. % of coastline inspected once/twice; % sandbags issued within period specified;
5. **achievements**, i.e. assessment of success against targets e.g. % targets reached, absolute total spending above or within budget.

The key implications of such an Action Plan are the availability of the required information, the commitment of elected members, the existence of supporting management systems, and the will to act on the results.

Jackson and Palmer's Action Plan for the development of effective indicators is consistent with the points noted above – it comprises:

1. **strategy and objectives**, including specification of measurable policy objectives;
2. **design of the measures**, including inputs, outputs and outcomes;
3. **collection of the data**, including the cost;
4. **presentation**, including avoidance of jargon, and consistency of presentation;
5. **organization and accountability**, including relationship to the budget process and to management systems (Jackson and Palmer, 1992, pp. 168–71).

The Performance, Review and Efficiency Sub-Committee is part of the **structure** of performance measurement on the corporate level. The Action Plan is part of the corresponding **process**, setting out clear roles for the elected member and the employee, together with a specification of targets and how they will be achieved.

resulted in a new policy and service review process, central to which was the creation of departmental position statements containing objectives, statements of service standards and levels, and performance indicators. A new committee structure was also evolved, which was based on the concept of identifying each of the main decision-making roles of a service committee, with separate sub-committees, so that each main committee could retain an exclusive focus on policy making (1990, p. 115).

In short, the Avon structure sought to place the policy-making (and, with it, the policy review) role of the elected member back at the heart of the political structure. The separate sub-committees referred to by Rogers are the Policy Advisory Sub-Committee, the Policy Implementation Sub-Committee, and the Policy and Service Review Sub-Committee. We need not elaborate these details further in order to see how performance review is in-built to a structure such as that of Avon.

In addition to the **structural** conditions for effective member involvement in performance measurement, several other factors assist the councillor in this role, including:

● commitment from the top of the officer side, i.e. the Chief Executive or equivalent;
● training in the use and interpretation of performance information for members;
● a corporate rather than departmental culture within the council as a whole.

The third point is particularly important. The effective participation of both members and officers in the overall process of performance review implies that some debate has already taken place about the corporate direction of the authority. Performance analysis of discrete departmental activities has a value, but all that has been said above about the principles/practice and problems of performance measurement implies a strong corporate ethos: an aspiration, if not a reality. The most effective role of the elected member is in contributing to this corporate culture.

There are obvious dangers in circumstances where councillors come to perceive the performance review process as officer-dominated, or as a 'technical' exercise in which the elected member has no role (Leach, Stewart and Walsh, 1994, pp. 160–1). Equally, managers may need to educate themselves to new councillor roles. Rogers talks of the

> uneasy relationship which can sometimes exist between politicians and managers. Councillors may be perceived as a constraint on management and are therefore held at arms-length as far as is possible – a situation which is achieved in part by providing them with large amounts of paper at regular intervals (1990, p. 113).

Performance measurement assessed: problems and prospects

Having examined the principles and practice of performance measurement in some detail, the discussion may be concluded by a review of problems and prospects. First, however, a diagramatic summary of the performance measurement process may be useful.

The first problem to consider in summarizing performance measurement is indicated within Figure 5.2. This is the reference to performance-related pay (PRP) and the question, already raised, of how far organizational performance measurement relates to individual performance. A key task in managing the introduction of a performance measurement or review system is in clarifying whether or not the information obtained will be used for PRP or associated schemes. Lack of clarity will feed the justifiable concerns of staff. The different levels of management within the local authority may have different interests in this matter. Performance measurement may be employed differently according to managerial function.

Burningham (1990) distinguishes the 'general manager' (corporate, Chief Executive department, strategic) from the 'professional' manager (someone with professional expertise in a specific service area who has then become a manager). In more general terms, the immediate line manager with a delegated budget may be more prone to (mis)use performance measurement systems for individual incentives or sanctions. These issues can be addressed by making explicit the purposes of a performance measurement system at the time of its introduction. Individual performance and organizational culture are linked. An increasing number of local councils do use some sort of PRP scheme (Wilson and Game, 1994, p. 241). However, mature managerial practice tends to look at the individual as a positive resource in solving problems, rather than as an individual problem (see Daley, 1992, pp. 42–3).

The second difficulty to consider in an overall review of problems and prospects is that of values. Jackson points out that performance measurement is not only concerned with indicators and procedures: it is also about the values of the organization, the 'images' of what the organization is about (1993, p. 9). This point is central to managerial practice in local government today, as debates about the relative merits of the new public management, the private-sector model, the bureaucratic model and so on are, ultimately, debates about values.

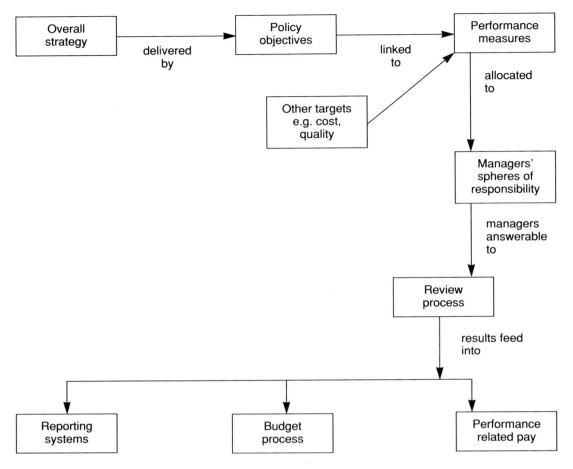

(*Source*: Jackson and Palmer, *First Steps in Measuring Performance in the Public Sector – A Management Guide*; published by CIPFA, London, 1989, p. 17.)

Figure 5.2   Designing the performance measurement system

As Jackson notes, performance measurement **may** be a means of managerial control (as, for instance, within the perspective of scientific management) but it may alternatively be a means of **learning**, not of control (1993, p. 10). The values of central government are also, of course, a crucial part of the normative framework for local government. Local managers can only work with what they have been given – and the normative stance of central government has often seemed punitive.

Concentration on X-efficiency, rather than allocative efficiency, has tended to shift the spotlight of accountability away from politicians to public service managers (Jackson, 1993, p. 14).

A third issue in summarizing performance measurement lies in recognizing its necessary limits. Not all inputs and outputs (and certainly not all outcomes) can be quantified. Even if such quantification **is** possible, **other factors need to be taken into**

account, as performance measurement does not tell us everything. Stewart and Walsh regard performance management as making the assumptions that managers can be allocated clear tasks and achievable performance targets, and can be held accountable for resources used to achieve these tasks (1992, p. 513). This may simply not apply.

> Performance management can confine the manager if it limits the capacity to learn and adapt. There is a value to ambiguity in enabling adaptation. The manager can, in any event, never be isolated from the political process, since actions taken in the public domain can and should be subject to public criticism, to which the political process should respond (Stewart and Walsh, 1992, p. 513).

Stewart and Walsh are thus making a point about the nature of public-service management rather than the nature of performance measurement. The management process cannot in their words be so easily 'bounded and measured' – the inherent limitations of performance measurement should not distort the practice which is being measured.

The fourth point to make in summarizing performance measurement is that while it necessarily refers to the political process, it is not linked to a strategy of 'cuts', savings or retraction of the public sector *per se*. Although performance measurement has grown through encouragement and legislation by successive Conservative governments, it is not containable within the political agenda of the Right alone. It is interesting to note the positive use to which predominantly Labour Party –controlled local authorities have come to put performance measurement, against initial suspicion of its true nature. After discussing the role of the Audit Commission under the Local Government Act 1992 in producing for the first time a comprehensive set of performance indicators (PIs) for local government (see below), the Local Government Information Unit points to the function of PIs in going beyond what the government may originally have intended and, indeed, in almost providing a **critique** of the 'official' indicators.

> The Audit Commission ... suggests that councils publish more than the minimum required PIs. Similarly the AMA and others advise that councils will benefit by producing additional non-statutory indicators that will enable councils to show some of the **unsung areas of achievement as well as providing a commentary on the statutory PIs** (Local Government Information Unit, 1994a, p. 5, emphasis added).

Thus performance measurement may (on the political level) be turned around by those who initially, with some justification, perceived it as an attack on non-Conservative local authorities, to become instead a tool in – for instance – extracting sufficient resources from central government. Moreover, whatever the political complexion of local or central governments in the future, there is a sense in which performance measurement must now be here to stay. It would be impossible to un-think the systematic process of performance review, the value of specific indicators or the **ethos** of the whole process, even in the very unlikely event of limitless resources suddenly becoming available.

The fifth and final point to make in reviewing prospects is that the **standardization** of performance measures will continue to increase, to the point where 'off the peg' measures for any conceivable area of local authority activity will soon be available. This means that local councils need not expend skills and time in endless formulations of their own indicators any longer, but it also means that standardization may become uniformity. Indicators, reflecting our earlier review of good practice, must still arise from local needs and reflect the concerns of those involved. This tension between standardized indicators laid down by central government, and particular indicators created by local councils to reflect their own needs, has not been resolved. It will continue to be problematic.

To draw this chapter towards a conclusion, this final point will be expanded to examine aspects of the work of the Audit Commission in the 1990s. In particular, between 1 April and 31 December 1994 local councils had for the first time to publish a comprehensive set of their performance indicators. These were produced with the intention that the Audit Commission would publish, in 1995, national league tables of local government PIs.

Under the Local Government Act 1992, the Audit Commission has to specify the particular indicators which local authorities themselves are then obliged to publish. The 1992 legislation is explicit in the need for **comparative** indicators (e.g. between local councils, and over time) and in its reference to **standards of performance** as a central concern. The requirement to publish these indicators is linked, by the government, to the overall concerns of its 'Citizens Charter' which emphasized responsiveness to service users, quality of service, choice, acceptable standards, and value-for-money. In a sense, local government has to produce such indicators as an operationalization of the government's Citizens' Charter – as a tool of government policy. However, as we have seen, local government has also gone beyond the minimal requirements of legislation, producing indicators which help the case for local government.

The work of the Audit Commission on performance indicators for the Citizens' Charter in local government has been presented in a series of working papers and guides (Audit Commission 1992a; 1992b; 1993a; 1994a). Within the twin contexts of the Local Government Act 1992 and the Citizens' Charter initiative, the Audit Commission draws five conclusions about possible draft indicators, in its first report of September 1992.

'1. The indicators must be of interest to citizens.
2. They should, so far as possible, deal with cost, economy and efficiency, as well as with quality and effectiveness.
3. They should support useful comparisons, over time, and between authorities.
4. They should deal with the main services provided by local government, and focus on those aspects that reflect the performance of individual authorities.
5. They should be reasonably acceptable, without laying down new norms or standards, and avoid incentives to distort' (Audit Commission, 1992a, p. 2).

In formulating **draft** indicators, the Audit Commission sought to ensure the indicators would be relevant to the public; would measure cost, economy, efficiency and effectiveness; would be comparable; would correctly measure the performance of the local authority and not some other variable; and would be acceptable to users (Audit Commission, 1992a, pp. 2–5). The draft indicators included at Table 5.4 refer to the library service (compare also to Case study 5.2).

It is to be emphasized that in the Audit Commission's own comments on this table there are numerous riders and reservations. For instance, it is pointed out that under indicator 3 – ease of travel to library – 'rural areas will fare less well on this indicator

Table 5.4   Draft library service performance indicators

Citizens' questions	Indicators
1. How many books and other items are issued by the libraries?	Issues per head of resident population divided into: ● books ● other media
2. How many people go to libraries?	Visits per head of resident population
3. How easy is it to get to a library?	% of resident population living within 2 miles of a library which is open at least 20 hours per week
4. How good is the library stock?	Acquisition spend per head of population: ● books ● other media
5. What does it cost the taxpayer to provide libraries?	Net expenditure per head on the library service

Source: Audit Commission, 1992a, p. 70.

than urban ones', irrespective of performance (1992a, p. 70). Following the draft indicators produced in September 1992, the Audit Commission published formal requirements for performance information from local authorities in December of that year (1992b, p. 3). It is instructive – as a general lesson from this exercise in constructing performance indicators – to note the Audit Commission's response to the comments received on its draft indicators. The Commission decided to:

● focus initially on a smaller number of services than proposed, with pointers toward future developments;
● focus upon topics of public interest, using available indicators;
● formulate indicators which relate performance to **local** policy priorities, 'leaving authorities with maximum discretion to explain the reasons for their policies when publishing their performance locally' (Audit Commission, 1992b, p. 3).

To illustrate the impact of the consultation process and the application of these principles, Table 5.5 presents the **revised** library service indicators, and continues the example introduced in Case study 5.2.

We are now able to see that the process of formulating such indicators in draft and final form, consulting, and then monitoring their implementation is ironically akin to the performance measurement process itself. The successive reports of the Audit Commission on this topic constitute an exercise in policy analysis in themselves. In 1993, the Commission produced a further report reviewing progress on the indicators, and setting out (relatively minor) changes for the 1994–5 indicators, to be published between April and December 1995. A general lesson may be learned from this continual scaling down of the required number of indicators on grounds of feasibility and cost. In its third report the Commission speaks of '**many** fewer indicators' in the final list than those originally published for consultation (Audit Commission, 1993a, p. 4, emphasis added).

Table 5.5　Revised library service performance indicators

Citizens' questions	Indicators
1. How many books do libraries issue?	The number of items issued by the authority's libraries: (a) books (b) other items
2. How long are libraries open?	The number of public libraries (a) open 45 hours per week or more (b) open 30–44 hours per week (c) open 10–29 hours per week (d) mobile libraries
3. How many people go to libraries?	The number of visits by members of the public to public libraries
4. How much is spent on libraries?	The amount spent per head of population on books and other materials
	The net expenditure per head of population on libraries

Source: Audit Commission, 1992b, pp. 15 and 24.

As a final note on effectiveness, and on the value of qualitative indicators, the Audit Commission refers to a standardized model for a consumer survey – which, if taken up by local authorities, will counter the piecemeal approach to the collection of consumer information discussed in Chapter 3.

> To facilitate comparisons between authorities concerning the quality of council services, the Commission will produce early in 1994 a manual for a standard consumer survey . . . The manual will provide standard questions relating to several local authority services and a standard method of rating the public's levels of satisfaction with those services. The questions cover areas which the Commission knows from its own surveys to be of concern to the public, **but which are not addressed through the mandatory indicators** (Audit Commission, 1993a, p. 13, emphasis added).

The specified Citizens' Charter indicators for the library service 1994–5 are the same as those already specified in the Audit Commission's previous publication (1993a, p. 30; 1992b, pp. 15 and 24). In terms of implementation, the statutory requirements and additional guidance about the local publication of indicators is provided in a further report (Audit Commission, 1994a). Overall, the performance information which local authorities must provide under the Local Government Act 1992 has appeared for the first time between April and December 1994. It must be disseminated in a newspaper (not a council publication): the details can be found in the Audit Commission's 'Publication of Information (Standards of Performance)' Directives 1992 and 1993, as well as the successive reports.

Concluding comments

The Citizens' Charter performance indicators provide an example of how performance measurement proceeds through the draft design stage, the formulation of final indicators, implementation, monitoring, review, and dissemination, while linked to an overall policy objective – which, in this case, is central government's Citizens' Charter project. From this example, it is possible to discern the principles and practice of performance measurement, as discussed above, together with pointers toward likely future practice, particularly in the standardization of qualitative measures.

In conclusion, do managers use performance measurement? As we have already seen, performance data can be used on a number of managerial levels for a variety of reasons. The departmental and corporate levels, as we know, may generate specific information needs, for their tasks are different. Palmer looked at existing practice of performance measurement in local government in relation to which indicators are currently used, the structure of performance measures, who uses the information, user perceptions of the process, and the link between indicators and management systems (1993, pp. 31–2). After collecting data from over 300 local council officers, she tentatively concludes that:

- **senior** managers were mainly interested in measures relating to cost, quality of service, achievement of goals, and demand versus provision – but were least interested in time targets and productivity indicators;
- **middle** managers were mainly interested in measures relating to cost, quality of service, productivity and volume of service –but were least interested in demand versus provision, or attainment of goals (Palmer, 1993, pp. 33–5).

Additionally, it was found that departmental management teams were concerned particularly with achievement of **goals** of the service – i.e. effectiveness. Seventy-two per cent of all Palmer's respondents indicated that quality-of-service measures were particularly relevant to decision making – but only 27% of departments measure or set targets for these (Palmer, 1993, pp. 33–5). So there is something of a gap between aspirations and reality.

In general, it remains true that what is most important – the ultimate outcome of a service, its impact on the public, effectiveness – is still most difficult to measure. However, relatively simple and routinely available measures (such as those for the library service) have a considerable role to play, provided the end-user is clear about their inherent limitations. The over-riding concern is to avoid confusing the easily measurable with the really important.

Summary

The development of performance review, measurement and management in local government has been traced to early techniques such as Programme Analysis and Review (PAR), to economic constraint in the 1980s and 1990s, to a changed culture of public sector management, and to the political programme of central government. For a number of such reasons, the 3 Es – economy, efficiency and effectiveness – have come to occupy a central role in the management of contemporary local government. The principles and problems of performance measurement have been considered in the light of relevant case studies. The practice of performance measurement has been seen to link-in to wider processes of information management, decision-making and political control. Structural arrangements for the measurement of performance, and the rather ambivalent position of elected members of the council, have been examined in seeking to identify best practice. Current problems and future prospects have been discussed in the context of Audit Commission indicators for the Citizens' Charter.

Discussion questions and guidance

1. *Outline the key elements of a performance measurement system for a local authority depart-ment/service of your choice. Specify in particular:*

- *inputs;*
- *outputs;*
- *outcomes;*
- *policy objectives and service targets;*
- *managerial responsibilities;*
- *implementation/action upon completion.*

The task here is to design a performance measurement system. Note the importance of the corporate and strategic dimensions despite the invitation to focus upon one department or service. Material from throughout Chapter 5 will be useful here, perhaps supplemented by the following observation.

> Performance Review involves setting policy objectives and measurable targets for their achievement. It requires the creation of uncomplicated key performance indicators and regular and systematic review of results by reference to those indicators (ADC/PPRN, 1991, p. 6).

2. *Describe and assess the ways in which consumer satisfaction ratings and other qualita-tive indicators of effectiveness might be incorporated within the performance measurement process.*

The question refers to effectiveness – the third 'E' – rather than to economy or efficiency. It is a question about outcomes rather than mere outputs. A descriptive review of just **how** we might listen to the views of service users is one element of the question, and here it would be useful to refer back to Chapter 3 where the 'consumer perspective' was discussed. Assuming such qualitative data exist, however, it then becomes necessary to consider how such information can be brought in to a performance measurement system. It is clear from Chapter 5 as a whole that the most important performance factors – the impact on service users – may be the least measur-able in quantitative terms. One view is that this difficulty constitutes a fundamental flaw in the whole project of seeking to measure organizational performance. Another view is that consumer-led information can and must be a central part of measuring performance – but how? Useful further reading would include Appendix I of Jackson and Palmer's study (1989, pp. 46–9), plus sources referred to in Chapter 3.

3. *'The dissatisfaction with PIs arises where they are used to evaluate outcomes, measure improvements in quality and provide a basis for calculating rewards and incentives – precisely the areas in which it is most difficult to construct reliable indicators'* (Palmer, 1993, p. 35). Discuss.

The topic here is akin to that posed by question 2. However, here the discussion is more wide-ranging. There is an implication that performance indicators may be **misused** – to evaluate outcomes (rather than simple outputs) or to determine individual rewards (rather than organizational effectiveness). The discussion would need to include an assessment of what, in general, performance indicators can tell us, and what such indicators cannot tell us. There is also a reference to 'dissatisfaction' with PIs. Thus it would be useful to consider sources of disatisfaction with PIs in your local authority, together with ways of overcoming these problems.

4. *'In practice, most of the performance indicators currently used by local authorities are designed primarily to be used by managers. Some of these may also interest citizens; others will not'* (Audit Commission, 1992a, p. 2). Discuss.

Here, the different **audiences** for performance measurement are the principal topic for discussion. The question implies a review of how far performance indicators in local government are indeed primarily 'used by managers' – which indicators, and how used? If citizens' interest in such indicators is indeed secondary, is this a fault of the particular indicators used, or a more general problem of conflicting professional/ lay interests? Other audiences might be considered too: e.g. central government. It will also be remembered that 'citizens' may have individual or collective interests in the matter.

5. *As performance review manager for your local authority, you have been asked by your Chief Executive to identify ways to support and extend the role of elected members in performance measurement. Write a concise report for the next meeting of the senior management team.*

The role of elected councillors has been considered above in the text of Chapter 5. Sources of tension between managers and councillors were discussed. A further element – not considered above – is the role of opposition councillors in contributing to performance review in general. The question demands a succinct account of possible structural changes, e.g. setting up a specialist sub-committee for performance review work, but the dangers and costs of large-scale reorganization should be remembered too. Cultural change is arguably more important than structural change, but impossible to legislate for. Informal officer/member groups may be relevant. The distinction between departmental and corporate performance review may be important too.

6. *'It is important that performance measures are matched to policy objectives, targets and activities for which specific managers have been allocated clear responsibility'* (Jackson and Palmer, 1989, p. 13). Do you agree?

Here, an exploration is sought of how performance **measurement** connects to wider policy issues, organizational objectives, and specific managerial tasks. In other words, the question invites a discussion of performance **management** rather than performance measurement alone. A clarification of such differences of terminology was provided early in Chapter 5. Specifically, the elements of a performance management system (and process) need to be identified and elaborated.

7. *To what extent does the private sector provide a model for performance measurement in the public sector?*

Throughout the discussion of managing local government today, the **influence of** the private sector is present – in relation to competition, performance, the 'customer', choice, or research and development. Yet, as we have seen, the influence of the private sector is not uniform, nor straightforward, nor direct. In Chapter 2, for instance, competition was seen to have changed the nature and skills of public-sector management, but not toward a crude imitation of the private sector. For this question, consider the similarities and differences between public- and private-sector performance measurement. This is mentioned at the beginning of the chapter, and also in the section entitled the Practice of Performance Measurement. Burningham notes (1990, p. 141):

> There can be no doubt that the public sector needs PIs, but if they are to have coherence and meaning they must be based on a close analysis of how public sector institutions operate and reflect what they are really trying to do.

What are they 'really trying to do'?

8. *Define and assess the key inputs, processes, outputs and outcomes of your local education authority.*

As evident in Case study 5.1, performance measurement in education is increasingly important (not least because it remains the single largest budget item of any local authority with education responsibilities), but its practice remains difficult. Part of the difficulty arises from the methodological problems of constructing a successful performance measurement system for such a complex service. Part of the difficulty arises from the fact that the values and objectives of the education service are a topic of political and moral contention. The problem of education performance measurement is, then, both methodological and normative. For this question, the distinction between quantitative and qualitative measures, discussed within Chapter 5, will be relevant. The limitations of any system of education performance measurement might also be part of the discussion. The terminology of the question can be clarified by reference back throughout Chapter 5, although Klein and Carter's definitions will probably suffice (1988, pp. 7–8) as follows:

- inputs: resources (e.g. staff, buildings) used in provision of a service
- processes: the way a service is delivered, including a measurement of quality;
- outputs: the activities of, or services provided by, the organization, including 'intermediate outputs': the number of school places might be an intermediate output, the occupation of those places an output proper (to complicate things, of course, we might suggest that in this example the intermediate output constitutes an input – a resource made available!);
- outcome: the impact of the service, a product of its effectiveness (notoriously difficult to measure for education).

9. *'Here, then, is the agenda for the 1990s: to rescue the concept of PIs from the experts and to see whether, and how, it can be integrated into the democratic process'* (Carter, Klein and Day, 1992, p. 183). *Discuss.*

The question refers not to the techniques of performance measurement, but to its political context, and to its current or potential uses by different groups in the policy process. The apparent ownership of the performance process by experts **may** be based on expertise, but may also be based on relations of power and control. Within local government, there would also be an issue here of the respective contributions of elected councillors and professional managers. The sections of Chapter 5 dealing with the Development of Performance Measurement in Local Government and with the Role of the Councillor would be relevant, but a wider discussion of political change in local government is implied too, perhaps using sources such as Wilson and Game (1994), Cochrane (1993), and the general summation in Chapter 7.

Suggested further reading

Cave, M., Kogan, M. and Smith, R. (eds) (1990) *Output and Performance Measurement in Government: the State of the Art,* Jessica Kingsley Publishers, London. Collection of readings combining theory and practice in performance measurement.

Carter, N., Klein, R. and Day, P. (1992) *How Organizations Measure Success: the Use of Performance Indicators in Government,* Routledge, London. Overall text on the development and use of indicators.

Jackson, P.M. and Palmer, B. (1992) *Developing Performance Monitoring in Public Sector Organizations: A Management Guide,* Management Centre, University of Leicester. A thorough practical guide.

Shaw, K. (1995) Assessing the Performance of UDCs: How Reliable are the Official Output Measures?, *Planning, Practice and Research,* **10**. Questions the value of some of the indicators used to assess the performance of the Urban Development Corporations.

Audit Commission (1995) *Calling the Tune: Performance Management in Local Government,* HMSO, London (January). Mainly refers to staff performance rather than organizational performance, but includes relevant examples, one of which refers to the authority considered in Case study 7.2.

Audit Commission (1995) *Local Authority Performance Indicators, Vols 1 and 2,* HMSO, London (March). The construction of the standard indicators was described in Chapter 5. These reports present for the first time national comparisons of indicators from over 400 local authorities.

THE MANAGEMENT OF INFORMATION   6

This chapter examines **information** in several senses. First, the development of management information systems as an aid to the management process is considered, bearing in mind technological opportunities and practical limitations; secondly, the formal requirements of access to information legislation are discussed in the context of the organization and politics of 'access'; thirdly, the central policy, research and intelligence function in local government is examined – the local council as producer of information for its own corporate needs. The production and consumption of information, and the differing roles of local and central government, are essential parts of the **management of information**. The conclusions of the Widdicombe Committee (1986) continue to be of relevance, and along with debates relating to 'political' publicity and 'twin tracking' demonstrate that the **politics of information** are central too.

Introduction

Effective management is impossible in the absence of effective information. Such information is process rather than commodity: the right information is needed at the right time as part of the planned flow of information throughout the organization. In the absence of the right information, the more senior manager may be able to demand it, a common (if haphazard and inefficient) practice. The real problems arise for lower-level and middle managers within local authorities who have significant decision-making responsibilities, but may have neither the information to inform their decisions, nor the authority to generate such information themselves. Management without information is akin to responsibility without power.

There are many problems and opportunities within information-management. This chapter will consider three aspects of practical relevance.

First, some elements of management information systems will be reviewed, drawing attention to areas of common experience and good practice. Information technology (IT) has direct effects upon managerial practice and organizational structure. These effects may include the reduction of uncertainty, assisting interdependence and co-ordination within the organization, and creating a greater flexibility (Lucas, 1994, p. 85). Equally, IT in general and management information systems in particular may increase central control. Technology itself may influence the culture of management.

Secondly, public access to information will be considered. Developments did not stop with the enactment of the Local Government (Access to Information) Act 1985. The Widdicombe Report – Report of the Committee of Inquiry into the Conduct of Local Authority Business 1986 – and subsequent legislation continued to reformulate the boundaries of public access to information produced or collected in local authorities. Public rights to specified information may initially be perceived as problematic by hard-pressed officers, but it will be argued that public needs for information are a positive corollary of management information needs. The information needs of local council and public may coincide. Equally, there are contrasting pressures which may drive a wedge between the public and the local authority. The commercially sensitive information associated with CCT under the terms of the Local Government Act 1988, for instance, sits unhappily with the 'access' ethos of earlier legislation.

Thirdly, the local authority as producer of information will be discussed. The 'management' of information-as-intelligence is crucially important in conditions of uncertainty, where appropriate data have actively to be collected or at least collated by the local authority. In addition to the minimal information elements written-in to statutory requirements for local authority annual reports, it will be useful to examine the role of active policy/research or strategic intelligence units within local authorities. Here, a central part of the organization is engaged in research and intelligence for the purposes of strategic and corporate management. 'Information' here can be seen to be close to the political and managerial centre of the organization (Fenwick, 1992).

Management information

Information is self-evidently essential for the process of management, but it has to be the right sort of information, suitable for operational purposes, and delivered at the right time. The problem in local government is not one of insufficient information. 'There is no **lack** of information as a rule; but an over-abundance of it' (Knowles, 1988, p. 114, emphasis in original). A system to meet the information needs of managers thus needs to provide a way of **making sense** of potentially limitless information.

The management information system

Within local authorities, sense may be made of information by the introduction of a Management Information System (MIS). The MIS, with its origins in private industry in the 1960s, will be regarded here as a computer-based means for the systematic storage, organization and delivery of information to managers. The information technology (IT) element of any MIS is an essential one, as it would be stretching the definition of a management information **system** rather too far if it were to include manual catalogues or stored documentary sources.

The local authority MIS may be general and all-embracing, or may be concerned with specific applications. Dockery (1992) provides a case study of developments in management accounting information systems in a London borough, 'enabling managers at all levels of the department structure to draw on computer-based on-line information to monitor, and thus control, expenditure across areas of immediate responsibility' (p. 277). The uses of such a system were evident in areas such as co-ordination of advice on budget strategy, review and monitoring of spending departments, and economy and public accountability (Dockery, 1992, p. 278).

It has been suggested that information, when locked into an effective MIS, represents a key corporate asset in itself, not just a means to other resources. Thierauf regards information as a 'sixth major corporate resource', alongside money, materials, machines/facilities, people and management (1987, pp. 4–5). Information delivered via the MIS 'can assist managers at all levels in performing their managerial functions of planning, organizing, directing, and controlling available corporate resources' (Thierauf, 1987, p. 5). This view of the MIS within organizations as a whole certainly has a relevance for local government, and in particular it can be suggested that the local authority MIS links-up clearly to the **corporate** dimension of management. The link between information and corporate management will be considered further in the third section of this chapter, dealing with the central policy research function.

Torrington, Weightman and Johns point out that an effective MIS presupposes that decisions have been made not only about specific MIS requirements, but also that the organization has developed a specific information **strategy** (1989, p. 341). Further, they draw attention to the key problems – the common failures – of the MIS, as follows (Torrington, Weightman, and Johns, 1989, pp. 345–6):

1. insufficient support amongst senior management;
2. lack of management support at the design stage;
3. ignorance of computing skills amongst managers;
4. inappropriate computer applications;
5. excessive concentration on routine data processing;
6. ignorance of management needs amongst computer specialists;
7. lack of attention to assessing and choosing the right system;
8. lack of information strategy;
9. no common appreciation of the rationale for the MIS, and little training;
10. inappropriate use of the MIS after implementation.

Any MIS will be useful, of course, to functional and departmental managers as well as to those at the centre of the organization. In discussing commercial organizations, Thierauf distinguishes various subsystems of an effective MIS, including corporate planning, but also, for instance, marketing, manufacturing and finance (1987, p. 374). It would be straightforward enough to apply these to a local authority in terms of MIS needs, e.g.

- leisure management;
- personnel;
- social services;
- education;
- housing;

- planning;
- corporate management.

Some of the relevant departmental information needs here will already perhaps have been met by established data sources, especially computerized social services or housing records, or the General Information System for Planners. Writing of the MIS generally, Cole distinguishes control systems (monitoring the organization's activities), database systems (storing and processing data), enquiry systems (producing reports on internal or external performance) and decision-support systems proper (1990, p. 249). However, it is within the strategic and corporate sectors that the MIS has tended to develop in local government. A further consideration of the broad features of any MIS tells us why.

Remenyi (1991), for instance, charts the development of the MIS from the 1960s, through the conceptual development of Decision Support Systems (DSS) in the work of Gorry and Scott-Morton (1971) and the notion of the executive information system (EIS) developed by Rockart and Treacy (1982). The DSS is an information system which informs 'semi or unstructured decisions' in areas of strategy, management control or operations while the EIS placed emphasis upon the people identified as information users (senior executives) requiring an accessible system (Remenyi, 1991, pp. 47–8). On these sorts of basis, **Strategic** Information Systems (SIS) were ultimately developed, essentially as a product of the 1980s. Following Remenyi's discussion of the SIS (1991), each part of the term seems crucial: it is 'strategic', and it is an 'information system' where appropriate (and accessible) technology is also crucial. Applying these elements to a local authority setting, let us now suggest that a Management Information System is properly considered as a subvariety of a Strategic Information System. The MIS is not merely an information retrieval device, and is not confined to departmental (or rather, in the post-CCT environment, 'client-side') needs.

Looked at in this way – the MIS as part of an overall SIS – an ironic consequence is that the MIS ceases to be of exclusive interest to managers. The MIS becomes relevant to all those with a strategic or corporate role within the authority. In particular, elected members develop an interest. An Elected Members Information System (EMIS) is, again, a particular form of the SIS. Case study 6.1 describes the EMIS developed in Gateshead Metropolitan Borough Council.

CASE STUDY 6.1 Elected Members' Computerized Information System

Such information systems for members have been developed in a number of local authorities. Gateshead Metropolitan Borough Council began to develop its computerized members' information system in the 1980s, consistent with the borough's early use of computerized systems in relation to social services client records, and an innovative high-tech shopping scheme for the elderly.

Established in the 1980s, the Gateshead Members' Information System was reviewed and superseded in 1993. The Gateshead system was innovative in providing elected councillors with direct computer access to information sources, thus removing or at least reducing the need to work through council officers or systems specialists.

The main menu included the following data:

1. **borough profile**: e.g. population and unemployment statistics;
2. **ward data**: e.g. relevant data by ward for education, housing, social services;
3. **finance**: e.g. income and expenditure, housing revenue;
4. **electoral details**: e.g. central, local and European;
5. **education**: e.g. schools, committee members, governing bodies;
6. **social services**: e.g. committee members, district profiles;
7. **housing**: e.g. committee members, housing stock, repairs, sale of houses;
8. **other committee data**: e.g. economic development, policy and resources.

An information system of this kind raises a number of questions: for instance,

- in what ways do the pressures of competition, listening to the public, or the development of the client – contractor split imply **new** information needs within any such system?
- can the system **adapt** to meet new information needs?

Information technology

For councillors and officers alike, it is essential that information systems are accessible to users. It is not unknown for a system to contain excellent data, but to depend upon frequent reference to IT experts in order to extract useful information. The availability of desktop personal computers for all relevant staff, linked, where needed, to a network of authority-wide data and to other users, may help to overcome the reliance upon technology professionals – so long as proper training on the use of 'accessible' hardware and software is provided too. Winfield (1991) refers to the work of Markus and Bjorn-Anderson (1987) in pointing to the **dangers** (as well as irrelevance) of a system which depends on specialist expertise, thus concentrating power in the hands of that specialist. Winfield was not writing here of local government, although the following passage might certainly apply:

An everyday organizational occurrence is the burning tension between system professionals and system users. Systems people (systems analysts, system designers, computer managers and vendors) can often function as 'gatekeepers': people have to go through them to access the system and to learn how to use it (Winfield, 1991, p. 95).

Further, it is unreasonable to expect that all managers will seek to extend greatly their own knowledge of the more esoteric areas of systems applications. Hence the emphasis above on accessible technology. As Thierauf notes,

> Overall, a close relationship is needed between MIS analysts and managers. Analysts must extend themselves into the manager's world, not the other way around (1987, p. 24).

It seems unrealistic to suggest (Westcott, Grayson and Hobson (eds), 1991) that technology is not an essential prerequisite in developing effective management information. Further, the growth of information technology has itself led to **new forms of management control** as the bureaucratic organization of the traditional local authority has given way to the kinds of contract management and multi-agency arrangements discussed in Chapters 2 and 7. Burns, Hambleton and Hoggett (1994, p. 271) suggest that information technology in local government provides an opportunity for the organization to develop simpler forms of managing complexity. There is, then, a technological base for our recurring concern with the decline of traditional local authority line-management.

Indeed, it is very difficult to conceive of any MIS in the 1990s and beyond becoming part of the strategic and corporate management function without an appropriate technological base. Correct decisions about hardware and software are crucial. These develop too quickly to summarize in any useful way, but two general points can be made. First, the use of ready-developed commercially available software even if **imperfectly** matched to organizational needs does have the great advantage of having a history: its performance elsewhere can be checked. Secondly, the growth of personal computers (PCs), their ease of operation by non-specialists, and the linking of several PCs by networks (see above), may gradually diminish the dependence on systems professionals. A concern with technology should not, however, obscure understanding of why management information is important in the first place.

> Information is required at every stage in the management process: to assess needs and thus help set objectives; to evaluate alternative courses of action and enable correct decisions to be taken; to control and measure performance against targets (Knowles 1988, p. 114).

Few would disagree with Knowles' view of the role of information within local authority management. To build on this, management information processes need to be based upon explicit decisions and choices within the authority. Some of these areas for decision, reviewed here, have been: establishing Management Information Systems; locating MIS within primarily corporate/strategic managerial structures, without losing sight of departmental needs too; recognizing the centrality of information technology and the appropriate hardware and software; identifying possible user system/professional conflicts; linking the MIS and SIS explicitly; including the elected member in corporate information systems; and, finally, regarding information not only as a means to an end (i.e. better decision-making) but also as an asset in itself – something valuable and worthwhile as process as well as product. For instance, the free flow of data and information assists in promoting a **culture** of openness and of vertical and horizontal communication.

Even where the MIS seems to meet formal requirements, however, individual managers may maintain their informal sources of information, as a 'buffer' to the formal MIS (Dockery, 1992, p. 291). Further, where information is held only by those with senior political or administrative authority, or where it is haphazard in its scope and availability, the management of the authority as a whole is adversely affected.

The implications of access to information are taken up in the following section of this chapter.

Access to information

Access to information continues to be a topical, sometimes contentious, issue. It includes, like the Management Information System, a technological element. In 1993, for instance, Oxfordshire County Council introduced a network of outdoor 'community information points' where information can be accessed via a keyboard and screen, not unlike a bank cash machine (ATM). This particular system was developed in conjunction with the private sector. There is even a grouping for local councils involved in such initiatives: the Society of Public Information Networks (SPIN).

Access to information, however, is about much more than technology. It includes matters of public access to meetings of local authority committees and sub-committees; to the documentation provided for those meetings; to background papers used in the preparation of committee and sub-committee reports; to the specific responsibilities of local government officers in adhering to relevant legislation; and to political arguments about openness and access in the broadest senses, including the question of whether central government practises the same openness as it prescribes for local authorities.

Public access

The pace of public access to council information and council business has increased in recent years. As long ago as 1908, the Local Authorities (Admission of the Press to Meetings) Act established a right of the Press to be admitted to council meetings. This initial legislation was superseded by the Public Bodies (Admission to Meetings) Act 1960 'which provided both the public and the press with a statutory right to attend meetings of local authorities' (Harrison, 1988, p. 1). The 1960 Act, incidentally, was presented to Parliament by Margaret Thatcher (Mallabar, 1991, p. 87).

The Local Government Act 1972, as well as setting up the new structures for the 1974 reorganization of local government, also established the right of public attendance at council committee meetings. This right was extended by the provisions of the Local Government (Access to Information) Act 1985, which granted public access to sub-committee meetings, and to supporting information, with the exception of confidential items relating for example to child care proceedings or tenders for services. This Act, resulting from a Private Members' Bill of Tory MP Robin Squire, attracted an interesting coalition of supporters across the political spectrum each imbued with their own notion of 'access', akin to the seeming unanimity provoked by references to 'the consumer', as discussed in Chapter 3.

Indeed, in relation to the consumer perspective, it can be argued that information and access *per se* are consistent with the spirit of a responsive local council, drawing closer to its public. For Bellamy and Taylor (1994), developing information systems can be consistent with 'more citizen focused public services' (p 59). Such developments, incidentally, are not confined to the UK, as Bellamy and Taylor point out in citing examples from Portugal and the United States (1994, p. 60).

The question of the relationship between public and local government was of course addressed by the deliberations of the Widdicombe Committee – the Committee of Inquiry into the Conduct of Local Authority Business – announced in 1984, reporting in 1986, forming the basis of the 1988 White Paper and legislation the following year in the form of the Local Government and Housing Act 1989. The importance of Widdicombe is universally recognized.

Young and Davies note that Widdicombe's origins – in political abuse between the second Thatcher government and supposedly inept and reckless Labour councils – were soon transcended by the Widdicombe Committee itself, 'Widdicombe having perhaps succeeded in moving the discussion away from the language of abuses and corruption towards the language of management practice in a political environment' (Young and Davies 1990, p. 8).

The phrase 'management practice in a political environment' is central to our interests throughout. Before examining the lasting impact of Widdicombe, however, it is worth exploring the 1985 legislation in a little more detail, to see if this Act represented minor incremental charge, or a more fundamental recasting of relationship between public, local council, and council officer.

Under the 1985 Act, the local authority is required to give access not only to committee and sub-committee meetings, but also to agendas and reports for these meetings, the background papers used in compiling the reports, and the minutes of the meeting. There are, as noted above, exempt items. Although the trend throughout the years of Conservative government has been to oblige local government to do less, and spend less, the 1985 Act required local councils to do considerably more in these important respects.

The reader who is seeking specific guidance on other access to information provisions may consult numerous sources. Hutt, for instance, summarizes in a readily accessible style the provisions of the Data Protection Act 1984 in relation to computer-stored information and the Access to Personal Files Act 1987 as it affects Social Services and housing records when they are not computer-stored (Hutt, 1990, pp. 119–22). There were hitherto supposedly self-evident reasons why tenants, clients or other service users could not have access to such personal information – reasons which seem now to have melted away, across the party political spectrum. Similar reasons were commonly given for the non-release of subject grades to higher education students in the award of their degree classifications. It was feared they might begin to 'calculate' their results. Heaven forbid.

Harrison (1988) provides a concise summary of the Data Protection Act 1984, the Local Government (Access to Information) Act 1985 and the Access to Personal Files Act 1987. It is relevant to point out that legal complexities surrounding the nature of committee and 'sub-committee' are not necessarily settled. Harrison notes that it does seem clear that in certain circumstances, member bodies can exist as working parties without them amounting in law to sub-committees so as to attract the provisions of the Access to Information Act, particularly where the body is concerned with matters not directly related to service provision (1988, p. 7).

In general, however, the 1985 Act was clear in its operationalization of the principles that advance notice must be given of the business of council committees and sub-committees, that only a strictly circumscribed category of business is to be considered in private, and that there is a general right of access to the background papers used in putting together committee and sub-committee reports (Harrison 1988, pp. 12–13; p. 30). It needs to be added – though it is frequently overlooked – that an elected councillor enjoys 'an **additional** right of access, certainly to local authority documents, by virtue of his official position' (Harrison, 1988, p. 47, emphasis added). The particular rights and duties of the elected member are spelled out by Harrison in a separate guide (1987).

Aside from the importance of 'access' to the local authority manager and the elected member, the advocacy of open access by community groups should not be overlooked. The successful enactment of the 1985 Act was, arguably, based on a broad foundation of support from the political Right (a Conservative member's bill), the non-centralist Left, and community groups, significantly via the active involvement of the Community Rights Project. A comprehensive and practical guide to freedom of information describes the 1985 Act as 'a unique "right to know", unprecedented in English law' (Northmore 1990, p. 27). However, the same guide expresses doubts about local authorities' **active** encouragement to the public to use their rights acquired under the 1985 Act (Northmore, 1990, p. 30).

Degrees of **enthusiasm** in implementing statutory access provisions vary, but **cost** is always important. The costs of openness are not universally recognized in discussions of access to information, whether referring to documentary and printing costs, accommodation for meetings or officer time. Local authorities, for instance, are required under the 1985 Act to identify a 'proper officer' responsible for assembling lists of background papers and judging which are to be included (Mallabar, 1991, p. 95n). Access, then, has a cost. It might be argued this is a price worth paying in terms of an informed and participative public, the (consequently) effective local council, and (thus) good management. Equally, some may still oppose the culture of openness as well as the implications it brings for resources. Where this is so, it is a problem of management, i.e. the problem of how to promote cultural change.

The politics of access

Knowles reminds us of the distinction between a local authority's general **power** to provide information, and a **duty** to do so (Knowles, 1988, p. 136). There is also, of course, the duty **not** to provide certain sorts of information, for example campaigning or political material deemed to be propaganda in terms of the Local Government Act 1986, subsequently amended by Section 27 of the Local Government Act 1988; any information promoting homosexuality (Section 28 of the Local Government Act 1988); and the restrictions upon council officers' own 'political' activities, which came into effect on 1 March 1990 under the terms of the Local Government and Housing Act 1989.

This final point has a number of aspects. It includes restrictions upon council officers serving as elected councillors for another local authority (or, of course, for their own authorities). It also includes limitations on senior officers (or more junior officers responsible for policy advice to committees, sub-committee or joint committees) engaging in political activity such as canvassing or publicly speaking on behalf of a party. Doubtless case law will continue to refine the precise application of these provisions, including perhaps the European dimension.

The 'twin-tracking' debates are ably summarized by Mallabar (1991). It might be added, however, that the central government perception of highly paid policy-oriented officers being elected councillors for neighbouring authorities with an alleged blurring of loyalties and responsibilities is a perception derived – rightly or wrongly – from a few urban authorities, especially in London. There is no basis for considering that 'twin tracking' in the roles of influential officer and elected councillor has ever been a widespread phenomenon, yet the consequent legislation has certainly affected the parameters within which all managers now have to work.

Irrespective of legislation, attitudes to openness and access still vary. 'Not all authorities . . . were enthusiastic about the demands for open government and some even today, not surprisingly, still feel it inhibiting to good management for policy issues to be formulated in public' (Knowles, 1988, p. 138).

In drawing a general lesson from the preceding discussion, there seem no obvious examples where **restricting** information and activity within a local authority (as in recent legislation) has led to a demonstrable improvement in service or effectiveness. In contrast, **increasing** information flow and public access – even where initially 'inhibiting', problematic, or costly – does demonstrably lead to subsequent improvement in the management of the authority. An example is provided by the experience of providing basic descriptive and performance information for annual reports, initially as specified in a code of practice deriving from the Local Government Planning and Land Act 1980.

At first a routine, perhaps tiresome, presentation of unexciting data, the subsequent development of such data into more advanced performance indicators and systematic measures of activity has become a crucial element of contemporary local authority management, as discussed in Chapter 5.

The difficulty found by some in local councils, however, is that both the restriction and the extension of varying types of information have been the product of the same central government's policies. It is difficult to form any judgement about the rationale for this in other than ideological terms. Arguably, the governmental agenda of the New Right contains both libertarian and centralizing elements, not readily compatible.

It is now fitting to consider the Widdicombe Report 1986 in more detail, in its concerns for information in general, and for managing in a politically difficult environment.

The Widdicombe Report

The Widdicombe Report – Report of the Committee of Inquiry into the Conduct of Local Authority Business 1986 – is significant for what did **not** result from it as well as for what did. The legislation, in the form of the Local Government Acts 1986 and 1988 and the influence on subsequent legislation, does not exactly mirror Widdicombe nor, of course, is there any formal or constitutional reason why it should. Gyford points out that the government's legislation of 1986 and 1988 'went further than the Widdicombe majority had suggested', especially in relation to local authority 'political' publicity (Gyford, 1991, p. 119).

The overall restrictions upon local authority 'political' publicity are reviewed by Parsons (1993): it might be added that these apply to voluntary agencies with local authority funding as well as to local councils themselves. The point is that Widdicombe has been significant in its influence upon the **culture** of local government, and upon the **terms of debate**, which should be distinguished from its partial formal translation into law. It could be suggested that the **former** sense in which Widdicombe has been influential – the overall cultural sense – is more important for the current managerial environment in local government than any specific enactment into legislation has been.

Widdicombe's view of the culture of local authority management was based upon pluralism, participation and responsiveness. Pluralism may be expressed here in Mallabar's words, indicating that 'a vibrant system of local government offers the possibility of policy diversity and of a political expression for the wishes of particular local communities' (Mallabar, 1991, pp. 182–3). The emphasis on participation has a self-evident meaning in terms of public involvement in the local political process, but as Mallabar rightly says, participation presupposes that local authorities do have some real influence over local spending and local provision. However, when 'local government becomes little more than local administration with the key policy decisions being made at the centre then participation at the local level becomes an exercise in political futility' (Mallabar 1991, p. 183).

The third value – responsiveness – denotes the necessary responsiveness of elected members to the electorate which put them there, and may remove them. Mallabar points, however, to the very low turnout at elections for local authorities (1991, p. 185). Indeed, to return to Widdicombe's second value of participation, we could say that the participation rate in local government is, at best, modest.

If pluralism, participation and responsiveness are indeed the key elements of Widdicombe's view of the public/local authority relationship, some questions need to be asked about subsequent legislation. In particular, there is a gap between this view of the public–local authority relationship, and the specific impact of subsequent legislation. While Widdicombe outlined a pluralist and open vision of the cultural context of local government, central government has pursued another vision. It is not readily apparent that pluralism, participation or responsiveness shape central government policy towards local government. Participation and responsiveness certainly decrease, not increase, in a situation where local authorities cumulatively have less and less direct control over their budgets and service levels. Not only is there a gap between the spirit of Widdicombe and subsequent legislation. There is also a gap between the vision for local government held out by Widdicombe, and central government's own existing, and continuing, agenda.

Central government's response might well be: so be it. The local authority *per se* may well decline in significance, and traditional forms of participation are now less important anyway, as local services become subject to new forms of organization and control. CCT opens up new forms of service delivery, the client–contractor relationship coming to characterize internal management structures, even those relating to non-CCT services. The public is now 'engaged' with local services in many different ways.

Thus, the themes of openness, access, information, and the relationship with the public, are fraught with complexity. The Conservative years have by no means seen these themes developing in a coherent or single direction. Greater access to information exists alongside restriction. Greater participation exists alongside fewer local government services in which to participate. These tensions are further evidence of the fundamental problem that the relationship between central and local government is not settled. Nor is it likely to be settled, given the parameters of current ideological debates and political power.

This unsettled context is the site for contemporary local authority management. The 'management of uncertainty' is a hackneyed term, but a crucial one here.

Another dimension of post-Widdicombe change is explored by Young and Davies who seek to measure the extent of 'political change' in local authorities since the Widdicombe inquiry was completed (Young and Davies 1990). By repeating (on a more limited scale) the research of the Widdicombe Committee itself, Young and Davies suggest that:

1. there has been a growth in 'politicization' within local government since Widdicombe's work was done;
2. this change is independent 'for the most part' of any actual change of political control within those local councils;
3. the distinction between types of local authority is relatively unimportant compared to contrasts between the (relatively politicized) urban authorities and the (less politicized) rural authorities (Young and Davies, 1990, p. 2).

If Young and Davies are correct, an initial picture emerges of the 'politicized' local authority generally, with the urban authority (metropolitan or non-metropolitan) particularly subject to increased politicization. Young and Davies take politicization to include: political competition; the 'formalization' of political direction; the polarization of politics; and member involvement in appointing officials (1990, p. 5). As Young and Davies themselves point out, Widdicombe did not see member involvement in appointments as having a **necessary** connection to politicization, but they suggest the practice may arise from 'a clear political impulse' (1990, p. 52).

Young and Davies find regional differences to be of some importance, the Welsh districts having close member involvement in even the most junior appointments (1990, p. 54). Overall, however, it would not be accurate to say that more appointments are now being made by officers either, for 'the upward shift in the level at which members are **routinely** involved in appointing officers has been counterbalanced by an increase in **occasional** involvement below this level' (Young and Davies, 1990, p. 56: emphasis in original). Again, the urban dimension is important.

> Overall, it is clear that councillors in the more urban authorities are far more likely to intervene in officer selection below their routine level: . . . they generally do so in support of those member-led initiatives where they are less likely to be willing to leave the choice of appointee to their officers (Young and Davies, 1990, p. 57).

Although the question is not explicitly addressed in Young and Davies' research, it seems reasonable to suggest that member involvement in appointments significantly affects management practice. Managing the local authority in a permanently or intermittently 'member-led' environment is likely to require political skills of a high order, and in the urban context referred to above, most probably party-political skills.

This takes us some way from the management of information. Yet the path is a necessary one. As we have seen, questions of information availability rapidly become transformed into questions of 'access' in a wider political sense, the precise boundaries of which remain contentious. Questions of publicity move inexorably from descriptions of what is or is not permissible to larger issues connected to the restriction of political activity among council officers. Access to information in local government stands in contrast to the restriction of central government information. Access to some types of local authority information contrasts to the increasing commercial sensitivity of documentation required for Compulsory Competitive Tendering, a process itself expanding during the fourth Conservative term. A consideration of information and its management within the terms of the Widdicombe Report inevitably leads to the controversial roles of members and officers re-considered; to the political environment of local authority management once more.

A third aspect of the management of information may now be considered. Information, when collected and used for strategic purposes at the heart of the authority's central activities, becomes transformed into **intelligence**. Such information also acquires a high political visibility. The final section of this chapter considers the local authority as producer of information and intelligence by an examination of the central policy, research, and intelligence functions.

Information and intelligence

Under the Local Government Act 1972, the newly established county councils were given the power (not the duty) to carry out research relating to the county area (Knowles, 1988, p. 114). The Report of the Study Group on the new Local Authorities Management and Structure 1972 – i.e. the 'Bains Report' – envisaged that a central research and intelligence unit would fulfil an information and forecasting role, a research and intelligence function, and would provide support for corporate planning (Knowles, 1988, p. 114).

Research and intelligence activity has developed unevenly throughout local government. There may be an established research and intelligence function, or none at all. Where it exists, it may be more, or less, centralized. Moreover, it may be oriented more towards information and intelligence, or more towards policy analysis and policy development. Each of these factors affects the management of the research and intelligence function; the corporate or departmental character of that management; and the proximity of their activity to the political (as distinct from administrative) heart of the authority. I have elsewhere drawn the following conclusion, in relation to central policy/research.

> The case for policy/research remains a strong one, provided its practitioners can withstand ambiguity and a high degree of exposure (Fenwick, 1992, p. 40).

Before exploring such issues in greater detail, let us first of all clarify the nature of the local authority intelligence function. What does a developed research and intelligence unit do? How does its output assist the effective management of the authority?

The research and intelligence function

Cleveland County Council developed a mature research and intelligence function, operating as a unit within a planned coherent programme of work, rather than merely responding to *ad hoc* demands. The Cleveland R and I unit worked to a set of 57 general aims and objectives grouped under eight headings as follows:

1. **Policy Co-ordination**: e.g: 'to increase and improve the value of the Authority's management information systems by ensuring adequate information is and will be available'; 'to provide information and analytical skills to aid the monitoring of the Council's Equal Opportunities programmes'.
2. **Environment**: e.g: 'to obtain consumer views of the service provided in this area of the Council's activities'.
3. **Economic Development**: e.g: 'to provide research assistance to help meet the challenges and opportunities posed by the Single European Market'.
4. **Community Development**: e.g: 'to help in the development and implementation of the Council's Unemployment Strategy'.
5. **Education**: e.g: 'to provide spatial and trend information on pupil and student numbers to assist in effective allocation of resources'.
6. **Social Services**: e.g: 'to help in the development of community care'.
7. **Public Protection**: e.g: 'to help evaluate and monitor policing methods by use of consumer surveys'.
8. **Research and Intelligence Unit Operation**: e.g: 'to provide appropriate information to members, officers and the public'; 'to develop a more pro-active input to policy issues' (Cleveland County Council Research and Intelligence Unit: General Aims and Objectives 1990/91).

Put more simply, a brochure produced by Cleveland R & I Unit asks 'what does the R & I Unit do?', and provides its own reply as follows:

> The R & I Unit provides research, information, advice and support to meet the needs of the County and the Boroughs (Cleveland County Council, no date).

Clearly, the work of such a Unit is central to any consideration of local government information systems in the broadest sense. Yet information is not synonymous with intelligence, and Units such as that in Cleveland do not produce 'information' of some abstracted kind; they produce 'intelligence' for use by policy makers. For those involved in policy-making within local government – i.e. those at the political and administrative centre – such intelligence may be crucial in shaping policy and priorities. The work done by the policy/research/intelligence unit or section impacts directly on management, especially corporate and strategic management.

CASE STUDY 6.2 County Council Research and Intelligence Unit Work Programme (Cleveland County Council)

The work programme for this R and I Unit in 1991–2 derived initially from discussions between the Director of R and I and other Chief Officers. A draft programme was generated and discussed with the Chief Executive and main committee chairs. The amended draft programme then passed to the Liaison Group, comprising committee chairs (all Labour) and Chief Officers. This is summarized below. Further, as Figure 6.1 illustrates, there is an additional formal stage where the programme is considered by the co-ordinating Committee – essentially the main Policy and Resources-type committee.

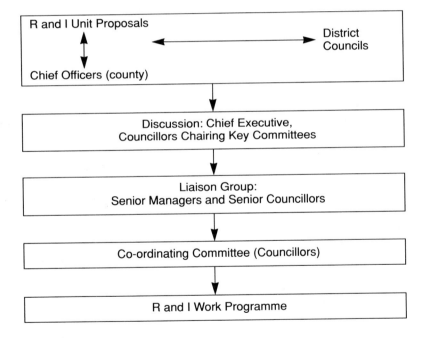

Figure 6.1   Formulating the R & I Unit Work Programme

This structure is a formalization, dating from 1991, of more informal managerial processes. It generates an agreed work programme, listing projected activity under the seven programme areas used in defining the Unit's Aims and Objectives. Over 120 new or continuing items of work were identified for 1991-92, including:

1. **Policy Co-ordination**: population estimates and forecasting, computer users survey; equal opportunities and anti-poverty monitoring; ergonomics of new technology;
2. **Environment**: housing database; environmental audit;
3. **Economic Development**: marketing advice centre;
4. **Community Development**: credit unions; after school care
5. **Education**: LMS allocation formulae; pupil projections;
6. **Social Services**: data for Children Act; out-of-hours evaluation
7. **Public Protection**: consumer views of policing; fire cover model.

The range of R and I activity in the draft 1991–92 programme is self-evident. Moreover, there are several distinct sorts of client or policy audience for the outputs of the R & I Unit, including senior managers of several councils, councillors, and the public. This diversity points to some of the strengths, and possible weaknesses, of such a Unit for the overall management of the council.

Smith describes the experience of running the R and I units of Cleveland and of Cheshire County Councils. In Cleveland, the normal group of county council departments exists, each led by a Chief Officer, but there is also a distinct group of 'management service units' (MSU). The Cleveland R and I Unit constitutes one such MSU, along with, for instance, Personnel, or the County Supplies Office.

The Cleveland R & I Unit is of interest, then, not only for the services it provides as a MSU to the councils' (county and district) managers as a whole, but also in terms of its own management. It has a discrete existence on a Unit, its Director having Chief Officer status – 'albeit a junior one' (Smith, 1992, p. 94) – yet cannot be independent in any sensible use of the term. It depended for its role, and its very existence, on the services offered to county council departments and district councils within the county. In 1992/93, the budget of the Cleveland R and I Unit was approximately £651 000, with a staff of 30 or so (Smith, 1992, pp. 94–5). In trying to specify ever more precisely just what is meant by R & I work, we can refer to the extracts above from the Cleveland Unit's aims and objectives, but Smith adds another, perhaps more problematic, element: 'R and I can exist at any point along the spectrum between policy and information' (Smith, 1992, p. 97). Managing R & I is not only a technical matter of 'managing' information and information needs, it is a process involving engagement with direct, and perhaps contentious, matters of policy.

It goes without saying that this brings the research/policy manager directly into contact with the politically controversial, with policy disputes. In conditions of political uniformity – i.e. one party control – the quasi-political policy role of officer management may not 'matter' in terms of any doubts about policy outcomes, but it does matter in the sense that it affects our understanding of 'management' itself – of what it means.

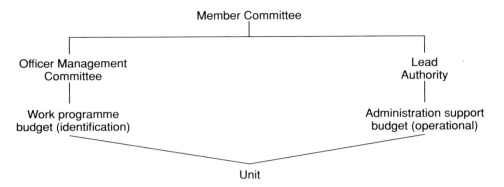

Figure 6.2 Joint Research/Information Units: management structure (Quicke, 1992, p. 88)

> Compared to equally senior, or more senior, officers in service departments, those responsible for policy/research at the centre are necessarily close to the political as well as the administrative heart of the authority. This may be less significant for R and I teams than for policy teams, but in all cases central location and the corporate dimension imply an obvious sensitivity to the expectations of the local political leadership (Fenwick, 1992, p. 36).

Perhaps few generalizations can be made in discussing the overall management of R and I and policy research. Cleveland's arrangements were perhaps those closest of any local authority in Britain to full-blown Departmental status. Arrangements in metropolitan areas vary, but the Chief Executive's Department is a key location for such activity. Quicke (1992) summarizes the arrangements for running R and I in the metropolitan county areas, following the abolition in 1986 of the elected authorities for those county areas. The five metropolitan county areas which continued to operate formal joint teams – that is, Greater Manchester Research; London Research Centre; Merseyside Information Service; Tyne and Wear Research; West Midlands Joint Data Team – may be characterized by broad (not strict) adherence to the management structure set out in Figure 6.2.

Arising from the absence of a metropolitan county authority, the managerial arrangements for such county-wide research and information units become complicated by the need to work to several constituent metropolitan districts. Thus, a 'lead authority' (one of the districts) provides support for and will tend to provide accommodation for the county-wide unit. The responsibility of managers to the elected councillor is also complicated by these arrangements, although as can be seen from Figure 6.2, there is in all cases an accountability to the political level.

Quicke describes the metropolitan county-wide units as 'data units, not policy units, providing information about metropolitan areas' (1992, p. 88). Such units are toward the 'information' rather than 'policy' end of the continuum identified above by Smith (1992, p. 97). Yet clearly the generation of data about the functional areas outlined by Quicke – transport, socio-economic data such as homelessness and housing, land use etc. – does not occur in a political vacuum. The data thus produced are taken up in the prosecution of political disputes, and the fact of party political uniformity in most of the metropolitan areas does not render the context apolitical.

The centre

The examples and case studies of the information/intelligence function considered so far in district and county, metropolitan and non-metropolitan areas, indicate diverse patterns of organization and management. It is to be emphasized, however, that this function may be well-developed even in the smaller district councils, and that the need for management information is no less in such areas. The diverse patterns of local council structures and the changed relationship with localities which will emerge from the deliberations of the Local Government Commission will thus be quite compatible with an organized information function. Case study 6.3 illustrates current arrangements in an existing district.

CASE STUDY 6.3 A Central Policy, Planning and Information Unit (Derwentside District Council)

The Management Team (established 1990) consists of the three most senior managers: Chief Executive, Director of Central Services, Director of Customer Services, none of whom has routine operational responsibilities. Their role is, instead, to 'think strategically and plan long term' (Derwentside District Council, undated). The central unit exists to support the Management Team in its strategic planning activity.

The unit is policy-driven: not pure 'research', nor data-led. It engages in policy analysis, review, and corporate strategy. It has a broad 'think tank' role as well as specific responsibilities (e.g. industrial and economic development) in support of the Management Team.

'The Management Team represents perhaps the most important element of the Council's administrative set-up and plays a central role in policy formulation, policy planning, performance review and service co-ordination' (Derwentside District Council, undated).

Structurally, the unit is part of the Chief Executive's Department. The information role for managers is driven by specific policy needs arising from internal (political) priorities or external (legislative or central government) demands. Its role is corporate and strategic rather than departmental or operational.

A developed function of this kind is thus tenable in a relatively small district. The urban or rural nature of the authority may be relevant in considering the role of the unit. It is also important to consider how far the authority perceives itself to be a corporate authority (Fenwick, 1992, pp. 35–6).

To complete the review of the many possible arrangements for the research, policy and information function, reference may be made to Norris' discussion of the 'central policy capability' in a metropolitan district (1989).

Norris points out that the role of the 'centre' in a local authority – the corporate, strategic heart of the authority – is changing in the face of (a) the shift from direct service-provision to the client and contractor distinction and (b) the growth of multi-agency local provision (1989, p. 9). (The former is part of our discussions in Chapter 2; the latter is considered in Chapter 7.) The centre can no longer have a directing or monopolistic influence on the management of the authority. Its role has changed. Norris suggests that the centre serves in the changed environment of contemporary local government to:

1. co-ordinate resource planning;
2. provide corporate strategic guidance;
3. 'articulate' corporate policies;
4. establish systems for performance review;
5. represent the authority externally;
6. provide services to main departments;
7. lead corporate efforts on specific policy developments.

This characterization of the role of the policy unit has taken us considerably further than the review of the mechanics of the management information system, or the response to access to information legislation. Yet the common threads are important. The use and management of information, intelligence and policy-related data are central elements of the strategic management of local government itself. Old-style monolithic 'strategy' may have gone (and the removal of the metropolitan county authorities were part of this) but this has made the strategic approach to the new circumstances (the enabling role, multi-agency provision, contracting-out) more, not less, important. Further, the preceding discussion has demonstrated that as we move from managing information in the sense of using a MIS, through to active involvement in central policy planning, management moves ever closer to the political as well as administrative centre. This seems inevitable. Without strategies for the generation and policy-related use of information in the broadest sense, local government will become ever more fragmented.

Research, policy and management

Relationships between research, policy and management within a local authority may now be sketched out diagrammatically. Figure 6.3 suggests a relationship between research/information activity, and the management process, within a county (two-tier) structure. The district tier may, of course, have its own such function, as we have seen.

Within such a two-tier structure, the inter-relationships between different users of and audiences for policy-related information are highly important. Management exists on several levels, within separate local authorities, within which are the client and contractor sides, and in each case an elected or political level is involved too. It should be possible, by using and extending such a diagrammatic scheme, to identify the points at which managerial intervention is likely to be most effective. There is also

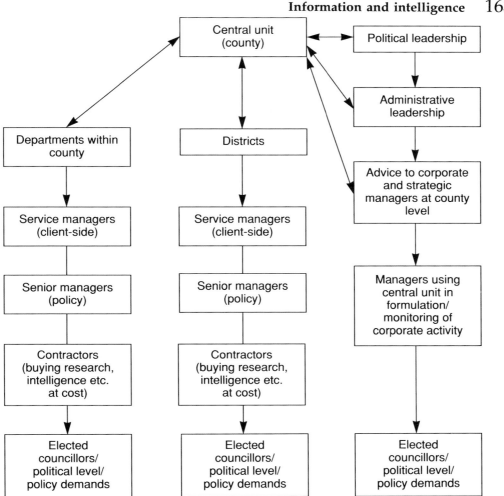

Figure 6.3   A research function within a county (two-tier) structure

the matter of exactly **where** such a function is located within the authority. Worrall, in his review of the district-level corporate R and I function, discovered it was not uncommon to find the research and intelligence function located in a planning (i.e. service) department (Worrall, 1990).

Relationships within a single-tier authority (the post-1986 metropolitan districts, or the new authorities emerging in the 1990s through the deliberations of the Local Government Commission) are likely to differ from the model outlined above. Figure 6.4 illustrates possible patterns of communication and influence within the single-tier council.

Figures 6.3 and 6.4 are not exhaustive. They illustrate, however, key administrative and political factors relating to research and information within the corporate authority. Exact relationships will vary from one council to another. Some specific problems for the service manager or for the corporate manager are as follows:

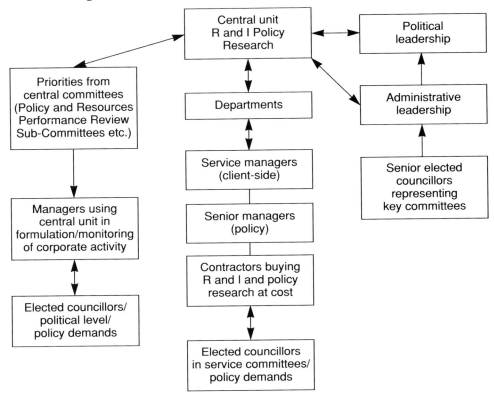

Figure 6.4 A research function within a single-tier structure

● **How is the central research/information function to be paid for?** The manager of a service activity may increasingly be expected to buy-in central services like research and information from within a finite budget. It is expected that all central services identified in the Government's 'Competing for Quality' (1991) are to be subject to Compulsory Competitive Tender by 1997 (see Chapter 2). Even without CCT, the manager of a central R & I-type service now needs to quantify different elements of the total workload, and different 'clients', especially distinguishing departmental and corporate work. Coupled with service-level agreements in advance of each year's work, the central research and information unit becomes almost an internal sort of management consultancy. (Leeds City Council even has a Project Management Group running an in-house Public Sector Management Consultancy.) This has a cost.

● **To whom is the central function accountable?** Figures 6.3 and 6.4 illustrate some of the complexities of accountability among different groups of managers and different elective parts of the organization. The traditional responsibility of service managers to their director, and thence to a specific 'service committee' as the guarantor of public accountability, has been fundamentally changed by CCT, the 'enabling' authority, and multi-agency provision. Consequently, the line-management responsibilities of the service manager have been eroded too, especially as a result of the client–contractor split. In the area of leisure services, for instance, the middle-manager's staff have in some cases evaporated as they transfer to the contractor side. In this context, new ways of seeking public consultation and listening to the 'customer' have arisen, as discussed in Chapter 3.

All these developments blur the lines of accountability of the central unit itself. Additionally, staff of such central units are likely to have extensive contact with the political centre of the authority. Many aspects of the work of such units are almost totally unknown to the public (Fenwick, 1992, p. 40). Taken together, these developments make the accountability of the central unit of paramount importance. The managers of such a function are not necessarily protected by traditional patterns of accountability.

● **Does a local authority need a specific research and intelligence operation?** Economic cost-benefit analysis may balance the costs of maintaining such a service against the costs of not running (or not buying-in) such a service. Not all of the latter are open to quantification: the effects of a poor decision made through lack of information cannot be compared to the hypothetical effects of a hypothetical good decision. However, insofar as the central function exists to improve the overall management of the authority, its role may be evaluated by the tools it provides toward this end, for instance policy analysis skills and processes, data interpretation, statistical and other analysis, measures of performance, original research, information systems, and internal management consultancy. These can be identified, and their cost and effect can (within limits) be measured. Alternatively, a comparison with private industry may be useful. How many private industries with the annual budget of a medium-sized local council would be prepared to forego a research and development capability, or to be defensive about its existence?

● **Is there a typical model for central research and information?** The diversity of arrangements has already been discussed. There is no uniform, model, structure. There is bad as well as good practice too. The central unit may stifle rather than expedite communication. It may restrict rather than accelerate the flow of management information. However, assuming a positive orientation toward the provision of management information, decisions about a wide variety of factors remain to be taken: size; organizational location; balance between research, information, intelligence and policy work; direct political accountability (insufficient or excessive); line-management responsibilities; workload and service level agreements; cost.

● **Does the central research and information function help local government to argue its case?** This is an important issue on which to draw the discussion to a close. A research and information function has a further rationale, which gains in importance with each successive central government decision about the powers and expenditure of local authorities. This can be conceived of as the local authority becoming **empowered** in its dealings with central government by having at its disposal a strong research and intelligence capability. Sharpe (1985) has documented the 'implementation gap' between the wishes of central government and the formally independent 'subnational' level of local (or, in other countries, regional) government.

Sharpe discusses the attempts of central government to persuade, co-opt or otherwise coerce sub-national government in order to implement central government policy, noting the readiness of government 'to change the conditions in which intergovernmental relations take place' (Sharpe, 1985, p. 375). Sharpe goes on to illustrate how central government has changed local–central relations by means of structural reform of local government, different forms of service delivery and new agencies of such delivery, and ultimately 'direct central control of decentral budgets' (Sharpe, 1985, p. 378).

The initial reluctance of local government to engage with performance measurement, indicators and performance review in the early years of successive Conservative administrations was soon replaced by an understanding that such information is a powerful means of defending local government as well as implementing restraint. The minimal indicators first required for annual reports gave way to an appreciation of the positive uses of such information.

Concluding comments

It could be argued that a developed research and information function for local authorities helps to redress the balance of influence and argument between local and central government. The corollary is that those concerned with the management of information in a period of debate, friction or outright hostility between local and central government are necessarily involved in hotly contested policy issues. This does not necessarily reflect party political differences alone. It also reflects the needs of government at two levels.

Information has been considered above in several distinct senses. The nature and problems of Management Information Systems were considered: the uses of technology; the differences between operational and strategic information needs; and, especially, the difficulty of providing information directly to those who need it, rather than filtering information needs through specialists or gatekeepers. The wider topic of access to information – and thus the relationship between the local authority and the public – was discussed in terms of the political context of local authority management post-Widdicombe. Management Information Systems and questions of access to information were also seen to raise long-standing questions about the respective roles of local authority managers and elected representatives.

Finally, detailed consideration has been given to the role occupied by the central research, information and intelligence function within local government. It has been suggested that this constitutes a considerable, and probably undervalued, aid to the strategic management of local authorities. In particular, structural reorganization of local government, multi-agency delivery of services, and the conflictual nature of local–central relations were held to add weight to the existing rationale for such a central function: it becomes an ever more important foundation for effective corporate and strategic management.

Summary

In Chapter 6, consideration has been given to information as **process**, in several forms: management information systems, access to information provisions, and the central research and intelligence capability within the local authority. These link **inter alia** to the 'closeness to the public' discussed in Chapter 3 and the measurement of performance discussed in Chapter 5. Information constitutes empowerment: for the public, for managers (and councillors) internally, and for the local authority as a whole in its dealings with central government. Effective production and dissemination of information therefore reinforces accountability within the local political process as well as assisting managerial effectiveness. Equally, information systems (and policy units) may **block** the flow of information: the way in which they are used, and the purposes for which they are used, are crucial.

Discussion questions and guidance

1. *How would you define a Management Information System and what would you regard as its principal uses and principal limitations for the local authority manager?*

Consider here the first pages of Chapter 6, especially the origins of such systems in private industry, the relation of Management Information Systems to wider strategic information networks, the different information needs of different levels of management within a local council, and the relationship between managers and elected councillors. Bear in mind the following observations of Torrington, Weightman and Johns. 'It is often the lack of top management involvement at the outset which is a key reason for the failure to develop systems which meet operating criteria. Substantial top management attention is needed at the start since the MIS network cuts across all departmental boundaries' (1989, p. 345).

2. (a) *Describe specific ways in which 'gatekeepers' may assist or hinder the flow of information to and from management, using examples from experience or individual study.*
    (b) *Evaluate the extent to which the influence of gatekeepers can be ascribed to their organizational location, their real or assumed expertise, or to inertia.*

The role of the gatekeeper is indicated above in Chapter Six in the quotations from Winfield (1991) and Thierauf (1987). You might consider strategies for turning a possibly obstructive role into one which assists the transmission of information: interpersonal skills, incentives, sanctions, structural changes, technology, and other approaches you may wish to adopt.

3. *Has the Local Government (Access to Information) Act 1985, subsequent legislation and, in particular, the Widdicombe Report 1986 contributed primarily to a changed climate for the use of information within local government? Is it accurate and useful to regard such cultural change as more significant for the local authority manager than the specific legislative consequences of such measures?*

It is important here to grasp that the overt provisions of legislation dealing with local government information are part, but only part, of the total picture. Government reports and legislation may contribute to changes in organizational culture. The acceptable boundaries of information availability, council/public interaction, and the norms of open management have changed considerably since the mid 1980s. Consider the opportunities and problems this presents for the individual manager. Read the section of this chapter – 'access to information' – again, comparing your own experience within your organization or, if not applicable, your knowledge of recent developments in local government.

4. *Can and should the senior local authority manager avoid political engagement?*

This question has numerous aspects. As discussed above, senior staff (defined by salary level or duties relating to policy advice) cannot participate in active politics. They may not be elected as councillors, even for another authority: see Mallabar (1991) for the 'twin-tracking' debates. Equally, the essential work of such staff is inherently, and probably increasingly, political. The restrictions are institutional as well as individual: general limitations also apply to council publicity information deemed to be political (Parsons, 1993). The question might alternatively be put in terms of how politics are to be 'managed' appropriately, and even positively, rather than avoided. An attempt to make sense of these complexities is being sought here, with apposite examples.

5. *'. . . recent transformations in the management of public services crucially depend upon innovations in the communication of information' (Bellamy and Taylor, 1994, p. 59). Discuss.*

The question invites an exploration of how far the New Public Management is linked to developments in technology and information. The question does not imply that political and economic factors are unimportant, nor does it imply a determinist role for technology and information. Rather, it asks us to consider the influence of information, in its own right. See the paper by Bellamy and Taylor (1994) from which the quotation is taken, plus the first section of Chapter 6 as a whole. Dockery's discussion (1992) is relevant too. The 'new' public management is referred to in Chapter 7 below.

6. *Is a management service unit (or similar central function) more effective than a fully fledged Department in meeting the information needs of the local authority's senior management? If so, why?*

The question refers in part to the best way of delivering information and intelligence to managers across the authority. The R&I function of Cleveland County Council in the early 1990s (see the section on 'Information and Intelligence' in this chapter (above, pp. 156–66)) was located in one of the several management service units providing common services within the council. Does this avoid some of the hierarchies, rivalries and empires associated with strong central departments, such as large Chief Executives' departments? The question also refers in part to the shortcomings of departments *per se*. As discussed in Chapter 2, the pressures of contracting (whether private or in-house) and the client–contractor distinction have undermined traditional departmental boundaries. North Tyneside Metropolitan Borough Council in 1992 confronted this in establishing a managerial structure around six executive directors (non-departmental), 16 heads of function and 45 managers at third level – with no Chief Executive (see Chapter 7, Case study 7.2, for details). The question is posed of where information provision properly sits within changed, perhaps obsolete, departmental structures.

7. *'By using its range of expertise the Unit should be aiming to help the Council achieve efficient and effective use of their resources, so that the right services for the right people can be provided in the right place at the right time' (Research and Intelligence Unit Provisional Work Programme 1991/92, Cleveland County Council, 1991). Is this a convincing rationale for the existence of a research and intelligence function in local authorities?*

It is useful here to refer to the examples of the central research function discussed in this chapter. It is necessary to distinguish between research, information, and intelligence, and to consider the organizational location of any such function. Of particular relevance is the use to which operational and service managers – and corporate management – might put such a facility, and the cost.

8. *Are the tensions between operational management and corporate management likely to be resolved by a strong policy research function within the local authority?*

Here it will be useful to explore the nature of **operational** management – which historically has meant managing a Department but has now become more diverse – and of **corporate** management –which may or may not be synonymous with strategic management. Possible conflicts between the two may be identified. Reference may then be made to the case-study material from this chapter, including the Derwentside case study of a central policy unit. Worrall indicates that R&I may be viewed as an 'expensive luxury' by some district councils, but, in others, 'as an essential part of strategic management' (1990, para 12). Is the research and policy work reviewed in the 'Information and intelligence' section (above, pp. 156–166) 'essential' for management of the contemporary local authority?

Suggested further reading

Blackman, T. (1995) *Urban Policy in Practice*, Routledge, London. Includes a chapter (pp 166–194) which deals specifically with local authority research and intelligence.

Fenwick, J. (1992) Policy Research in Local Government, *Local Government Policy Making*, **18** (4) (March) pp 35–41. Describes differing approaches within the policy-research function.

Isaac-Henry, K. (1993) The Management of Information Technology in the Public Sector, in K. Isaac-Henry, C. Painter and C. Barnes (eds), *Management in the Public Sector: Challenge and Change*, Chapman & Hall, London, pp 95–114. This review of IT and public management as a whole includes a case study of Birmingham City Council.

Bellamy, C. and Taylor, J. A. (1994) Reinventing Government in the Information Age, *Public Money and Management*, **14** (3) (July–September), pp 59–62. The implications of technological change for the process of government.

Dockery, E. (1992) Management and the Usefulness of Information, in L. Willocks and J. Harrow (eds), *Rediscovering Public Services Management*, McGraw-Hill, London, pp 275–293. Examines information use within public sector management.

Parsons, S. (1993) *The Right Side of the Law*, Local Government Information Unit, London. Discusses 'political' publicity and council information.

MANAGING THE NEW LOCAL GOVERNANCE

7

This final chapter brings together some important strands of the preceding discussion. The key themes are briefly restated, before considering the implications of local government reorganization in the 1990s. It is argued that reorganization fails to address the changed agenda of local government management. The growth of multi-agency provision and the non-elected local state are then considered. Within this new pattern of local provision, local government increasingly forms part of a wider network of local governance, with consequences for both the management of local councils and the politics of local democracy. Some future prospects are finally considered: the future for local political leadership, the future for the internal structure of local councils, and thoughts on the future of the management process in local government.

Introduction: a new management for local government?

Key themes

The following themes have now been explored:

- competition;
- the public as consumers;
- comparative local government;
- performance management;
- information and intelligence.

Taken together, these themes represent the framework within which local authority management will, for the foreseeable future, adapt and develop. The focus throughout the discussion of these themes has been upon **process**; upon **change**; upon the implications of such changes for **practice**; and upon the necessarily **political** context within which local government is managed.

In this final chapter, some overall observations are made about multi-agency local provision, local government reorganization, the internal structure of local councils and future prospects. How can the changes in local government be characterized overall? It is useful to remind ourselves of Stewart and Walsh's summary (1992) of the 'organizational assumptions' which have been challenged throughout the public services:

- the assumption of 'self-sufficiency', where the public organization responsible for a certain service function carries out that function itself, using its own staff, has been challenged by contracting out and the increased role of other agencies;
- the assumption of 'direct control', where the activity of the organization is supervised by direct continuous hierarchical management, has been challenged by the growth of contracts and performance specifications;
- the assumption of 'uniformity', where the same service is provided uniformly to all users, has been challenged by an increased number of providers and the ostensible choice thereby created;
- the assumption of 'accountability upwards', where the accountability of public officials is through the political process, has been challenged by a notion of accountability to customers;
- the assumption of 'standardized establishment procedures', where staffing issues are handled by standard authority-wide procedures, has been challenged by a stress upon motivation and reform of pay structures (Stewart and Walsh, 1992, pp. 509–10).

Such challenges to the traditional assumptions of local government lie behind many of the specific changes discussed in previous chapters. The managerial structures arising from the challenge of competition, and the cultural changes associated with the rediscovery of the public, are specific examples of how the new assumptions about public service provision have to varying degrees replaced accepted wisdom. 'To varying degrees' is an important rider, for the pace and scope of change in local government proceeds unevenly.

Within such changes to local government practice and culture can a 'new' public management be discerned, and if so, does it represent the future? Dunleavy and Hood (1994, pp. 10–12) suggest that the idea of a new public management can be criticized from four distinct, perhaps contradictory, directions: the **fatalist** critique that it cannot readily resolve the inherent problems of public management; the **individualist** critique that it does not go far enough along the road of privatization and individual contract relationships; the **hierarchist** critique that it is insufficiently guided from the centre and may have a destabilizing effect on public provision; and the **egalitarian** critique that it may undermine accountability, and, contrary to the way it is presented, may primarily serve the interests of service providers.

The conflicting and contradictory nature of such criticisms makes it difficult to propose some fixed overall definition of the new public management. Yet given the nature of the changes so far discussed, and our review of the 'key themes' shaping local government now and in the future, it seems important to try to pin down the 'new' management of local government more precisely.

As suggested below, it is perhaps easier to define the 'new public management' in terms of what it is not rather than what it is. It is not the 'old' paternalism of monopolistic bureaucratic provision (see Figure 1.1). Nor is it the methods of private industry crudely transferred across to public service. The 'new' public management, if it exists at all, is a sometimes uneasy combination of market-led reforms, a public service commitment, a de-scaling of the actual **size** of service provision, and a willingness to listen in however imperfect a way to the public. Defined in this way, the new public management does offer much for the future of local government, provided it is not subsumed within a narrow ideological framework which would emphasize the market elements to the exclusion of all else.

In evaluating the impact of our 'key themes' on the future of local authority management, it is important to make the distinction between the ideologically defined terms of reference laid down by central government, and the terms of debate as defined in local government. The two are not synonymous. The difference between the two will determine the particular form of the 'new' public management which will ultimately prevail.

What then have been **central government's** own guiding themes in its approach to public sector management since 1979?

Thomson (1992) describes seven main themes in central government's approach:

1. privatization;
2. delegation;
3. competition;
4. enterprise;
5. deregulation;
6. service quality;
7. curtailing trade union powers;

which are 'underpinned' by the three principles of efficiency, effectiveness and economy (see Chapter 5), plus two 'governing assumptions' from which the lists above originate: first, an assertion that Britain's poor economic performance derived not just from particular economic policies but also from the nature of state management of the public sector; second, that the collective organization (of services, and of parts of the economy) had failed and that the market provided the better discipline (Thomson, 1992, p. 33).

The ideologically driven agenda of central government can be distinguished from the wider concerns of a 'new' public management which are not constrained by a prior political imperative. The exact shape of the local government management of the future lies within these debates, constraints and opportunities.

Reorganization for a new local government?

It is easy now to see why local government was reorganized in April 1974. Reorganization at that time was the product of debates set in motion by the creation in 1966 of the Royal Commission on Local Government or 'Redcliffe-Maud' Commission (Report of the Royal Commission on Local Government in England, 1969) and mediated by the electoral defeat of the Labour Government in 1970 (and indeed the subsequent defeat of the Conservatives in February 1974).

The urban and rural districts, counties and county boroughs, essentially deriving from the nineteenth century, were self-evidently ill-suited for the growing cities of post-war Britain as traditional boundaries were left behind, or the massive growth of the local and national state as economic prosperity in the period up to the early 1970s promised an ever greater number of things for local government to do. Although it is not always interpreted in this way, the eventual shape of reorganization stood Redcliffe-Maud's initial recommendations for unitary councils as the norm on their head. Instead of unitary local government everywhere except for three urban areas with a two-tier system, the 1974 reorganization brought two-tier local government everywhere, with a rather different distribution of functions between the two tiers in six 'metropolitan' counties.

Although the reorganization of April 1974 took place under a Labour government, it derived from the Local Government Act 1972 of a Conservative government. It would be reasonable to say that the post-1974 system had a large measure of consent across the party-political divide, especially on the local level. Where there was dissent locally – notably with the legitimacy of new councils such as Humberside and Avon – this was, at this stage, not an essentially party-political dispute.

In due course, the nature of political discourse about the organization of local government changed. Local government *per se* became a problem for central government. The next substantial 'reorganization' of local government – the abolition of the Labour-dominated metropolitan county councils (not in fact the abolition of the metropolitan **counties**) and the Greater London Council in April 1986 – is entirely comprehensible as a political act of an ideologically driven Conservative government irritated by persistent opposition. As in 1974, a motivation for the changes of 1986 can be discerned.

It is interesting to note here two aspects of the 1986 abolition. First, the Redcliffe-Maud proposal for a single-tier or unitary authority (supported at the time by Labour) ironically appeared in the metropolitan areas in 1986 for the first time – created by the Conservatives, and opposed by Labour. Secondly, the abolition of the metropolitan county councils had implications for the management as well as the politics of local government in those areas. Abolition came to be seen as a counter-move against the expansion of an over-reaching corporate management, derided as social engineering or the province of much-maligned 'planners'.

Thus in their different ways the changes in the organization of local government in 1974 and 1986 have a comprehensible basis, part managerial, predominantly political. However, the most striking characteristic of the fundamental review of the organization of local government in the 1990s is that it has no evident rationale.

Formulating proposals for local government reorganization in the 1990s has been a lengthy and at times puzzling process. All authorities in Wales and Scotland will be unitary authorities. In England, proposals were in place by September 1994 for the final county to be considered by the Commission, Cornwall. In broad terms, these proposals became, eventually, that some county councils would be replaced by unitary authorities, while other counties would remain two-tier, and that within this structure there would separately be 13 unitary towns, responsible for all their own services.

What is the rationale? The government initially had a presumption that unitary councils would be the norm, but the Local Government Commission has exercised its remit to consult the local public and to make recommendations accordingly. Consequently two-tier authorities are suggested for considerably more parts of the country than intended originally by government. Unitary councils are more common than two-tier authorities under the Commission's proposals, but the picture is complex. Additionally, some historic counties keep their name, but cease to have functions as local elected authorities. Further, there are large population areas of England – i.e. the metropolitan county areas – which were outside the consideration of the Local Government Commission at this stage. The exclusion of the West Yorkshire metropolitan area, for instance, makes the Commission's proposals for restoring the 'ridings' of Yorkshire implausible.

Jones and Stewart (1993, pp. 68–9) draw attention to the government retreat from the unitary principle in its successive consultation and policy papers. That would not be a problem if the original focus upon the unitary principle had been replaced by an alternative emphasis, but the direction or justification for structural change has become unclear.

> The commission's main problem is it has to produce a structure without knowing the purpose of the structure (Jones and Stewart, 1993, p. 70).

If the unitary principle is not universal, some may argue that 'public opinion' has become the guiding principle of a diverse new structure for local government, and that such diversity is a strength not a weakness: after all, why should the system of local government be uniform throughout England when local needs vary considerably? This would be a stronger argument if there had not been so many changes and counter-proposals as the suggested structures have emerged, and if the government had adopted an arm's-length approach which gave primacy to public consultation. However, government has made its own agenda evident (though not clear, for it has changed over time). It would also appear from this logic that local needs somehow do not vary in Wales or Scotland, given that the structure there is to be unitary throughout.

It should be noted that the popular basis of the proposed authorities is meant to be based not only upon what the public thinks, if that indeed is knowable, but also upon an objective assessment of community and identity. It is this area which has proven particularly contentious for counties such as Humberside and Cleveland, held by their critics to be artificial products of the planners' imagination (perhaps especially so for Cleveland, given the previous and short-lived 'Teesside' dating from 1968 to 1974). By far the longest section of Cleveland County Council's submission (1992) to the Local Government Commission is concerned with 'community identity'.

> In the Policy Guidance to the Local Government Commission, it is stressed that local authorities should be based on communities and that, in gauging community identities, 'peoples's expressed preferences' should be considered (Cleveland County Council, 1992, p. 38).

The question of measuring community identity thus presumably becomes a technical one of finding the right indicators, and then acting upon them. In the case of the Cleveland submission, 'community' is explored through analysis of historical settlement, shared interest, public opinion polls, geography, industry, demographic factors, and retail and travel-to-work data, in a body of information which was ultimately unsuccessful in shaping the Commission's recommendations.

Perhaps a rationale for local government reorganization can be found in the very processes discussed in this book: i.e. that as the nature of running local government has changed under the impact of competition, the consumer, performance measurement and all the other changes referred to, so local government requires an overall structural reorganization. Such a reorganization would **re-align** local government with its public and its changed responsibilities. However, although potentially this could be a very convincing argument for **a** reorganization, it is not so obviously applicable to **this** reorganization. If this were the agenda, the reorganization would need to go considerably further, and accommodate the growth of other local agencies and the changed role of councillors.

These wider changes are beyond the remit of the present Commission. Perhaps a new 'Bains Report' is needed: an update of the 1972 report on the structure and management of local authorities, often still discussed in relation especially to the chief executive role (Report of the Study Group on the New Local Authorities Management and Structure, 1972). There is no evidence that the proposed local authorities of the 1990s reorganization reflect or assist the changed management of local government. Leach (1994) suggests that the **enabling role** could have been a rationale for the whole reorganization process, but the opportunity was lost. Instead, reorganization has addressed a number of objectives, changing over time, and failing to link to broader changes in the role of local government.

> The problem is not a lack of objectives, but too many objectives. There are the declared objectives of the government, published in various forms over time, supplemented by inferred hidden agendas and conspiracy theories. There are the objectives which appear to be involved in the work of the Local Government Commission for England. There are the contrasting objectives of other players in the game, particularly the Local Authority Associations, and individual councils. The commitment to extensive consultation gives these other players some hopes of capturing the process and imposing their own alternative agendas (Leach, 1994, p. 2).

Wilson and Game (1994) begin to draw out the possible relationships between models of local government and their likely structural counterparts. This relationship in turn may be developed to point to typical features of how such local authorities would be run, politically and administratively. The models of local government and some of their characteristics are described by Wilson and Game as follows (1994, pp. 342–55):

- **traditional hierarchical authority**: mainly a direct service provider; a representative model of accountability; traditional patterns of management and hierarchical structures;
- **residual enabling authority**: 'provider of last resort'; specifies and monitors contracts; free-market notion of accountability with individual charging; small single-tier authorities with some need to co-operate; a clear client/contractor split in management terms;
- **market-oriented enabling authority**: agent for local economic development; specifies and monitors contracts but with a more active 'bargaining' role; local

business culture; corporate notion of accountability; geographical council boundary based on economic coherence – much larger than residual model; a private-sector/ entrepreneurial management model would seem to fit;

- **community-oriented enabling authority**: identifies community needs and meets them, not necessarily directly; redistributive element; social goals; participative; community notion of accountability; a unitary system with local neighbourhood devolution, or a two-tier system with small local tiers; decentralized management model with local participation.

The typology suggested by Wilson and Game is useful in beginning to connect the overall themes of this book to possible structures. In reality the reorganization of the 1990s is likely to fit uneasily with both the changed nature of the local government task and the changed nature of the management process.

A residual sort of rationale for reorganization, in the absence of any overall guiding principle, is simply that it will save money, through rationalization, joint-work and elimination of now redundant structures. Making savings in the total cost of local government is of course a consensual goal, but there is no agreement about the actual costs or actual savings involved in this reorganization. Wilson and Game point out that the estimates of savings in public expenditure claimed for the implementation of the first wave of reorganizations are hotly disputed (1994, p. 301). There is also the cost of the Commission itself, and of transitional arrangements, to consider. At present, total costs are simply not known with any precision.

Local governance I: Multi-agency local provision

The term 'multi-agency local provision' is jargon, but jargon with a meaning. It is not synonymous with the growth of non-elected agencies, although these too might form **part of** a network of local provision. Multi-agency local provision refers to joint work by the local authority and other local bodies, ideally led by some local need rather than being led by producer needs. Joint work by police and local councils in areas seen as problematic in some way is a good example. The development of Community Care policies (see Case study 1.1) brings together health and social services providers, and 'joint commissioning' between these is increasing. The example of community care also reminds us that multi-agency local provision may include the private sector as well as local public agencies, and that this private element may include private companies as well as voluntary organizations.

Multi-agency local provision also tends to involve the rather overworked term 'partnership', but, looking beyond the terminology, there is no doubt that joint working arrangements between local councils and other local bodies are here to stay.

Problems arise with multi-agency arrangements. There may be disagreements between different groups of 'professionals', notoriously keen to preserve traditional empires. There may be lack of clarity about the purpose at hand. Gray (1994) writes of Community Care in the following terms.

The problem of reaching agreement between the participants in this process, in particular between health and local authorities, has been primarily a result of the conflicts over defining what community care actually is, and the financial issues that have been generated as a consequence of re-directing policy along one path rather than another (Gray, 1994, p. 145).

Local councils are also limited by what they can legally do – on the one hand, they cannot dispose of some statutory responsibility onto the shoulders of a specially created local group; on the other hand, they may be constrained from acting altogether once they get much beyond their statutory duties. Hence, the range of activities and services for which a joint-agency approach is appropriate or possible may be quite narrow. The creativity allowed by the 'free local government' experiments in Scandinavia (Case study 4.4) would allow considerably more scope for multi-agency initiatives. However, this tends to run counter to the centralist culture of British government. Another drawback of multi-agency approaches is that, rather than being led by local needs, they may be led by available funds, perhaps available from central government for certain purposes only. Initiatives may thus be led by resources, not needs. The City Challenge programme of the 1990s is a good example.

The final problem of multi-agency local provision is one of accountability. The fragmentation of local service delivery with which we have been concerned throughout, the changed balance of public and private provision, the growth of multi-agency provision and the rise of the non-elected local state, have served to blur patterns of accountability. Traditional accountability of locally elected council members for locally delivered services has fundamentally changed within the new multi-agency framework. Similarly, at central government level, the Parliamentary accountability of ministers for the work of the 'next steps' agencies in the 1990s is by no means clear. As Gray notes in relation to the introduction of the poll tax or 'community charge' in 1990 – since of course abandoned in favour of a 'council tax' – a political concept of accountability has been partly superseded by an economic notion of what accountability means.

> By shifting accountability from democratic to economic channels the entire collective nature of local service provision came under attack as the relationship between paying for services and the receipt of services moved to centre-stage. Similar moves have also been introduced with the attempt to introduce more market-based criteria for service delivery in services such as housing, education and health care (Gray, 1994, p. 65).

The difficulty of an economic notion of accountability in local services is, of course, that economic power is unequally distributed. Economic accountability therefore inevitably implies different degrees of eligibility for local services. Once again, this tends to come up against the values of local government which, while not narrowly political, have implied since the nineteenth century a general ethos of social and public service. These debates about accountability can in turn be related back to the discussion of the links between models of accountability and models of local government structure.

Local governance II: The non-elected local state

> The crucial issue raised by the growth of appointed boards is that of accountability (Stewart and Davis, 1994, p. 32).

The existence of a network of local service providers, including a variety of public agencies and an element of private provision both voluntary and commercial, is essentially what is meant by a move from local government to local governance. As Cochrane (1993) points out, the **enabling authority** concept, with which we have become familiar, correctly points to the 'fragility' of local government's own role within this multi-agency network, but it also implies a leading role for local government, in the following terms.

> It emphasizes the need for those working in and elected to positions within local government to work for the right to be seen as representative of their communities and to be the agencies around which others should cluster. In that sense it does give the strategic managers a role, if they can take it; just as it gives the local politicians a role if they can win it (Cochrane, 1993, p. 79).

However, the problem is that multi-agency local provision, with a changed but far from residual local government, is increasingly giving way to a local governance of the non-elected. As noted in Chapter 1, the rise of the QUANGO has been at the expense of elected authorities. The development of a **non-elected local state** has far-reaching implications for local accountability, the representative basis of public service provision, and the future of local government.

It is difficult to evaluate the extent and impact of appointed local bodies. Their growth has been gradual, and the government tends to adopt a definition of such agencies which excludes most of them from consideration (Stewart and Davis, 1994, p. 30). What then is the non-elected local state? The implication of the term is the removal of **large scale functions** from **elected** and **local** bodies in circumstances where appointed agencies take over those functions. The growth of the Development Corporations in urban areas is a particularly visible example of how the responsibilities of the elected local authority in development and planning matters are superseded by appointees. This particular example is 'visible' also in the sense that, being led by resources made available to them, the Development Corporations tend to make a physically visible impact. The detachment of the elected tier of local authority members from the National Health Service, and the existence of political appointees to the chairs of NHS trusts, form another significant plank of the non-elected local state.

The Local Government Information Unit (1994d) suggests eight 'democratic tests' to use in comparing QUANGOs and local councils:

1. open to public scrutiny;
2. declarations of interest;
3. fiduciary duty;
4. access to information;
5. open accounts;
6. access to meetings;
7. monitoring and auditing a council's affairs;
8. complaints and maladministration.

Clearly the point should not be over-emphasized. Local government did not provide 'access to information' other than through legislation (initiated by a Conservative member). The investigation of complaints and maladministration is also a statutory matter, externally directed. The argument should not be over-simplified. However, the point is that the obligations falling to local government in these eight senses, whatever their origins over a period of time and whatever the then attitude of local government to their introduction, do not fall upon QUANGOs in any comparable form. These are quite fundamental differences.

Alongside the growth of the non-elected tier has been the change in the meaning of accountability already referred to. Representative political accountability has given way to an individual-contractual market model of what accountability is meant to mean. The growth of Citizen Charters (see Chapter 5) becomes more comprehensible alongside the growth of QUANGOs, for the Charters fundamentally represent an individualization of accountability – even leaving aside the question of whether they 'work' in their own terms. A market-led notion of the local population as comprising individual consumers (see Chapter 3) rather than a collectivity reflects the same shift in accountability.

> There are now more and more appointed bodies, locally, who are taking over the powers of local government. Nobody knows who they are, they don't know who they're accountable to, and yet there they are, in fact, spending more money across the country than the whole of local government put together (Lady Elizabeth Anson, former chair of Association of District Councils, quoted in Local Government Information Unit) (1994c).

The future of local political leadership

The local authority elected member has in recent years experienced a rather contradictory **curtailment** of responsibilities as services are contracted out and spending capped, and an **expansion** of responsibilities as legislation about local government has multiplied and the demands of the role have become more complex. The Audit Commission suggested in 1990 that legislation and central government's reforms were influencing the 'environment within which elected members operate' in five principal ways, defined as follows (1990, pp. 9–10).

- a growing emphasis on quality and the customer;
- the distinction between client and contractor, or purchaser and provider;
- councils decreasingly being direct providers, increasingly being involved in partnerships and contracting out;
- changes in committee representation and growth of for instance member involvement in staff appointments;
- the community charge, as then was, increasing the pressure for value for money – a pressure, we might add, not reduced by the subsequent introduction of the council tax.

Certainly there is no reason to consider that the pace of change has at all slowed down during the 1990s. The emphases on quality, upon the 'customer', and upon a relatively narrow concept of value for money have increased not decreased. CCT has been driven forward, as we have seen, into further services. Local government finance has gone through yet more change.

All this is evident enough, and the nature of the changes affecting the local authority member can be itemized under each chapter heading in this book. However, the nature of the change affecting the elected member is of a more fundamental kind. The question of local political **leadership** is the key question for the future. The logic of the continuing changes to local government is that the role of the elected member becomes closer to that of the officer: the councillor becomes more of an administrator, less of a politician, for all the familiar reasons – contracting out, the decline of a representative concept of accountability, the constraints of legislation. Thus the quantitative accumulation of successive legislation leads to a qualitative change. The nature of local political leadership alters to accommodate the new system of governance described above.

These fundamental changes to the role of the local councillor do not mean that the role has become irrelevant. However, it has changed. The desirability or otherwise of such changes is, of course – like much else in local government – a matter of values and of politics. Some local authorities may, in seeking a positive outcome from the inevitability of externally generated changes, adopt an active approach to restructuring their own administrative and political systems. Case study 7.2 below has particular implications for the local councillor, arguably giving the elected member an enhanced not reduced role.

Yet do such examples only further confirm that local leadership must essentially be reactive? Leach and Stewart, in a guide to political leadership for local councillors, refer to the 'crisis management' which became characteristic of local political leadership in the 1980s, whether imposed by central government through its many policy initiatives and pieces of legislation or driven by local socio-economic problems such as urban disorder or large-scale industrial closures (1990, pp. 9–10). We might add that the latter set of factors arguably derive from the former, and that the 'crisis management' of the local political leaders has thus largely been centrally determined.

Is crisis management still the norm? The controversies of political leadership in Liverpool or in former outposts of municipal socialism like Sheffield have moved on, partly because central government did eventually force such authorities to change (e.g. Sheffield's public transport system) and partly because the agenda changed with the departure of Thatcher. However, caution is necessary. Crisis management on the political level may seem to have mellowed only because it has become normal. It has not gone: we have simply become used to it.

The future internal organization of the local authority

In a climate of rapid cultural change and external political and financial pressure, the internal organization of the council tends to adapt in response. Restructuring the political and administrative organization of the council may of course be fundamental

CASE STUDY 7.1 A corporate centre

The Chief Executive Department of Sunderland City Council, a single-tier metropolitan authority, contains several functional units:

- **Strategic Planning**: a central policy/research unit dealing with strategic and corporate planning and research (see Chapter 6 for discussion of central policy units);
- **Economic Development**: responsible for attracting investment and running the council's industrial activity;
- **European Affairs**: concerned with European grants and wider participation of the City in Europe;
- **Regeneration**: involved in developing and attracting funding for regeneration initiatives;
- **Public Relations and Marketing**: including PR, the press office, corporate marketing and tourism;
- **Elections**: responsible for the council's election and registration functions.

This structure is a part of Authority-wide organizational change. An Assistant Chief Executive is responsible for the units listed above, and for: monitoring a cycle of performance review activity across the Authority; strategic and corporate planning; CCT; customer care; and liaison with external agencies.

It is interesting to note that these specific responsibilities, and the changed structure associated with them, mirror the themes which have proven so important throughout the book. Case study 7.1 represents an Authority which has, in its managerial roles and formal organizational structure, adapted significantly to these changes. The direction of such adaptation is clearly toward the strategic and corporate.

in its scope, or relatively superficial. Can any generalizations be offered about the likely shape of the future internal organization of local authorities?

The local authority discussed in Case study 7.1 represents one form of adaptation: toward a strong centre, based in a Chief Executive's department, with a range of support units around an essentially corporate management. Aspects of the central policy function discussed in Chapter 6 are relevant to this kind of structure, and links can also be made to the characteristics of the central corporate manager (in contrast to the client-side and contract managers) considered in the discussion of competition in Chapter 2. This sort of internal structure potentially gives the local authority the ability to deal with change through the strategic policy element, as well as to raise resources through the economic development elements. The structure also places

– potentially – expertise at the centre so that future changes, for instance to CCT, can be managed more smoothly. What drives the creation of this kind of internal structure? As already noted, internal adaptations are largely a response to the pace and nature of the external pressures on local government. More specifically, the kind of structure represented by Case study 7.1 is driven by:

- the search for **resources** (European; economic development more widely; public–private partnerships);
- the need for **more co-ordination of services and policy** (the corporate and strategic management elements);
- the need to manage a **changed relationship with the public** based on the demands of CCT, the push to 'customer care' and so on.

There are possible problems, however, with this kind of structure – indeed, with any avowedly corporate structure in the contemporary local authority. First, there is the question of how far a corporate approach implies a centralist approach, and the dangers of locating (or being perceived as locating) too much influence at the centre. To take the point further, a paternalism of the kind discussed in Chapter 3 may be repackaged, not replaced, by centralist structures. Secondly, in addition to the danger that corporatism goes too far is the danger that it does not go far enough.

There are limits to corporatism: the very uncertainty which makes it necessary makes it difficult to achieve, as we have already noted, and even the best structures are bound in the contemporary climate to be reactive. Thirdly, there is a continuing tension between the fragmentation of services and their management in the departments or units concerned with their delivery, and the need for more effective overall co-ordination. These three problems pull local authorities in different directions: attempt to solve one, and another becomes more difficult. Attempts to grapple with

CASE STUDY 7.2 A non-departmental corporate structure

The restructuring of North Tyneside Council, a single-tier metropolitan authority, took place during 1992. The main innovation is the creation of the posts of **Executive Director** and **Head of Function** within a non-departmental and explicitly corporate structure.

Executive Directors: six executive directors were specified in the original proposal (five subsequently in place), each to have corporate responsibilities across a number of service areas (functions), across policy areas, and across geographical areas of the authority. The job description for the Executive Director includes:

- translation of policy into specific action plans for delivery of services;
- monitoring and evaluation;

- 'leading the climate for cultural change, by direct communication with all levels within individual functions';
- communications;
- no line management responsibility but 'to discuss and agree with heads of function their proposals for meeting targets and timescales consistent with service and budget targets. Day to day operational matters will be delegated to heads of function who will be accountable to the Executive Directors for the results. Executive Directors will be ultimately accountable to the Council.' The latter accountability is exercised through weekly meetings with the Leader or Deputy Leader;
- human resources strategy;
- advising the council and its committees;
- 'networking across functions: formation of task specific teams which will not be impeded by attitudes of "departmentalism"';
- outside representation;
- integration of services within geographical areas.

Heads of Function: 16 heads of function were established (on chief officer scales) for the following:

1. Education Services
2. Environment
3. Development
4. Assessment
5. Care in the Community
6. Childcare Enterprise (under 8s)
7. Property Services
8. Community Services
9. Corporate Finance
10. Information Technology
11. Housing Technology
12. Customer Services
13. Public Works
14. Transport and Engineering
15. Corporate Services
16. Corporate Policy

Even those Functions without the word 'corporate' in their title are intended to cut across traditional department/service boundaries: 'assessment' for instance includes elements of education, housing and social services as traditionally conceived.

Within the structure there are no Departments, hence no Directors of Deputy Directors of Departments. There is no Chief Executive.

There is no legal requirement to have a post of Chief Executive, but there are certain statutory posts in local government including:

Head of Paid Service
Chief Finance Officer
Monitoring Officer
Public Analyst and Trading Standards Officers
Director of Social Services
Chief Education Officer

These statutory roles are formally allocated to named officers in post at the Executive Director or Head of Function level.

(*Sources*: North Tyneside Council, 'job description for executive directors', 'brief description of each function', 'statutory officers', 1992.)

these conflicting pressures produce internal adaptations, new patterns of working, or perhaps complete new structures.

The management structure presented at Case study 7.2 represents not only a considerable departure from the traditional line management systems and service committees of local government, it also provides an alternative to corporate authorities where greater emphasis is placed upon a more powerful Chief Executive department. There is no Chief Executive department within this structure as there is no Chief Executive.

The questions which most immediately arise in relation to Case study 7.2 are, first, why would such a structure be adopted, and, secondly, does it work?

Reasons for adopting this structure are on the general level clear enough, and unsurprising: finding the right structure to cope with change, and linking the senior management of the authority to the political leadership and to corporate policies. The specific reasons are perhaps evident in the item of the Executive Director job description where reference is made to not being 'impeded' by a 'departmentalism'. The management structure of this council cuts right across traditional service areas, and across traditional areas of influence. This propels the authority towards a corporate approach. There is no departmentalism where there are no departments.

Whether the structure 'works' implies a prior question: works in doing what? There is no body of evidence to refer to here, but it would be fairly clear that the structure has almost by definition 'worked' in removing some of the barriers to change, because it has forced change to happen. The structure also appears to allow a more direct influence of the political leadership over the operational affairs of the council, blurring the 'political' and 'managerial' even more than is usual, for good or ill. In any evaluation, there would also be the very important question of what sense the public (or other councils) make of a structure which differs so markedly from historical experience of contacting 'the council': a 'function' is hardly a term with a self-evident meaning here.

The management structure outlined in Case study 7.2 involves further vertical change throughout the authority. Within each function, there are new **third-level** managers too, e.g. financial services manager, cleansing manager, property manager. A total of 45 third-level manager posts came into existence within the new structure.

Thus Case study 7.2 represents a substantial form of 'adaptation' to the pace of political and managerial change. Its applicability in whole or part to other authorities is a matter for further debate. The relationship of such a new structure to the committee system must also be considered. There needs to be changed organization of the councillor side too, corresponding to changed managerial structures, in addition to any changes on the member side already implied by CCT.

The changed officer structure in Case study 7.2 was followed in 1993 by a committee structure comprising:

- six **standing committees**, of between 19 and 29 members, ie: policy and resources; performance review and monitoring; external affairs; education; social affairs; contractor;
- five **policy liaison committees**, of 15 or 19 members, i.e. women's issues, older persons' issues, young people's issues (reporting to policy and resources) plus health issues and voluntary organizations (reporting to external affairs);
- two **standing sub-committees**, of 15 or 19 members, dealing with appeals and with development/planning issues, and reporting to the Social Affairs Committee;
- plus ad hoc 'task groups' reporting to the Policy and Resources Committee or the relevant standing committee.

It might also be noted that since Case study 7.2 refers to a metropolitan authority already responsible for the range of services – resembling the 'unitary' council which will be more common if reorganization is implemented as recommended – the structural issues raised by its reorganization will tend to become more rather than less relevant.

The future of local authority management: concluding comments

Mallabar talks of management in a local authority in terms not only of organization, planning, control and implementation, but also of the development of an organizational culture which fits the formal structures of the authority, and of a strategy for that organization's own survival (1991, pp. 108–9). This last point is worth a little more thought at this concluding stage.

What strategies exist for maintaining the existence of local government other than political ones prosecuted on a national stage? The future management of local government is of a reduced sector of elected local and public administration alongside an increased sector of appointed agencies of central government and mixed 'partnership' bodies. The exact scope of local government proper at the end of the twentieth century and beginning of the twenty-first depends upon unpredictable political developments, but local government is unlikely ever to resemble the form of the pre-Thatcher years.

Whatever structures and direct service responsibilities obtain, officers will be 'managing' a local government permanently changed in size, complexity and scope.

Any attempt to define the characteristics of such a management brings into play once again the relationship between public and private, and the particular features of managing the public service sector. Writing of public-sector management as a whole, Willcocks and Harrow advocate a **contingency approach** to public sector management where environmental factors impinge upon a 'dominant coalition' of forces to produce particular management functions, which in turn influence the 'technical core' of equipment skills etc available to the manager (1992, pp. xviii–xix). This model implies that private-sector management is itself rather more complex than traditionally conceived and, further, that comparisons between public and private management are contentious.

> In summary, there emerges no coherent, systematic, agreed view of management or what managers do, or what they should be doing in private sector organizations. There is some irony, then, that in a period when the nature of management has been questioned as never before, the UK public services have found themselves judged against 'traditional' management criteria, which are themselves suspect, and has been found wanting (Willcocks and Harrow, 1992, p. xix).

Thus, to emphasize an earlier point once more, there is no simple process of public management becoming more like private management. Indeed, to take Willcocks' and Harrow's point, there is no simple model of private-sector management to which the private sector itself, let alone the public sector, adheres.

Is it useful, then, to talk of a 'new' public management at all? We have already referred to what it is **not**: it is not the methods of the private sector straightforwardly transferred across to local government, not least because of the distinguishing value systems, culture and social ethos of the public services. We have explored some of the **elements of** the new public management, as applied to local government, particularly the growth of the consumer perspective. But does the new public management have an enduring meaning in local government, and is it any different from 'old' methods of running public services, particularly the 'paternalist' view that service providers know best?

Dunleavy and Hood (1994) suggest that the new public management principally differs from the old public administration on two axes: first, public officials have a growing discretion, more devolved responsibility, in areas such as budgets and staffing; secondly, the public sector has become 'less distinctive as a unit from the private sector' (Dunleavy and Hood, 1994, p. 9). Conceivably the first area of change may be a subsidiary consequence of the second.

The other features of the new public management referred to by Dunleavy and Hood – e.g. the growth of the principal–agent relationship, the concern with measurable performance outputs, the competition between providers – remain significant (1994, p. 9). Dunleavy and Hood suggest that there is unlikely to be a single uniform future for 'new public management' *per se*: there are instead a number of futures (1994, p. 13). This is relevant to our concluding observations, for, applied to local government, a number of competing versions of the future management of local authorities are opened up. Returning to Dunleavy and Hood's terminology, they propose four possible futures of public management, as follows (1994, p. 14).

- A 'gridlock' model: a large number of general rules; a low degree of separation between public and private providers; the example given is that of (pre-Clinton) US health care, with a hugely influential private sector, but a 'heavily rule bound' mode of operation, driven by the fact or threat of litigation.
- A 'public bureaucracy state': a large number of general rules; a large degree of separation between public and private sectors; represented in practice by strong public-service organizations with clearly defined bureaucratic roles.
- A 'minimal purchasing state': a small number of general rules; a low degree of separation between public and private providers; the 'contract' local state, dominated by private provision, which, we might add, so influenced the initial rationale in the 1970s of Conservative policy toward local government.
- A 'headless chicken model': a small number of general rules; a high degree of separation between public and private providers; a feeling that 'no-one is in charge', old ways of managing have been relaxed, but the force and weight of predominantly public provision remains in place.

Dunleavy and Hood consider that current reforms in public management are tending to push it in a 'headless chicken' direction, either as a general state of affairs or as a transitional stage (1994, p. 14). If this model indeed describes the characteristic mode of organization of local government, what are the future prospects?

It would seem necessary here to distinguish short/medium-term prospects from the longer-term future. The immediate and currently foreseeable future for managing local government lies in the changed skills, the forms of adaptation, upon which we have concentrated – the growth of resource management and decline of line management, the distinct skills of the client-side and contractor-side manager, the attempts to cope with change through a stronger corporate centre. Indeed, some of these changes are contradictory.

The possibility that this pattern of management is but a transition on the road to some other set of arrangements, which in turn will require distinctive managerial methods, is worth consideration. It may be that eventually 'local government' comes to consist of an arrangement of contracts, presided over by an arms-length group of managers, augmented by various appointed agencies. It may in contrast be that local government takes over responsibilities it does not currently have, perhaps in the health area, or that a regional level of local government is created. Or it may be that local government continues in its currently uncertain mode of operation, responding to frequent legislative and financial change, permanently. Whatever the outcome, it will be determined politically. The future management of local government is a function of future political change.

Prospects for the future management of local government are reviewed by Smith (1993). She summarizes the main themes deriving from a panel of senior local authority officers co-ordinated by the Local Government Management Board, as: responsiveness to the public, increased competition, the client–contractor split, limited resources, the impact of what is now the European Union, an increased political environment in local government, technological change, and further legislation in major service areas (Smith, 1993, p. 111). It is interesting to note how closely these themes – generated by practitioners – mirror those considered throughout this book. There is clearly a level of consensus about the kinds of **issues** likely to continue to face local government managers.

However, what do these issues mean for the practice of local authority management? Smith refers, tentatively, to 'a growing recognition that professional and technical training on its own is no longer an adequate grounding for management in local government. More generic managerial competences are needed' (1993, p. 111). Smith goes on to refer to the development of 'flatter' and less hierarchical structures in local councils, and a greater degree of team working (1993, p. 112). We could add that these changes are compatible with the expansion of project and contract management already discussed. The fact of change is also of course here to stay. The **broad** direction of such changes in the way local authorities are run at present, and are likely to be run in future, now seems clear enough. However, there are areas of contention, of conflict, and these are once again about values.

A key issue for resolution is the nature of the 'generic' skills appropriate for the council manager of the future, as the role of the manager trained solely in the professional area of their (former) department declines. The dominant view of central government in the Conservative years from 1979 has been that the skills and values of private industry are appropriate for local government too. The alternative view, probably still dominant in local government, is that while there may be general skills applicable to local government, these skills are distinct from those of commercial organizations on the level of values, social goals, accountability to the public and public purpose. This is a difference of philosophies, of values, and of politics (though not necessarily simple party politics) and it impacts directly upon management practice.

The total effect of competition, compulsory tendering, budgetary devolution, management by contract, the growth of the purchaser–provider (and client–contractor) relationship, and the successive changes in the way in which local government finances are determined is one of a progressive **fragmentation** of local authority management. The future of local authority management is in the growth of **distinct and particular skills** based upon the precise role being performed, such as client, contractor or corporate manager (see Fenwick, Shaw and Foreman, 1994).

Further, as the boundary between public and private sectors becomes more blurred, so the skills of the private-sector manager become perceived as more applicable to local government itself. The tension arises when it becomes clear that local government traditionally represents a set of values at odds with a shallow managerialism bought in from outside. The legislative changes affecting local government throughout the 1980s and 1990s have eroded the value-base of local government but have not swept it away. Hence, the process of change continues to be characterized by conflict and dissent. This is entirely unsurprising given the ideological agenda pursued by central government since the end of the 1970s.

Thus the future of local government management lies on one hand in the gradual fragmentation of patterns of service-delivery and the corresponding changes in the skills required to run the new pattern of services. Against this trend are efforts by local authorities to restructure their systems of political and administrative management in order to increase their corporate strength. It has been noted above that as the need for local government to act corporately increases, so the ability to do so decreases. It is in these **adaptations** to uncertainty and fragmentation that local councils are evolving new management structures, some of which are more successful than others.

There are, then, two contrasting pressures shaping the future pattern of local authority management, and the contrast is largely one of values rather than Party politics. There is the externally driven pressure towards fragmentation. There is the internally generated pressure toward corporatism. The way in which this tension will ultimately be resolved is not yet clear.

Summary

The exploration of contemporary local government has concluded with a review of local government reorganization, the growth of local governance, and the internal restructuring of local authorities. All such processes are in a state of continuing change. It is concluded that the externally driven trend towards fragmentation of local services, documented throughout the book, exists alongside renewed attempts by local government to achieve corporate management and to evolve corporate structures. The future shape of local authority management lies in the way in which continuing tensions are ultimately resolved: the conflict between internal and external pressures, between the fragmentation and corporatism, and between the *ad hoc* and the strategic response to local needs.

Discussion questions and guidance

1. *Bearing in mind the changed functions of local councils, and the changed management of local services, what recommendations would you make for the structural reorganization of local government?*

The question invites an exploration of how local government reorganization matches up to the new demands of running local services. It has been argued in Chapter 7 that the reorganization proposals of the 1990s do not address the changed nature of local government, nor could they, given their terms of reference. The changes in local provision are precisely those which have formed the central 'themes' of this book, summarized again at the beginning of this chapter. A discussion is required of how different forms of structure would assist the process of managing the new pattern of local services. There is also the theoretical dimension to consider: the **model** of local government which lies behind descriptions of change. Wilson and Game (1994, p. 343) link different models of local government to different forms of organizing local provision, and then go on to relate this to possible structures. This can be developed. The actual proposals of the 1990s reorganization should be considered in detail too. What model of local provision is implied?

2. *Identify the challenges and opportunities created for local government by the growth of multi-agency local provision.*

It would be useful to begin here by defining the nature and extent of multi-agency provision. As noted in Chapter 7, the term may denote various types of partnership between the local authority and other public or private agencies around local needs. Such joint approaches may follow in the wake of central government funding initiatives, or may be part of a longer-term trend towards joint working as between, for instance, health and social services. The term may also include public but unelected agencies, taking over the role of local authorities in defined circumstances, e.g. the Urban Development Corporations. QUANGOs were discussed initially in Chapter 1.

After forming an accurate picture of the extent of multi-agency local provision in all its forms, it is necessary to assess its implications – its 'challenges and opportunities' – for local government. There are for instance the purely managerial implications of running services across traditional boundaries (and empires): what are the likely problems and possible solutions? There are also major implications for the accountability of local services when provision is a mix of elected and non-elected public bodies, together with the private sector. Accountability is discussed in this context in Chapters 1 and 7.

3 (a) *Evaluate the internal managerial structure of North Tyneside council following its reorganization.*
   (b) *Does the North Tyneside structure provide a model for other local authorities?*

It will be necessary to refer to Case study 7.2 to identify the key aspects of the restructuring in North Tyneside. The resulting non-Departmental structure is quite different from that of most local authorities. An evaluation of the structure should address aspects such as lines of communication, the management of specific services in the absence of departments, the nature of 'functions', the corporate ethos underpinning all this, the political dimension and the likely problems. The more general question of whether the structure thus provides a model for others to follow may then be addressed. Does the structure deal effectively with the themes of contemporary local authority management – competition, the consumer and so on – which have been considered throughout this book? What would other authorities have to gain (or lose) from adopting such a structure?

4 '. . . the business model has been appropriated within local government for the organization of its own activities – from strategic policy-making and mission statements, down to the making of business plans, the issuing of contracts and the monitoring of service provision. In the 1960s the language of management was utilized to justify expansion, but this time it is being taken up in the context of contraction' (Cochrane, 1993, pp. 106–7). Discuss.*

The quotation addresses the 'business' model in local government, and implies a broad discussion of what such a model might be, and whether it is applicable to local government. The discussion should review the changing boundaries of the public and the private, touched on throughout the book. It would also be useful to consult Cochrane (1993, ch. 6) for a fuller exposition of his argument. The 'context of contraction' is certainly an important part of any assessment of recent and current changes in local government management. Consideration might be given to the financial and political bases of such contraction, and the changed role thus implied for local government. The question also invites some discussion of the wider role of the business sector within the non-elected local agencies which have gradually taken over functions hitherto the responsibility of local government: see Stewart and Davis (1994) for a critical review.

5. What is the 'new public management' in local government?

The question of the 'new' public management in general, and its applicability to and implications for local government in particular, requires a wide perspective drawn from the book as a whole. The new public management does not have a precise definition about which everyone is agreed. Thus its meaning is open here to exploration, and then to critique. The discussions in the first and last sections of Chapter 7 may provide a starting point, along with direct reference to Dunleavy and Hood (1994) in Chapter 7. The discussion of the 'consumer perspective' in Chapter 3 is relevant too, and some of the original sources referred to in that chapter might be consulted including Richards (1992), Pollitt (1990) and Gyford (1991; 1993a). The managerial implications of competition, discussed in Chapter 2, are also applicable. The comparison of 'old' and 'new' management suggested at Figure 1.1 may be of interest. The parameters of a 'new' public management – if one exists – can be compared to the characteristics of 'old' public service paternalism: see Hambleton (1992). It may also be possible to make a link to traditional models of management discussed in Chapter 1.

Suggested further reading

Stewart, J., Greer, A. and Hoggett, P. (1995) *The QUANGO State: an Alternative Approach*, Commission for Local Democracy, Research Report 10.

Weir, S. and Hall, W. (eds) (1994) *EGO Trip: Extra-Governmental Organizations in the United Kingdom and their Accountability*, Charter 88 Trust, London.

Lamb, C. (1995) QUANGOs and Sub-national Executive Agencies: Problems of Unconstrained Power and Some Remedies, *Local Government Policy Making*, **21** (4) (March), pp 61–68. All three 'QUANGO' references deal with the growing influence of the non-elected state. This is increasingly important to all those with an interest in the future of local government.

Greenwood, J. and Wilson, D. (1994) Local Government and the Contracting State, *Parliamentary Affairs*, **47** (3) (July), pp 405–419. Examines the growth of the contractual relationship within local government, and the lasting implications.

Dunleavy, P. and Hood, C. (1994) From Old Public Administration to New Public Management, *Public Money and Management*, **14** (3) (July–September), pp 9–16. An exploration of the characteristics of a 'new' public management. Perhaps useful to consider this alongside the discussion of changing management paradigms in Richards (1992).

Wilson, D. and Game, C. with Leach, S. and Stoker, G. (1994) *Local Government in the United Kingdom*, Macmillan, London. This discussion of contemporary issues and problems in local government, suggested as preliminary reading at the end of Chapter 1, may now repay attention on the basis of the further reading and exercises which have been suggested above.

BIBLIOGRAPHY

Anderson, A. and Sims, R. (1990) Managing for quality: getting the right management framework for information technology. *Public Money and Management*, **10**(3) (Autumn), 33–8.

Andreassen, T.W. (1994) Satisfaction, loyalty and reputation as indicators of customer orientation in the public sector. *International Journal of Public Sector Management*, **7**(2), 16–34.

Armstrong, G. (ed.) (1993) *View from the Bridge*, Institute of Personnel Management, London.

Association of Direct Labour Organizations (1993) *A Tale of Two Cities: A Study of Client/Contractor Relationships for Grounds Maintenance*, ADLO, Manchester.

Association of District Councils (1990) *Closer to the People*, ADC, London.

Association of District Councils/Policy and Performance Review Network (1991) *Performance Review Guide for Elected Members*, ADC/PPRN, London.

Audit Commission (1988) *The Competitive Council*, HMSO, London.

Audit Commission (1990) *We Can't Go On Meeting Like This: The Changing Role of Local Authority Members*, HMSO, London.

Audit Commission (1992) *Competing for Quality: Comments on the Government's Proposals*, HMSO, London.

Audit Commission (1992a) *Citizen's Charter Performance Indicators* (September), HMSO, London.

Audit Commission (1992b) *Citizen's Charter Indicators – Charting a Course*, HMSO, London.

Audit Commission (1992c) *Publication of Information (Standards of Performance) Directive*, HMSO, London.

Audit Commission (1993) *Phoenix Rising: A Study of New Zealand Local Government Following Reorganization*, Occasional Paper 19 (June), HMSO, London.

Audit Commission (1993a) *Staying on Course: the Second Year of the Citizen's Charter Indicators*, HMSO, London.

Audit Commission (1994a) *Read All About It: Guidance on the Publication by Local Authorities of the Citizen's Charter Indicators*, HMSO, London.

Audit Commission (1994b) *Behind Closed Doors: the Revolution in Central Support Services*, HMSO, London.

Audit Commission, Local Government Training Board, and Institute for Local Government Studies (1985) *Good Management in Local Government: Successful Practice and Action*, Local Government Training Board, Luton, 1985.

Baddeley, S. (1992) The local government role in the developing European market. Paper presented to Association of Direct Labour Organizations Seminar 'The European Challenge: Competition in a European Framework', November, Edinburgh.

Bains, M. (1972) *The New Local Authorities: Management and Structure*, HMSO, London.

Batley, R. and Stoker, G. (eds) (1991) *Local Government in Europe: Trends and Developments*, Macmillan, Basingstoke and London.

Beeton, D. (ed.) (1998) *Performance Measurement: Getting the Concepts Right*, Discussion Paper 18, Public Finance Foundation, London.

Bekke, H. A. G. M. (1991) Experiences and Experiments in Dutch Local Government. In R. Batley and G. Stoker (eds), *Local Government in Europe: Trends and Developments*, Macmillan, Basingstoke and London, pp. 123–33.

Bellamy, C. and Taylor, J. A. (1994) Reinventing Government in the Information Age. *Public Money and Management*, **14**(3) (July–September), 59–62.

Bingham, R. D. *et al.* (1991) *Managing Local Government: Public Administration in Practice*, Sage, Newbury Park California.

Blackman, T. (ed.) (1992) *Research for Policy: Proceedings of the 1992 Annual Conference of the Local Authorities Research and Intelligence Association*, LARIA/City of Newcastle, Newcastle upon Tyne.

Blackstone, T. and Plowden, W. (1988) *Inside the Think Tank*, Heinneman, London.

Bogason, P. (1991) Danish Local Government: Towards an Effective and Efficient Welfare State. In J.J. Hesse (ed.), *Local Government and Urban Affairs in International Perspective*, Nomos Verlagsgesellschaft, Baden-Baden, pp. 261–90.

Boyle, R. (1989) *Managing Public Sector Performance*, Institute of Public Administration, Dublin.

Braunig, D. (1992) Management of local authorities in Germany and the Netherlands. *Local Government Policy Making*, **19**(3), (December), 29–35.

Burningham, D. (1990) Performance indicators and the management of professionals in local government. In M. Cave, M. Kogan and R. Smith (eds), *Output And Performance Measurement in Government: the State of the Art*, Jessica Kingsley Publishers, London, pp. 124–42.

Burns, D., Hambleton, R. and Hoggett, P. (1994) *The Politics of Decentralization: Revitalizing Local Democracy*, Macmillan, London.

Butcher, H., Law, I. G., Leach, R. and Mullard, M. (1990) *Local Government and Thatcherism*, Routledge, London.

Byrne, T. (1994) *Local Government in Britain: Everyone's Guide to How it All Works*, 6th edn, Penguin, Harmondsworth.

Caring for People: Community Care in the Next Decade and Beyond (1989), White Paper, HMSO, London.

Carley, M. (1988) *Performance Monitoring in a Professional Public Service: the Case of the Careers' Service*, Policy Studies Institute, London.

Carter, N., Klein, R. and Day, P. (1992) *How Organizations Measure Success: the Use of Performance Indicators in Government*, Routledge, London.

Cave, E. and Demick, D. (1990) Marketing the school. In E. Cave and C. Wilkinson (eds), *Local Management of Schools: Some Practical Issues*, Routledge, London, pp. 70–80.

Cave, M. and Kogan, M. (1990) Some concluding observations. In M. Cave, M. Kogan and R. Smith (eds), *Output and Performance Measurement in Government: the State of the Art*, Jessica Kingsley Publishers, London, pp. 179–87.

Cave, M., Kogan, M. and Smith, R. (eds) (1990) *Output and Performance Measurement in Government: the State of the Art*, Jessica Kingsley Publishers, London.

Cave, E. and Wilkinson., C. (eds) (1990) *Local Management of Schools: Some Practical Issues*, Routledge, London.

Chandler, J. A. (ed.) (1993) *Local Government in Liberal Democracies*, Routledge, London.

Chandler, J. A. (1991) *Local Government Today*, University Press, Manchester.

Chandler, J. A. (1993) The United States of America. In J. Chandler (ed.), *Local Government in Liberal Democracies*, Routledge, London, pp. 138–58.

Chapman, R. (1989) Core public sector reform in New Zealand and the United Kingdom. *Public Money and Management*, **9**(1) (Spring), 44–9.

Chartered Institute of Public Finance and Accountancy (1984) *Performance Indicators in the Education Service*, CIPFA, London.

City of Newcastle upon Tyne (1985) *West City Consumer Survey First Report*, Performance, Review and Efficiency Sub-Committee (October), Newcastle upon Tyne.

City of Newcastle upon Tyne (1985) *West City Consumer Survey Second Report*, Performance, Review and Efficiency Sub-Committee (December), Newcastle upon Tyne.

City of Newcastle upon Tyne (1986) *West City Consumer Survey Third Report*, Performance, Review and Efficiency Sub-Committee (February), Newcastle upon Tyne.

City of Newcastle upon Tyne (1987) *Three Wards Consumer Survey Final Report*, Performance, Review and Efficiency Sub-Committee, Newcastle upon Tyne.

Clarke, M. and Stewart, J. (1985) *Local Government and the Public Service Orientation*, Local Government and Public Service Working Paper no. 1, Local Government Training Board, Luton.

Clarke, M. and Stewart, J. (1988) *The Enabling Council: Developing and Managing a New Style of Local Government*, (November), Local Government Training Board, Luton.

Clarke, M. and Stewart, J. (1991) *Choices for Local Government*, Longman, London.

Clarke, S. (ed.) (1989) *Urban Innovation and Autonomy: Political Implications of Policy Change*, vol. 1, Sage, London.

Cleveland County Council (1992) *A City for Cleveland: the Case for a Single Unitary Authority*, submission to Local Government Commission, (November), Cleveland County Council, Middlesbrough.

Cleveland County Council (undated) *General Aims and Objectives of Research and Intelligence Unit 1990–91*, Cleveland County Council, Middlesbrough.

Cleveland County Council (undated) *Research and Intelligence*, brochure, Cleveland County Council, Middlesbrough.

Cleveland County Council (1991) *Research and Intelligence Unit Provisional Work Programme 1991–2*, Cleveland County Council, Middlesbrough.

Cochrane, A. (1993) *Whatever Happened to Local Government?*, Open University Press, Buckingham.

Cole, G. A. (1990) *Management: Theory and Practice*, 3rd edn, DP Publications, London.

Coppell, C. and Brown, R. (1993) Beat the Buy Out Blues. *Local Government Chronicle*, 30 April, p. 19.

Council of Europe (1993) *The Role of Competitive Tendering in the Efficient Provision of Local Services*, Report no. 49 of Steering Committee on Local and Regional Authorities (CDLR), Council of Europe Press, Strasbourg.

Daley, D. M. (1992) *Performance Appraisal in the Public Sector: Techniques and Applications*, Quorum Books, Westport and London.

Darke, R. and Walker, R. (eds) (1977) *Local Government and the Public*, Leonard Hill, London.

Department of Education and Science (1988) *Circular 7/88*: Local Management of Schools, HMSO, London.

Department of the Environment (1991) *Competing for Quality*, HMSO, London.

Department of the Environment (1993) *Compulsory Competitive Tendering of Housing Management: A Consultation Paper* (June) HMSO, London.

Department of the Environment (1991) *The Internal Management of Local Authorities in England: A Consultation Paper* (July) HMSO, London.

Derwentside District Council (undated) *The Chief Executive's Department*, information sheet, Derwentside District Council, Consett.

Dobson, N. (1993) Tendering law's double whammy. *Municipal Journal*, **20**, 21–27 May, pp. 24–5.

Dockery, E. (1992) Management and the usefulness of information. In L. Willcocks and J. Harrow (eds), *Rediscovering Public Services Management*, McGraw-Hill, London, pp. 275–93.

Dommel, P. R. (1991) Intergovernmental relations. In R. D. Bingham *et al.* (eds), *Managing Local Government: Public Administration in Practice*, Sage, Newbury Park, pp. 135–55.

Downes, P. (1988) *Local Financial Management in Schools*, Blackwell, Oxford.

Dungey, J. (1993) Putting the customer into customer care, *Local Government Information Unit Briefing no. 67* (March), p. 8.

Dunleavy, P. and Hood, C. (1994) From old public administration to new public management. *Public Money and Management*, **14**(3) (July–September), 9–16.

East Cumbria Health Authority (1992) *Involving the Community in Health Needs Assessment*, East Cumbria Health Authority Health Education Unit, Carlisle.

Education Reform Act (1988).

Elcock, H. (1994) *Local Government: Policy and Management in Local Authorities*, 3rd edn, Routledge, London.

Etherington, D. and Paddon, M. (1991) The free local government initiative in Denmark: modernization, innovation or control. *Local Government Studies*, **17**(4) (July–August), 6–13.

Farnham, D. (1993) Human resources management and employee relations. In D. Farnham and S. Horton (eds), *Managing the New Public Services*, Macmillan, London, pp. 99–124.

Farnham, D. and Horton, S. (eds) (1993) *Managing the New Public Services*, Macmillan, London.

Farnham, D. and Lupton, C. (1994) Employment relations and training policy. In S. P. Savage, R. Atkinson and L. Robins (eds), *Public Policy in Britain*, Macmillan, London; St Martin's Press, New York, 1994, pp. 96–115.

Fenwick, J. (1989) Consumerism and local government. *Local Government Policy Making*, **16**(1) (June) 45–52.

Fenwick, J. (1992) Policy research in local government. *Local Government Policy Making*, **18**(4) (March) 35–41.

Fenwick, J. and Harrop, K. (1990) The customer and local services: a model for practitioners. *Public Money and Management*, **10**(1) (Spring) 41–5.

Fenwick, J., Harrop, K. and Elcock, H. (1989) *The Public Domain in an English Region: Aspects of Adaptation and Change in Public Authorities*, Studies in Public Policy 175, Centre for the Study of Public Policy, University of Strathclyde, Glasgow.

Fenwick, J., Shaw, K. and Foreman, A. (1993) Compulsory competitive tendering in local government: a study of the responses of authorities in the north of England. Research Report, Department of Economics and Government, University of Northumbria, Newcastle upon Tyne.

Fenwick, J., Shaw, K. and Foreman, A. (1994) Managing competition in UK local government: the impact of compulsory competitive tendering. *International Journal of Public Sector Management*, 7(6), 4–14.

Fenwick, J., Snape, S., Ranade, W. and Harrop, K. (1994) Competition without compulsion. *Local Government Management*, 1(9) 14–15.

Gilbert, C. (ed.) (1990) *Local Management of Schools: A Guide for Governors and Teachers*, Kogan Page, London.

Gill, J. and Johnson, P. (1991) *Research Methods for Managers*, Paul Chapman Publishing, London.

Gorry, A. and Scott-Morton, M. (1971) A Framework for Management Information Systems. *Sloan Management Review*, 13(1) (Fall) 55–70.

Gray, C. (1994) *Government Beyond the Centre: Subnational Politics in Britain*, Macmillan, Basingstoke and London.

Griffiths, W. (1993) Facing the future: supporting change at Kent County Council. In G. Armstrong (ed.), *View from the Bridge*, Institute of Personnel Management, London, pp. 36–54.

Gyford, J. (1991) *Citizens, Consumers and Councils: Local Government and the Public*, Macmillan, London.

Gyford, J. (1993a) Putting the question. *Local Government Management*, 1(5) (Spring), 18–19.

Gyford, J. (1993b) Professionalism, managerialism and politics: an uneasy co-existence. In G. Stoker (ed.), *The Future of Professionalism in Local Government*, Belgrave Paper no. 10, Local Government Management Board, Luton, pp. 12–21.

Hadly, R. and Young, K. (1990) *Creating a Responsive Public Service*, Harvester Wheatsheaf, Hemel Hempstead.

Hague, B. (1989) *Local Authorities and a Public Service Orientation: Ideas into Action*, Local Authority Management Unit, Discussion Paper 89/3, Department of Economics and Government, Newcastle upon Tyne Polytechnic.

Ham, C. and Hill, M. (1993) *The Policy Process in the Modern Capitalist State*, 2nd edn, Harvester Wheatsheaf, Hemel Hempstead.

Hambleton, R. (1992) Decentralization and democracy in UK local government. *Public Money and Management*, 12(3) (July–September), 9–20.

Hambleton, R. (1993) Enabling U.S. style. *Local Government Chronicle*, 12 March, pp. 16–17.

Hambleton, R. (1991) Ideas and alarm bells: learning from American local government. *Local Government Policy Making*, 18(3) (December) 3–9

Handy, C. B. (1985) *Understanding Organizations*, 3rd edn, Penguin, Harmondsworth.

Harlow District Council (1990) *A Consultation Guide to Good Practice*, Harlow Policy and Planning Division, Harlow.

Harrison, T. (1988) *Access to Information in Local Government*, Sweet & Maxwell, London.

Harrison, T. (1987) *Danger Zones: A Guide for Councillors and Officers*, LGC Communications, London.

Harrow, J. and Shaw, M. (1992) The manager faces the consumer. In L. Willcocks and J. Harrow (eds), *Rediscovering Public Services Management*, McGraw-Hill, London, pp. 113–40.

Harrow, J. and Willcocks, L. (1990) Risk and the public service manager. *Public Money and Management*, 10(3) (Autumn) 61–4.

Harvey-Jones, J. (1988) *Making it Happen*, Collins, Glasgow.

Hender, D. (1993) *Managing Local Government Services*, ICSA Publishing/LGC, Hemel Hempstead.

Henderson-Stewart, D. (1990) Performance management and review in local government. In M. Cave, M. Kogan and R. Smith (eds), *Output and Performance Measurement in Government: the State of the Art* Jessica Kingsley Publishers, London, pp. 106–23.

Hesse, J. J. (ed.) (1991) *Local Government and Urban Affairs in International Perspective: Analyses of Twenty Western Industrialized Countries*, Nomos Verlagsgesellschaft, Baden-Baden.

Hogwood, B. W. and Gunn, L. A. (1984) *Policy Analysis for the Real World*, University Press, Oxford.

Huczynski, A. A. (1993) *Management Gurus: What Makes Them and How to Become One*, Routledge, London and New York.

Hutt, J. (1990) *Opening the Town Hall Door: An Introduction to Local Government*, 2nd edn, Bedford Square Press, London.

Isaac-Henry, K., Painter, C. and Barnes, C. (eds) (1993) *Management in the Public Sector: Challenge and Change*, Chapman & Hall, London.

Jackson, P. M. (1993) Public service performance evaluation: a strategic perspective. *Public Money and Management*, **13**(4) (October–December), 9–14.

Jackson, P. M. and Palmer, B. (1992) *Developing Performance Monitoring in Public Sector Organizations: A Management Guide*, Management Centre, University of Leicester.

Jackson, P. M. and Palmer, B. (1989) *First Steps in Measuring Performance in the Public Sector: A Management Guide*, Public Finance Foundation with Price-Waterhouse, London.

Jesson, D. and Mayston, D. (1989) Measuring Performance in Authorities and Schools. *Education and Training UK*, 17–25.

Jones, G. (ed.) (1993) *Local Government: the Management Agenda*, ICSA Publishing, Hemel Hempstead.

Jones, G. and Stewart, J. (1993) Retreat from the unitary option. In G. Jones (ed.), *Local Government: the Management Agenda*, ICSA Publishing, Hemel Hempstead, pp. 68–70.

Keller, L. F. and Perry, D. C. (1991) The structures of government. In R. D. Bingham *et al.* (eds), *Managing Local Government: Public Administration in Practice*, Sage, Newbury Park, pp. 31–58.

Kelly, J. (1992) Private sector and public sector views of customer care and quality. In T. Blackman (ed.), *Research for Policy*, LARIA/City of Newcastle, Newcastle upon Tyne, 5–15.

Kerr, A. and Radford, M. (1994) TUPE or not TUPE: competitive tendering and the transfer laws. *Public Money and Management* **14**(4) (October–December), 37–45.

Kershaw, P. (1977) Developments in Sunderland. In R. Darke and R. Walker (eds), *Local Government and the Public*, Leonard Hill, London, pp. 215–28.

King, D. S. and Pierre, J. (eds) (1990) *Challenges to Local Government*, Sage, London.

Kingdom, J. (1991) *Local Government and Politics in Britain*, Philip Allan, London.

Klein, R. and Carter, N. (1988) Performance measurement: a review of concepts and issues. In D. Beeton (ed.), *Performance Measurement: Getting the Concepts Right*, Public Finance Foundation Discussion Paper no. 18, London, pp. 5–20.

Knowles, R. (1988) *Effective Management in Local Government: An Introduction to Current Practice*, revised edn, ICSA Publishing, Cambridge.

Kolam, K. (1991) Neighbourhood councils in the Nordic countries. *Local Government Studies*, **17**(3) (May–June), 13–26.

Kooiman, J. and Eliassen, K. A. (1987) *Managing Public Organizations: Lessons from Contemporary European Experience*, Sage, London.

Labour Party (1988) *Social Justice and Economic Efficiency: First Report of Labour's Policy Review for the 1990s*, Labour Party, London.

Lane, J-E. (1993) *The Public Sector: Concepts, Models and Approaches*, Sage, London.

Lauritzen, B. and Hague, B. (1993) Performance measurement and social citizenship: an Anglo-Danish comparison. Paper to 23rd Annual Conference, Public Administration Committee of Joint University Council, September, University of York.

Lavery, K. (1992) The 'council manager' and 'strong mayor' forms of government in the USA. *Public Money and Management*, **12**(2) (April–June), 9–14.

Leach, R. (1994) Reorganizing for enabling? Restructuring local government for an altered role. Paper to 24th Annual Conference, Public Administration Committee of Joint University Council, September, University of York.

Leach, S. and Stewart, J. (1990) *Political Leadership in Local Government*, Local Government Training Board, Luton.

Leach, S., Stewart, J. and Walsh, K. (1994) *The Changing Organization and Management of Local Government*, Macmillan, London.

Leasehold Reform, Housing and Urban Development Act 1993.

Lewis, P. (1994) *Information Systems Development*, Pitman Publishing, London.

Leonard, M. (1988) *The 1988 Education Act: a Tactical Guide for Schools*, Blackwell Education, Oxford.

Likierman, A. (1993) Performance indicators: 20 early lessons from managerial use. *Public Money and Management*, **13**(4) (October–December) 15–22.

Local Government (Access to Information) Act 1985.

Local Government Act 1972.

Local Government Act 1988.

Local Government Act 1992.

Local Authorities (Admission of the Press to Meetings) Act 1908.

Local Government Chronicle (1993) *US Mayor Says Managers are Barrier to Competition*, 23 April, p. 6.

Local Government (Direct Service Organizations) Regulations 1993.

Local Government and Housing Act 1989.

Local Government Information Unit (1993) *LGIU Guide to Local Government Finance*, LGIU, London.

Local Government Information Unit (1993a) *Special Briefing* no. 43, February.

Local Government Information Unit (1993b) *Briefing* no. 73, October.

Local Government Information Unit (1994a) *Briefing* no. 77, March.

Local Government Information Unit (1994b) *Briefing* no. 81, July.

Local Government Information Unit (1994c) *QUANGO File* no. 3, September.

Local Government Information Unit (1994d) *QUANGO File* no. 4, September.

Local Government Management Board (1992) *Citizens and Local Democracy*, LGMB, Luton.

Local Government Planning and Land Act 1980.

Lodden, P. (1991) The 'Free Local Government' experiment in Norway. In R. Batley and G. Stoker (eds), *Local Government in Europe: Trends and Developments*, Macmillan, Basingstoke and London, pp. 198–209.

Loughlin, M. (1992) *Administrative Accountability in Local Government*, Joseph Rowntree Foundation, York.

Lucas, H. C. Jnr (1994) *Information Systems Concepts for Management*, 5th edn, Mitchell McGraw-Hill, San Francisco.

Mallabar, N. (1991) *Local Government Administration: in a Time of Change*, Business Education Publishers, Sunderland.

Markus, M. L. and Bjorn-Anderson, N. (1987) Power Over Users: Its Exercise by System Professionals. *Communications of the Association for Computing Machinery*, **21**(1), 24–33.

Maysey, G. (1992) Women CCT and the Social Charter. Paper presented to Association of Direct Labour Organizations Seminar, June, Dundee.

McCarthy, A., Shaw, K., Fenwick, J. and Foreman, A. (eds) (1992) *Compulsory Competitive Tendering in British Local Government: An Annotated Bibliography*, Earlsgate Press, Winteringham.

McCarthy, U. (1993) European Community Developments. In C. Trinder and P. Jackson (eds), *The Public Services Yearbook 1993*, Chapman & Hall, London, pp. 41–56.

McKevitt, D. and Lawton, A. (eds) (1994) *Public Sector Management: Theory, Critique and Practice*, Sage, London.

Meacher, M. (1993) Reviving socialism. In S. Wilks (ed.), *Talking About Tomorrow: A New Radical Politics*, Pluto Press in association with New Times, London, pp. 13–19.

Monaghan, C. and Ball, R. (1993) Gearing up for performance review. *Local Government Policy Making*, **20**(3) (December), 11–18.

Morris, H. (1992) Braving the elements. *Surveyor*, 12 Nov., p. 20.

Mouritzen, P. E. (1989) Fiscal policymaking in times of resource scarcity: the Danish case. In S. Clarke (ed.), *Urban Innovation and Autonomy: Political Implications of Policy Change*, vol. 1, Sage, London, pp. 100–27.

Mullins, L. J. (1993) *Management and Organizational Behaviour*, 3rd edn, Pitman Publishing, London.

Murgatroyd, S. and Morgan, C. (1993) *Total Quality Management and the School*, Open University Press, Buckingham.

National Consumer Council (1986) *Measuring Up: Consumer Assessment of Local Authority Services – A Guideline Study*, NCC, London.

National Health Service and Community Care Act 1990.

Neale, F. (ed.) (1991) *The Handbook of Performance Management*, Institute of Personnel Management, London.

Newcastle upon Tyne City Council (1989a) *Local Management of Schools: Draft Scheme of Delegation for Statutory Consultation* (March), Newcastle upon Tyne.

Newcastle upon Tyne City Council (1989b) *Local Management of Schools: Proposed Scheme of Delegation* (September), Newcastle upon Tyne.

Nissen, O. (1991) Key Issues in the local government debate in Denmark. In R. Batley and G. Stoker (eds), *Local Government in Europe: Trends and Developments*, Macmillan, Basingstoke and London, pp. 190–7.

North Tyneside Council (1992) Job description for Executive Directors/description of Functions, North Tyneside Council, Wallsend.

Northmore, D. (1990) *Freedom of Information Handbook*, Bloomsbury, London.

Norris, G. M. (1989) The centre: what shape for the 1990s. *Local Government Policy Making*, **16**(1) (June), 9–14.

Norton, A. (1994) *International Handbook of Local and Regional Government: A Comparative Analysis of Advanced Democracies*, Edward Elgar, Aldershot.

Organization for Economic Co-operation and Development (1990) *Public Management Developments: Survey 1990*, OECD, Paris.

Organization for Economic Co-operation and Development (1991) *Public Management Developments: Update 1991*, OECD, Paris.

Organization for Economic Co-operation and Development (1992) *Public Management Developments: Update 1992*, OECD, Paris.

Organization for Economic Co-operation and Development (1993) *Public Management: OECD Country Profiles*, OECD, Paris.

Organization for Economic Co-operation and Development (1994) *OECD in Figures*, 1994 edition, supplement to the OECD Observer no 188 (June–July), OECD, Paris.

Open University (1992) Local government change: managing the challenges, TV programme for course B887, *Managing Public Services*.

Painter, C. (1993) Managing change in the public sector. In K. Isaac-Henry, C. Painter and C. Barnes (eds), *Management in the Public Sector: Challenge and Change*, Chapman & Hall, London, pp. 37–57.

Painter, C., Isaac-Henry, K. and Barnes, C. (1993) Conclusion: the problematical nature of public management reform. In K. Isaac-Henry, C. Painter and C. Barnes (eds), *Management in the Public Sector: Challenge and Change*, Chapman & Hall, London, pp. 171–86.

Palmer, A. J. (1993) Performance Measurement in Local Government. *Public Money and Management*, **13**(4) (October–December), 31–6.

Parker, D. and Hartley, K. (1990) Competitive tendering: issues and evidence. *Public Money and Management*, **10**(3) (Autumn), 9–16.

Parry, G. (1990) The legal context. In E. Cave and C. Wilkinson (eds), *Local Management of Schools: Some Practical Issues*, Routledge, London, pp. 81–97.

Parsons, S. (1993) *The Right Side of the Law*, Local Government Information Unit, London.

Patel, A. (1994) Quality assurance (BS5750) in social services departments. *International Journal of Public Sector Management*, **7**(2), 4–15.

Peters, T. J. and Waterman, R. H. (1982) *In Search of Excellence*, Harper & Row, New York.

Pollitt, C. (1990) *Managerialism and the Public Services: the Anglo-American Experience*, Blackwell, Oxford.

Public Bodies (Admission to Meetings) Act 1960.

Quicke, G. (1992) Metropolitan counties' experiences of joint research and intelligence work. In T. Blackman (ed.), *Research for Policy*, LARIA/City of Newcastle, Newcastle upon Tyne, pp. 87–92.

Rees, W. D. (1991) *The Skills of Management*, 3rd edn, Routledge, London.

Reinermann, H. (1987) Information and public management. In J. Kooiman and K. A. Eliassen (eds), *Managing Public Organizations: Lessons from Contemporary European Experience*, Sage, London, pp. 173–88.

Remenyi, D. S. J. (1991) *Introducing Strategic Information Systems Planning*, NCC Blackwell Ltd, Oxford.

Report of the Committee on the Conduct of Local Government (1974) – *the Redcliffe-Maud Report* – Cmnd 5636, HMSO, London.

Report of the Committee of Inquiry into the Conduct of Local Authority Business (1986) – *the Widdicombe Report* – Cmnd 9797, HMSO, London.

Report of the Royal Commission on Local Government in England 1966–69 (1969) – *the Redcliffe-Maud Report* – Cmnd 4040, HMSO, London.

Report of the Royal Commission on Standards of Conduct in Public Life (1976) – *the Salman Report* – Cmnd 6524, HMSO, London.

Richards, S. (1992) *Who Defines the Public Good? The Consumer Paradigm in Public Management*, Public Management Foundation, London.

Ridley, N. (1988) *The Local Right: Enabling Not Providing*, Centre for Policy Studies, London.

Rigg, C. and Trehan, K. (1993) The changing management of human resources in local government. In K. Isaac-Henry, C. Painter and C. Barnes (eds), *Management in the Public Sector: Challenge and Change*, Chapman & Hall, London, pp. 77–93.

Rockart, J. and Treacy, M. E. (1982) The CEO goes on-line. *Harvard Business Review*, **60** (Jan.–Feb.), 82–88.

Rogers, S. (1990) *Performance Management in Local Government*, Longman, Harlow.

Rose, L. E. (1990) Nordic free-commune experiments: increased local autonomy or continued central control? In D. S. King and J. Pierre (eds), *Challenges to Local Government*, Sage, London, pp. 212–41.

Rouse, J. (1993) Resource and performance management in public service organizations. In K. Isaac-Henry, C. Painter and C. Barnes (eds), *Management in the Public Sector: Challenge and Change*, Chapman & Hall, London, pp. 59–76.

Savage, S. P., Atkinson, R. and Robins, L. (eds) (1994) *Public Policy in Britain*, Macmillan, London; St Martin's Press, New York.

Segerlund, C. (1994) Developing citizens' offices in Nordic countries. *Local Government Policy Making*, **20**(4) (March), 57–60.

Sharpe, L. J. (1985) Central co-ordination and the policy network. *Political Studies*, **33**, 361–81.

Shaw, K., Fenwick, J. and Foreman, A. (1993) Client and contractor roles in local government: some observations on managing the split. *Local Government Policy Making*, **20**(2) (October), 22–7.

Shaw, K., Fenwick, J. and Foreman, A (1994) Compulsory competitive tendering for local government services: the experiences of local authorities in the north of England 1988–1992. *Public Administration*, **72**(2) (Summer), 201–17.

Smith, G. (1992) Research and intelligence in shire counties and districts. In T. Blackman (ed.), *Research for Policy*, LARIA/City of Newcastle, Newcastle upon Tyne, pp. 93–9.

Smith, L. (1993) Management's new breed. In G. Jones (ed.), *Local Government: the Management Agenda*, ICSA Publishing, Hemel Hempstead, pp. 110–12.

Snape, S. (1994) *Contracting Out by Dutch Municipalities*, research report for marketization in Europe project, Department of Economics and Government, University of Northumbria, Newcastle upon Tyne.

South, L. (1986) Education management: measuring quality in education. *Local Government Policy Making*, **13**(1) (June), 9–19.

Steele, K. (1991) Service appraisal in the Health Service. *Consumer Policy Review*, **1**(4) (October), 211–19.

Stewart, J. (1994) *Issues for the Management of Local Government*, Institute of Local Government Studies, University of Birmingham.

Stewart, J. and Davis, H. (1994) A new agenda for local governance. *Public Money and Management*, **14**(4) (October–December), 29–36.

Stewart, J. and Stoker, G. (ed.) (1989) *The Future of Local Government*, Macmillan, London.

Stewart, J. and Walsh, K. (1992) Change in the management of public services. *Public Administration*, **70** (Winter), 499–518.

Stoker, G. (1989) Creating a local government for a post-Fordist society: the Thatcherite Project? In J. Stewart and G. Stoker (eds), *The Future of Local Government*, Macmillan, London, pp. 141–70.

Stoker, G. (1991) Introduction: trends in Western European local government. In R. Batley and G. Stoker (eds), *Local Government in Europe: Trends and Developments*, Macmillan, Basingstoke and London, pp. 1–20.

Stoker, G. (1993) (ed.) *The Future of Professionalism in Local Government*, Belgrave Paper no. 10, Local Government Management Board, Luton.

Stoker, G. and Wolman, H. (1991) *A Different Way of Doing Business: the Example of the US Mayor*, Belgrave Paper no. 2, Local Government Management Board, Luton.

Stoker, G. and Wolman, H. (1992) Drawing lessons from US experience: an elected mayor for British local government. *Public Administration*, **70** (Summer), 241–67.

Terry, F. (1993) Managing relations with the European Community: the case of local government. In Isaac-Henry, C. Painter and C. Barnes (eds), *Management in the Public Sector: Challenge and Change*, Chapman & Hall, London, pp. 151–69.

Thierauf, R. J. (1987) *Effective Management Information Systems*, 2nd edn, Merrill Publishing Company, Columbus, Ohio.

Thomson, P. (1992) Public sector management in a period of radical change 1979–1992. *Public Money and Management*, **12**(3) (July–September), 33–41.

Torrington, D., Weightman, J. and Johns, K. (1989) *Effective Management: People and Organization*, Prentice-Hall, London.

Trade Union Reform and Employment Rights Act 1993.

Trinder, C. and Jackson, P. (eds) (1993) *The Public Services Yearbook 1993*, Chapman & Hall, London.

Transfer Of Undertakings (Protection of Employment) Regulations (1981) (Statutory Instrument 1981/1794).

Walker, P. (1994) What happens when you scrap the welfare state? *Independent on Sunday* (London), 13 March, p. 17.

Walsh, K. (1993) Citizens and markets. Paper to 23rd Annual Conference, Public Administration Committee of Joint University Council, September, University of York.

Walsh, K. (1991) *Competitive Tendering for Local Authority Services: Initial Experiences*, HMSO, London.

Walsh, K. and Davis, H. (1993) *Competition and Service: the Impact of the Local Government Act 1988*, HMSO, London.

Webster, B. (1991) *Customer Service in the Counties*, Association of County Councils, London.

Whiteoak, J. (1992) Making it pay. *Local Government Chronicle Supplement*, 13 March, pp. 8–9.

Wilks, S. (ed.) (1993) *Talking About Tomorrow: A New Radical Politics*, Pluto Press in association with New Times, London.

Willcocks, L. and Harrow, J. (1992) Introduction. In L. Willcocks and J. Harrow (eds), *Rediscovering Public Services Management*), McGraw Hill, London, pp. XIII–XXXI.

Willcocks, L. and Harrow, J. (eds) (1992) *Rediscovering Public Services Management*, McGraw-Hill, London.

Willmore, C. J. (1988) *Letting People Know: Local Government, Publicity and the Law*, 2nd edn, Association of Metropolitan Authorities, London.

Wilson, D. and Game, C., with Leach, S. and Stoker, G. (1994) *Local Government in the United Kingdom*, Macmillan, London.

Winfield, I. (1991) *Organizations and Information Technology: Systems, Power and Job Design*, Blackwell Scientific Publications, Oxford.

Wistrich, E. (1992) Restructuring government New Zealand style, *Public Administration*, **70** (Spring), 119–35.

Worrall, L. (1990) *Research Skills Audit*, Association of District Councils, London.

Yokota, M., Leggett, D. and Kasatani, N. (1992) Imaginative solutions to meet diverse needs: a Japanese perspective. Paper presented to Association of Direct Labour Organizations Seminar, June, Dundee.

Young, K. and Davies, M. (1990) *The Politics of Local Government Since Widdicombe*, Joseph Rowntree Foundation, York.

INDEX